About Island Press

Since 1984, the nonprofit organization Island Press has been stimulating, shaping, and communicating ideas that are essential for solving environmental problems worldwide. With more than 1,000 titles in print and some 30 new releases each year, we are the nation's leading publisher on environmental issues. We identify innovative thinkers and emerging trends in the environmental field. We work with world-renowned experts and authors to develop cross-disciplinary solutions to environmental challenges.

Island Press designs and executes educational campaigns, in conjunction with our authors, to communicate their critical messages in print, in person, and online using the latest technologies, innovative programs, and the media. Our goal is to reach targeted audiences—scientists, policy makers, environmental advocates, urban planners, the media, and concerned citizens—with information that can be used to create the framework for long-term ecological health and human well-being.

Island Press gratefully acknowledges major support from The Bobolink Foundation, Caldera Foundation, The Curtis and Edith Munson Foundation, The Forrest C. and Frances H. Lattner Foundation, The JPB Foundation, The Kresge Foundation, The Summit Charitable Foundation, Inc., and many other generous organizations and individuals.

The opinions expressed in this book are those of the author(s) and do not necessarily reflect the views of our supporters.

Building Community
Food Webs

Building Community
Food Webs

Ken Meter

ISLANDPRESS | Washington | Covelo

Library of Congress Control Number: 2020943013

All Island Press books are printed on environmentally responsible materials.

Manufactured in the United States of America
10 9 8 7 6 5 4 3 2 1

Keywords: Agricultural policy, Civic agriculture, Civic movements, Commodity crops, Community food systems, Economic development, Environmental planning, Equity in agriculture, Farm labor, Farmland conservation, Food banks, Food insecurity, Food security, Food systems, Local food, Regenerative agriculture, Resource economics, Rural development, Sustainable agriculture, Sustainable development, Urban and regional planning

Ken Meter's ORCID designation is 0000-0001-5221-6987.

*To the next generation of visionaries
who are devoted to crafting
community food webs globally*

Contents

Acknowledgments

This book literally represents a life's work. It has been gestating for 40 years. I am indebted to a vast web of supporters for helping inspire, and contributing to, this effort, primarily by sharing their experiences honestly with me. The people named in this book, and countless others, have given me a profound education.

Members of the Community Food Security Coalition (CFSC) were paramount. This umbrella organization brought diverse voices together to ensure that low-income consumers became engaged in shaping more responsive food systems. Its annual meetings regularly attracted about one thousand motivated food leaders who spurred extraordinary community activity and shared insights openly. Through CFSC I made strong connections with grassroots leaders across the US and Canada. Tragically, the organization closed its doors in 2010. I miss it dearly.

Long before this coalition formed, several insightful farmers played key roles in my education. With extreme patience they welcomed me to their farms and explained how the economy functions from their perspectives. The first courageous souls to take me on, when I was a neophyte learning about agriculture, were Bill and Dorothea Harjes, Roger and Holly Harjes, Gordy and Sherry Bates, Ken Narr, Art Berger, Jim Kreger, and Dennis Tuchtenhagen. Most of these farmers launched their operations at the same time, and they took exceptional care to collaborate. They shared equipment, guided accomplished children through 4-H, challenged each other's thinking, and swapped rich stories. They literally overturned my notions of economics. Their insights profoundly shape my work.

One small step removed from farming, but playing a key role in my education, was the late Dean Harrington (1950–2019), president of what is now called Foresight Bank, in Plainview, Minnesota. Dean showed me how a banker in a town of 3,300 could serve as a community-builder dedicated to a "steady-state" economy and as a champion of literature and theater. Similarly, in Viroqua, Wisconsin, Sue Noble modeled how an economic developer can create community among entrepreneurs, bringing people together to frame a common vision that helped construct strong businesses that complement each other.

Educators added incisive insights. I am deeply indebted to Sara Berry for taking me under her wing as a graduate student, deconstructing some false approaches I had taken, and then guiding me to reassemble a blend of farmers' pragmatic insights with scholarly research. Berry also introduced me to the diligent network-building of African villagers.

Two books especially inspired me in writing this work. One, another Island Press title, is Gary Paul Nabhan's *Food from the Radical Center*. The second is Sue Futrell's *Good Apples*. Both illuminate critical issues in deeply humane ways, through the voices of those who labor in farms, fields, and scholarship. A third, Michael Pollan's *Omnivore's Dilemma*, motivated me to publish the economic story that operates as a silent current beneath his explication of consumer food choices.

Linda Barret Osborne and Gary Nabhan played key roles in helping me to negotiate the intricate path of publishing a book. Adam Diamond graciously connected me to Island Press. Jesse Wilson offered astute commentary on rough early drafts, while Amanda Robinson suggested incisive ways to make the writing more precise. Carolyn Carr, who has supported this endeavor since its early days, homed in on important gaps in logic. David Conner offered critical suggestions from a professor's point of view. Helen Schnoes and Sarah Laeng-Gilliatt provided professional insights from their community food practice. Deb Slee arranged my professional work elegantly on the Crossroads Resource Center website.

Nancy Matheson and Barbara Rusmore offered particular guidance in refining the Montana chapter. Al Kurki, Pam Mavrolas, Jan Tusick, Jonda Crosby, Neva Hassanein, and Crissie McMullan added significant details to my understanding of this vibrant network. In Hawai'i, I am grateful to Alicia Higa, Moulika Anna Hitchens, Tina Tamai, Betsy Cole, Kristen Albrecht, Kaiulani Odom, Kasha Ho, Tammy Chase Brunelle, and Silvan Shawe for helping improve my account of the islands.

Elsewhere, exceptional editing suggestions were made by Susan Andrews, Robert Ojeda, Diana Teran, Moses Thompson, Tim Ferrell, Jeremy Call, Anneli Berube, Terry Freeman, Kate Radosevic, Cindy Gentry, Rosanne Albright, Kristen Osgood, June Holley, Leslie Schaller, Janet Katz, Richard Barnes, Nick Jezierny, Courtney Frost, Al Singer, Pat Garrity, Lori Tatreau, Sue Futrell, Angel Mendez, Michael Rozyne, Blaine Hitzfield, Brooks Hitzfield, Sue Noble, Brian Wickert, Bud Vogt, and Norm Conde. Emily Turner at Island Press took on the challenge of shepherding awkward early drafts, injecting delicate suggestions one by one until the manuscript took on a more cogent shape.

My colleague Megan Phillips Goldenberg served as a steady collaborator and trusted friend for six years. Aided by her husband Zach, sons Reuben and Jakob, and daughter Ella, she helped ground the work I do. Henry Heikkinen introduced me to both the rigor and the uncertainties of science. Randy Neprash and Sara Barsel kept finding creative ways to support the writing process, often involving food and music. My parents, Clarence and Margaret Seidl Meter, and my brothers Don and Dave, valued ideas that make a difference.

Introduction

It is difficult to imagine how meager food choices were 50 years ago. At that time, I could find no organic food items at the supermarket. Today organic food sales have soared to $45 billion per year. White bread was mainstream; it was nearly impossible to buy whole grains for home cooking. Today I can purchase bulk grains in any quantity I desire, grown by a farm I have visited. Back then grass-fed beef was an exotic import. I didn't yet know that some of the beautifully marbled cuts of beef I ate would later cause my heart distress, and it was decades until I learned that cattle were not meant to eat grain. The only farmers I knew were my cousins in Nebraska, who were suspicious of my suburban upbringing. My family trekked 8 hours to visit them each Labor Day, in part because my father wanted me to know what a ripe watermelon tasted like. He also sought to show me what an austere farm upbringing he had had, and how far my cousins had progressed. Now I can find sweet melons at my co-op grocery. A farm family I cherish delivered meats, cheese, and vegetables to my front door during the coronavirus pandemic.

These new food choices were sparked by the vibrant community foods movement that emerged across the US around 1969. That movement has set a deep taproot in diverse locales across the US. While its promise seems straightforward—that all people should have good food—adherents hold a wide range of motivations. Some join to cure themselves of a disease. Others seek to protect themselves from illness by eating the purest foods possible. A few hardy souls want to dig in the dirt so they can feed their neighbors while caring for the earth, and connect to consumers who will support their quest. Cultural enclaves renew their ancestral heritage of growing food for all. Entrepreneurs launch businesses in a quest to make money, while thousands of food-security leaders dedicate themselves to ensuring that those lacking wealth, low-income and other marginalized people have the best food available. Some organize their neighbors to take action, knowing that a democracy cannot survive unless it feeds itself. Most promising to me, food leaders collaborate across all shades of the political spectrum, convinced that food cannot be a partisan concern.

All of these viewpoints, and more, drive the work of community food webs: overlapping networks of grassroots leaders who are determined to define their own food choices. I use this term in kinship with two community food groups, the Ten Rivers Food Web and the North Coast Food Web, in Oregon, which incorporate the term into the names of their organizations following the inspiration of the visionary farmer Harry MacCormack. While it is meant to express an awareness of our interdependence with, and care for, the environment, the term carries a different meaning here than it does in the scientific work of ecologists.

Often this movement is referred to as the "local foods" movement, but I have found its strength runs far deeper than that (I will say more about this in chapter 11). "Local food" efforts are often limited to the privileged, or hollowed into meaningless marketing campaigns. This movement is more inclusive. It gains its most lasting victories when it builds community. Indeed its competitive advantage is that it builds strong relationships of trust among those who engage. Most critically, it builds mutual loyalty between farmers and consumers, because farmers face special risks no one else faces (including severe weather events, climate change, fickle markets, and bodily harm). They need consumers and policy makers who will help mitigate these risks. The movement is fueled by a conviction that we need to forge the food systems we deserve, rather than merely accept the food systems we inherit.

Despite the extraordinary pressures stacked against its success, and the intense resistance it faces, the community foods movement persists. Its dogged spirit is one of the most compelling reasons I have for writing this book. Exceptional victories have been won by taking slow steps over decades, but these achievements seldom reach the daily news cycle, nor do the movement's leaders gain national prominence. Rather, the work of building community food webs plays out on remote farm fields, inside the coolers of a local grocery store, and at spare conference tables in municipal halls.

This book is based on work I have shouldered over the past two decades, on the invitation of local foods leaders in more than 140 regions across North America. I've partnered with food webs in 41 states and two provinces, and with four Native American tribes. It has been a rare privilege to be invited in, and the richest educational experience of my life. This book will bring to light some of the best food webs I know of, showing the steps each took to become more effective. Many of these stories are simply not available anywhere else.

One central paradox drives people to construct community food webs. This paradox both creates the need for community food webs and frustrates our efforts to build them. Although our highly productive commodity farming has extensive global reach, and a small number of farms have become quite large and efficient, the prevailing food system systematically extracts wealth from rural and urban communities alike.

This book traces a loss of $4 trillion of potential wealth from rural areas over the past hundred years. That is nearly one-quarter of the current annual gross domestic product for the US. It also amounts to more than the current value of all US farms combined—$3 trillion. The massive subsidies given to farmers help input suppliers and lenders a great deal, but play a strong role in drawing wealth from the rural economy. Losses such as these have fed deep divisions in the countryside over recent decades, which exploded politically in 2016.

US farmers largely raise commodities for industrial processing, while even farm communities import most of the foods they eat. It is typical for 85 to 95 percent of the food people consume in any state to be grown outside of the state boundaries, while 95 percent of the commodities farmers raise are shipped to distant buyers. Urban communities lose wealth as well, spending billions of dollars each year purchasing food sourced on distant farms or processing plants.

Food Systems Have Also Eroded in Recent Years

This extraction means that over the past seven decades I have also witnessed erosions of the food systems I depend on. I will discuss some of these in the next chapter, but let me begin in a more personal manner. My mother, Margaret, an RN, prepared such great meals and kept such a cogent household that I went for six straight years without missing a day of school to illness. She taught me subtle cooking touches, such as how to add ingredients in the proper order to enhance the flavors of each. Our home meals were so well crafted that eating out held little interest for me. Even today it is rare for a restaurant chef to outdo my mother's daily fare.

One of Margaret's unfulfilled quests was to re-create the immense round loaves of dark rye bread her grandmother Anna had crafted in a wood stove, as Anna had learned in her home country. I have this recipe in the wooden box of hand-written recipes I inherited. Margaret never felt she had the bread just right, even after hours of consultation and mutual baking efforts with her sisters and friends. As I continue that quest, I find that my efforts improve when I turn to heritage grains and natural leavening. But even these efforts are probably not as nutritious or as flavorful as they would have been during Anna's time, because nutritional quality has been sacrificed for commercial appeal.

My father, Clarence, who was born in a log home on a farm in Nebraska, inherited his grandfather's farming genes. He became a respected science teacher and then a labor lawyer, but he always missed the land. During World War II, at the end of his workday, he took over two vacant lots near the duplex apartment they rented so he could grow a Victory Garden. He grew enough so that he could give fresh vegetables to several neighbors. My parents loved to tell the story of how they scrubbed their bathtub with cleanser one year, using the vessel to ferment a hardy crop of cabbage. The apartment stunk for two weeks, and my parents imposed on the neighbors upstairs when they needed a shower. They paid them in sauerkraut. The canned stuff, Clarence added, was never as good.

When I was young he nurtured tomato plants on the south side of our house until they stood 8 feet tall and strained under the weight of bright red globes. I live in that same house today, and I tend the same compost pile—though I have shifted the garden to the front yard as the tree canopy expanded.

I try to carry forward food traditions that are harder and harder to maintain as our lives have become uprooted. As just one example, I cook oxtail soup each year at Christmastime, as Margaret did. None of my childhood friends had any idea what oxtails were, but for me the soup conveyed a rich story as well as winter nourishment. During the Depression, a few years after Margaret's father died suddenly from an unrecognized heart defect when she was 16, her uncle, Louis Kreuz, owned a meatpacking house in the same town. On Saturdays, he would bring oxtails to give to her family, 10 children with a single mother, at the end of his workday. It was one of his ways of easing their burden. Margaret's carefully crafted holiday ritual served as a warning to her sons on multiple levels: people sacrificed so you could be here today. Be ready, because hard times may come again. Clarence underscored the message with his own stories. His first wife and an infant son had both died in childbirth, and he had lost all of his savings when his rural bank closed, in the span of one week in 1931. No packaged foods could convey such heritage.

Does the United States Truly "Feed the World?"

In our public discourse, it is difficult for us to comprehend the extractive nature of the food system because we carry an image in our minds that the US "feeds the world." The reality is far more nuanced.

Our country has constructed some of the most productive agriculture, and some of the grandest supermarkets, on the planet. Technological advances have fashioned attractive packaging that extends shelf life to a remarkable extent. American consumers spend $1.7 trillion each year purchasing food, an amount roughly equivalent to the value of the Apple corporation.

Yet the US food system endures a tortuous crisis. In this country that "feeds the world," SNAP (Supplemental Nutrition Assistance Program) benefits (food stamps) have escalated from $7 billion in 1969 (in 2017 dollars) to $60 billion in 2017. In many farm communities where I work, more net income is earned through food stamp benefits than by farming, and even farm families find they need SNAP. In some areas of the Heartland, farmers spend more purchasing farm chemicals (to grow commodities for export) than would be required to feed all of the residents of their county for a year.

One of every 8 Americans—40 million people—is food insecure, meaning that at some point during the year, they are not sure where their next meal is coming from. At the same time, people who eat too little are getting fat because their diet is out of balance. Two of every three Americans are either overweight (35%) or obese (31%).

Diet- and exercise-related illnesses, such as diabetes, have become epidemic. Americans now spend $327 billion each year paying the medical costs of diabetes. This amounts to 90 percent of the $359 billion farmers earned by selling crops and livestock in 2018. In a very real way, for each dollar we spend buying commodities from a farmer, we give a second dollar to our health care system to treat us for the consequences of the food we eat and our lack of physical activity.

In 2017, long before the deeper disruption caused by the coronavirus pandemic, net farm income was lower than at the onset of the Great Depression. US farmers earned a net cash income of only $4 billion in 2017, far less than the $56 billion (in 2017 dollars) the sector earned a century ago, even though farmers more than doubled productivity. The number of farms declined from 6.4 million to 2 million, so there are far fewer rural families holding a sense of ownership in their communities. Meanwhile farming has become the most dangerous occupation in the country.

This is all a consequence of constructing a food system in the US that subsidizes commodities but holds that communities should fend for themselves. Farmers raise tons of cash crops and livestock that are industrially processed or exported, but sell only a small fraction of what they produce ($2.8 million, or 0.7%) directly to US households. Meanwhile consumers search further and further for the foods we eat. More than half of the fresh fruit eaten in the United States was imported in 2016, up from 23 percent in 1975. Fresh vegetable imports rose from 5.8 percent to 31.1 percent over the same period.

Speaking socially, youth have become an export crop of farm communities, nurtured carefully just like field corn, and then shipped to urban centers. The intense competitive pressures placed upon farmers producing for global markets sets farm family against farm family and limits many aspiring commodity farmers' notions of success to, "What is the biggest equipment I can buy?" or worse, "How can I purchase my neighbor's farm?"

Consumers are similarly atomized. The average American knows less about where their food comes from, or how it was produced, than their ancestors a century ago. Schools have steadily dismantled programs in agricultural education and home economics. Few Americans hold even a rudimentary understanding of food safety, and thousands do not even have pots or pans in their kitchens. But almost all shoppers recognize corporate food logos.

What Should a Food System Accomplish?

Those who launch community food webs are challenging the prevailing food system at a fundamental level, asking for better outcomes. What, then, should a food system *accomplish*?

For many food investors or businesses, the principal purpose is to reward shareholders with dividends. Such a confining definition of success inevitably distorts our understanding of the food system by giving us a shallow view. It overlooks important concerns that do not fit into that limited purpose. Thinking only of monetary margins and returns, farmers and business managers often focus solely on cutting costs or increasing sales. While important, the outcomes described above make it clear that this is insufficient.

Overlooked in this notion of success are the environmental costs associated with raising food as cheaply as possible. These may be invisible today, but they will haunt our grandchildren in the future. Overlooked are the cultural celebrations that help place farmers and consumers in a productive, rooted context and keep spirits strong. Overlooked is the central importance food plays in cultivating health, and the distribution of wealth that results from the food choices consumers make. Overlooked is the need to direct the healthiest food we can produce to those who can least afford it, for the sake of public health.

My own definition of the purpose of any food system is that it should build four key strengths in each community where it operates: health, wealth, connection, and capacity. Implicit in each of these is the imperative of creating equity.

Health

Foremost, an effective food system should build health among its constituents. Eating the most nutritious food possible is, after all, the number one strategy any of us has for staying healthy. This is the way we bring essential vitamins, minerals, micronutrients, protein, and carbohydrates into our bodies. This is how we feed the microbiota we depend upon to stay healthy. If our food is tainted with disease-bearing microbes or chemical residue, or if it lacks nutritional value, we are likely to suffer complications later on in our lives.

On the producer side, raising food should also involve physical labor that makes us stronger. A successful food system cannot be built on the backs of farmers or farmworkers who contract cancer from exposure to chemicals, or who must shoulder repetitive, boring tasks that deplete the soul. The work has to hold meaning and help connect us to others. It must also be spiritually and financially rewarding. That brings me to the second purpose: wealth.

Wealth

It is also immediately apparent that a food system must build wealth in communities. This is particularly true for farm communities. If farm families do not build wealth by farming, and do not trade with those who live nearby, the food system will be unstable. A food system centered on a few wealthy individuals or corporations that own almost all the land, trade largely outside of their communities, and hold disproportionate political power is a type of feudalism—not a democracy.

On the surface, it may appear that consumers benefit from low prices paid to farmers at the farm gate, and that this advances their own prosperity. Yet purchasing food items grown by distant farmers sends money away from the communities where consumers live, and it limits local farmers' income in ways that are overlooked by national data sets. Grocery stores can only exercise independent judgment if the stores are locally owned and responsive to farmer and consumer needs. In general, the greater the consolidation of power and finance, the fewer options communities hold. After all, the primary reason a supermarket chain enters a given community is the promise of drawing profits from consumer purchases. Ultimately, when this happens, wealth is built by outsiders, at the expense of local choice. To counter this, consumers can help build their community's wealth by purchasing food at a fair price from farmers they know.

Connection

Less visible in our civic discourse is the need for a food system to connect people more closely to each other. This is one of the reasons serving culturally resonant foods is so important—people come together at such meals to strive for a sense of belonging, to celebrate their heritage of working the land, and to honor ancestors who carved out successful lives amid great adversity.

Ample research has shown that those communities holding the most equitable social connectivity are those most able to respond to crisis. And food is an exceptionally potent connector. Sadly, most policy discussions completely overlook our need to connect around food.

Capacity

Finally, an effective food system builds the capacity of its community members to make smart choices and take effective action on their own behalf. Those who engage with an effective food system will know how food is grown (and this understanding is central to people's making healthy food choices as consumers). Such knowledge will help them prepare safe, healthful, and savory foods. Knowing how food is grown also enables consumers to make informed decisions as they shop and eat.

Unfortunately, an industrialized society such as our own suppresses our personal skills in handling food safely because of the multitude of prepackaged items we enjoy. Many people are so distant from farms that they cannot recognize common raw vegetables. Few understand what is involved in growing food. Consumers often rely on a frozen-food container or canned-food label to tell them how to prepare a product, never learning to construct a nutritious meal for themselves. As a people, we have come to accept, and even expect, simple answers. The ease of selecting from a menu has often become preferable to the complexity of learning from the fits and starts we experience as we make things with our own hands.

Building a Culture of Collaboration

As I have already discussed, the prevailing US food system fails on all four of these counts. We are compelled to create alternatives. Although none of the emergent community-based food webs covered in this book have achieved global success, each has progressed on all four fronts. Each cluster of food leaders takes deliberate steps forward until larger opportunities open up. Each identifies at least one key "lever" to shift, creating larger impacts in their community food system. Each has, in its own way, built a local culture that fosters greater collaboration—by connecting personally to build trust, by heightening a sense of mutual respect, and by keeping a focus on where they are trying to move over the long term. It is these cultural webs that unify the diverse campaigns to build health, wealth, connection, and capacity.

Many of the groups that are represented here are telling their stories for the first time. Each spells out the pragmatic steps they took, but each of those steps was taken in a unique context at one particular time. I trust readers will sift through these stories looking for clues about how to adapt the strategies portrayed here in their own communities.

No single book can capture all of the stories that could be told about this vibrant movement. Indeed, it was difficult to limit myself to the stories presented here. Many others could be told: From 2003 to 2010, I attended annual meetings of the Community Food Security Coalition, where as many as 1,000 food animators convened to share insights. Each of them would have similar stories to convey. The ones I include here are the ones I can tell the best, because I am the most closely connected to them, and because people volunteered their time to share their experiences and refine my account. That said, it is also true that my colleague Megan Phillips Goldenberg and I have been invited to assist some of the most farsighted community foods initiatives, so these rank among the most inspiring stories I know.

Moreover, this book focuses on food initiatives that have flourished since the mid-1980s. But the latest iteration of this movement began about 1969–70, and claims roots that go back to Reconstruction and beyond. Among the first visionaries guiding the current wave were members of the Federation of Southern Cooperatives, who mobilized tens of thousands of Blacks against terrifying opposition to build wealth in their community. FSC members pooled their savings so Blacks could purchase farmland, built solid savings accounts, and formed cooperative food businesses. FSC invited me to their offices and fields for interviews in 1986, but their own members can tell a more complete story. In northern metro areas, the food movement expressed itself through young farmers who relocated to rural areas to grow food for people to eat. They collaborated with urbanites who formed cooperative grocery stores. Urban gardening and greenhouse efforts emerged in ethnic neighborhoods of cities such as Chicago, Detroit, Los Angeles, and New York.

A Preview of This Book

This book has three basic parts. First, I present a financial accounting of the ways that the prevailing commodity system has extracted wealth from rural communities. In the second part, I highlight several of the most impactful efforts to build community food webs that I have had the privilege to partner with. Finally, I will summarize several critical themes that guide this work, again drawing on specific field examples.

Chapter 1 includes a series of charts that will show how cynical policy makers took advantage of the 1973 OPEC energy crisis to transform a farm economy that was somewhat balanced into one that inherently extracts wealth from rural America (and urban America, as well, although this is more difficult to document). This occurred just after a community foods movement began to emerge. Further, the chapter identifies four periods over the past century when US farmers reached brief moments of prosperity, and explains why that occurred. It will show how volatile farm income has become, and how consistently net income eroded, even in a commodity industry that is highly favored in policy circles and heavily subsidized. This is critically important to understand, because the primary justification for the prevailing food system is that it generates wealth. Truly, it does, but only for some and at the expense of others. Its core impact is to extract wealth from rural communities, especially.

Chapter 2 opens the second part of the book with an account of how rural Montanans devised ways, amid the Farm Credit Crisis of the mid-1980s, to bring farmers and researchers together to cultivate more sustainable farming practices, and ultimately to grow more food for Montana consumers. Local groups formed neighborhood by neighborhood, collaborating to devise practical ways for improving soil health and to fashion new markets. These co-learning groups, in turn, were carefully networked by AERO, an organization that had initially focused on alternative energy, into a statewide force that crafted enduring policies. Guiding this effort was a group of compassionate leaders who formed strong bonds of trust with each other, adapted to change, and unleashed tremendous creative energy. In one remote town of 2,000, a $5 million food processing business emerged from this process to become a national leader in community foods production.

Hawai'i also forged a statewide network of community foods leaders, as chapter 3 shows. This network was born out of a crisis of a very different kind: the chronic vulnerability that Hawai'i faces as a group of islands that lie 2,500 miles from the farms where most of their food is produced. Once again, a group of leaders began by establishing strong trust with each other. In this case, they partnered with low-income people who were the most threatened by the fragility of the food supply. A food bank, a research and policy organization, a Native Hawaiian-managed health center, and a state department of health official collaborated, making innovative use of public programs to connect more closely with their communities. The food bank assembled farm-fresh produce into boxes that were sold at a reduced price to low-income residents. New farm enterprises were launched to grow traditional foods. The clinic served low-cost, healthy meals to its low-income constituents. SNAP Education funds allowed me and my colleague Megan Phillips Goldenberg to assess the strengths and weaknesses of the state's food system. An innovative farmer-training program was launched on the site of a former plantation, in partnership with a second health center, that is refashioning itself to serve as a community gathering point. One of the core insights propelling this work is that recovering traditional cultural practices helps to overcome the state's divisive legacy of plantation agriculture.

A food bank in Tucson also instigated far-reaching change by inventing new models of food banking, as chapter 4 spells out. Weary of being stuck in a pattern of handing out food to a rising number of hungry people, leaders at the Community Food Bank of Southern Arizona set a new course of encouraging their constituents to take civic and policy leadership roles. One low-income woman began working with her neighbors at a farm-training program; she challenged neighborhood leaders so effectively that she was elected to serve as a municipal official. One food bank client fashioned a thriving food business using an old family recipe. A school counselor engaged low-income students in planting a school garden, in the process learning that he could reach them in deeper ways than his academic training had taught. He built a solid network of support among their parents, who rallied to save the school when it was threatened with closure. Now the food bank is challenging its constituents to engage in the governance of the food bank itself. Supporting this effort, I analyzed the region's farm and food economy.

Chapter 5 highlights a food initiative mounted by economic developers in northeast Indiana, who gained transformative insights by listening closely to community members. After an initial attempt to bring commodity farmers and nationally prominent food processors into a collaborative network floundered, members of the Northeast Indiana Regional Partnership discovered, through a study I wrote, that a network of farmers were already growing food for household consumers. They also connected themselves to a long-standing community effort to engage low-income residents in building a more responsive food supply. Separately, these developers embraced a deeper vision—one which explicitly states that the region needs new immigrants to keep its economy vital.

Economic development also propelled the formation of a local food network in Southeast Ohio, highlighted in chapter 6. Over four decades, this effort has matured into one of the more advanced food-business efforts in the US. A cadre of young leaders moved to Athens, Ohio, decades ago because they sensed an openness to change. Working closely with low-income residents, these leaders altered their own course after realizing that creating a space where people could launch their own food-processing businesses would do the most to reduce poverty in their region. The ACEnet Business Incubator has become one of the country's most accomplished resources for food business development. ACEnet further expanded into a second operation in Nelsonville, Ohio, where woodworking equipment, office space, and warehouse storage provide places where residents can create their own economic opportunities. At the center of this process, ACEnet leaders told me, was the formation of a broad network of civic support that helped foster better economic development efforts.

On the other hand, narrow-minded economic development can also pose a dire threat to food networks, as chapter 7 spells out. Pressure for building new housing subdivisions and commercial properties in Phoenix is intense, despite evidence that water supplies are limited, and despite a lack of planning to ensure that new residents will have food. The price of land has skyrocketed, meaning that established and highly productive farms cannot afford to purchase land with water rights. So developers have bought vast tracts of farmland, waiting for an opportune moment to build. Several farms serving Phoenix consumers have been forced to relocate or close. The Maricopa County Food System Coalition asked Megan and me to map the networks their work had constructed. We found that farmers felt isolated, not only from each other but from the wider community. By bringing these findings to city officials, the coalition sparked a municipal effort to purchase food from these farmers and to engage them in planning a better food future for the region.

Potential conflicts between agriculture and suburban development were addressed elegantly in Brighton, Colorado, as chapter 8 documents.

After two farmers asked public officials to protect the rural quality of their town from encroaching development, fierce opposition broke out from landowners who wanted to sell their properties at high prices. Undaunted, city staff collaborated closely with Adams County staff to host public meetings as part of a comprehensive planning process so concerns could be aired. Taking a bold step based on our market research, the City purchased one farm property at its development value but reserved the land for agricultural use. This action sent a signal that the agricultural heritage of the community would also frame its future. Now this district has been rebranded as the Historic Splendid Valley. The land best suited for farming has been protected, and development was channeled to other properties. Brighton now hopes to develop a cluster of food businesses that will depend on these local farms.

The final food web story also involves protecting land. In Dakota County, Minnesota, an extensive network of greenways has been built patiently over 35 years, even as suburban development advanced. This effort was sparked by a group of environmentalists who intervened to protect the water quality of the Mississippi River and ensure that wildlife could thrive. One savvy county staff person worked quietly behind the scenes to shepherd the process of building civic support for protecting greenways. Attending thousands of meetings with residents' groups and township boards, he took deliberate steps to help public support coalesce. Although developers were initially skeptical about protecting open space, they have come to realize that home values are now higher because buyers want to live near these greenways for the open space and recreational opportunities they provide.

The third section of *Building Community Food Webs* identifies key themes that arise as communities try to construct effective food webs. Chapter 10 opens this section by describing how three community foods efforts have forged solid connections between farmers and consumers, to ensure that farmers build power in the marketplace. This chapter argues that this farmer-to-consumer connection is the most important one for food webs to make. Only if farmers hold the power to set prices and to build a network of support among community members can a food web be effective in the long term.

Chapters 11 and 12 tackle two related issues. Chapter 11 suggests that the most effective community food webs are those that set a course committing themselves to building resilient community-based food systems, not simply promoting local food items. This is because effective civic coordination is required to ensure the health of our soils, waterways, and people. This is especially true given the stark inequalities in our society.

Chapter 12 asks whether large-scale food system initiatives can even be helpful, given that so many of the difficulties we face are caused by large-scale economic systems that have become remote from their constituents. As the COVID-19 pandemic has shown, some of our largest systems are the most vulnerable when conditions change unexpectedly. Smaller-scale efforts have proven responsive to their constituents, but they are often financially stressed. The answer is to think critically about scale at each juncture, and to ensure that when one firm or network benefits from scaling up into a larger operation, the benefits of that size are shared broadly across the network.

In the Conclusion, the insights gleaned from these accounts are summarized in three ways. First, effective collaboration, built on considerable mutual respect and trust, drives the possibility of forming a culture of collaboration. As such a culture is fostered, effective networks form, creating new efficiencies in community food trade. This in turn strengthens local economies. Second, each of the initiatives covered in this book has further identified key "system levers," metaphorical levers that, when shifted, create larger, more lasting change. Since the issues community food webs face are so complex and the resistance so strong, it is critical that community food leaders identify these strategic leverage points and take action that reaps multiple rewards. Third, converting spontaneous food initiatives into lasting economic structures requires clustering local businesses so firms see that the success of the entire cluster is as important as the survival of their own business. The chapter ends by identifying the four key balance points that community food webs strive to address as they solidify their efforts to define food choices for themselves.

The pandemic, combined with the frightening political polarization that has taken root as our nation relives the social fragmentation that led to the Civil War, also illuminates the limitations of a society built on an individual notion of success. Although founded on the theft of Native lands, the institution of slavery, and denial of women's rights, the US Constitution did advance a collective concept of freedom: "We the People." It established a government intended to promote the "general Welfare," not simply an individualistic ethic. Indeed, freedom is inherently intertwined with responsibility and impossible to attain without equity. Yet how these collective and responsible notions of freedom have eroded over time!

Working with the groups covered in this book has kept me inspired despite the schisms that are erupting. I trust their stories will do the same for you. But first, a journey through the economic realities that impinge upon, and make necessary, this inspiring movement to build community food webs, in chapter 1.

CHAPTER 1

The Extractive US Farm Economy

Although US population and spending power have increased steadily, net farm income has declined dramatically. Farmers were far better off a century ago. While farmers earned 40 cents from every dollar of sales in 1910, net income from producing crops and livestock has fallen to Depression-era levels. Farmers now earn only one penny from each dollar they sell—a decline of 98 percent. In the country that claims to "feed the world," more of our food is imported than ever before. The economic structures that divide farmers from consumers systematically extract wealth from our communities. Each era in which farmers have won significantly more sales has led to further decline, not a more sustainable agriculture. Over time, the thrust of farm policy shifted from supporting market mechanisms to compensating farmers for the fact that markets were fundamentally unfair.

I have been invited to a wide range of rural communities over the past two decades, and welcomed by dogged leaders who work against great odds to weave stronger community fabrics and create healthier food systems. I am inspired by what these web weavers have accomplished with so few resources. You will read about some of their work in later chapters. At the same time, I often wonder why this work is so difficult to do, in a land of such prosperity.

I drive along midwestern Main Streets and see empty storefronts. Schools now carry hyphenated names because districts have been forced to merge to maintain a student population. I meet high school graduates who moved from rural communities to larger cities hoping to find greater opportunity. Often the county seats still boast a stately brick or stone courthouse, built more than a century ago by local craftsmen. Or they may host a grand church built by Italian stonemasons, imported for their exceptional skills—an expression of the community's aspirations for global importance. Each edifice speaks proudly of a bold future once imagined by remote small towns that barely had automobiles. That vision is long dispelled. Today, immense pole barns shelter half-million-dollar combines, within sight of lonely main streets. Trouble signs are the deepest where farms are largest, and where the myth that "America feeds the world" is the strongest. This chapter explores how rural America became hollowed out.

More Mouths to Feed, More Money to Spend, and Fewer Farms

The US population expanded from 92 million in 1910, about the time those aspiring civic edifices were built in midwestern towns, to 328 million in 2019. Personal income rose even faster, from about $1 trillion in 1910 (in 2017 dollars) to $17 trillion in 2017. Today consumers spend more than $1.7 trillion of that income buying food each year. That amounts to $850,000 per each of the farms that survive in the US.

With more mouths to feed, and the average household having more money to spend, it would seem that the US is well poised to support farmers generously, and to create whatever food system it chooses to create. Yet 12 percent of US households are now considered food insecure by the US Department of Agriculture (USDA). That tally measures the number of households that wonder, at some point during the year, whether they will have enough to eat.

Meanwhile, curiously, much of the political discourse about agriculture focuses on ways to export more food. In 2017, US farmers exported $47 billion of bulk commodities. This was only 13 percent of the commodities farmers sold. In the same year the US imported $33 billion of bulk food commodities. That is, net exports totaled $14 billion, only 4 percent of the value of the commodities farmers sold.

If our farmers are indeed feeding the world, it is not working out that well for farmers. By 2018, the net cash income from producing crops and livestock fell to $4 billion, lower than Great Depression–era levels, and only 1 percent of sales. USDA economists report that midwestern corn farmers are losing more than $60 *per acre* growing corn, losing $100 per acre of wheat, and gaining only $10 per acre growing soybeans. These are three of the main US export crops. I will offer more detail on this later.

Even though policymakers pursue new export markets, opportunities for new farmers wane. As Figure 1.1 shows, the US has hosted a fairly steady number of farms since 1990, about 2 million. This was a marked decline from the 6.3 million farms that grew food in the US in 1910. In some respects this demonstrates a triumph of efficiency. We have one farm for every 164 people today, compared with one farm for every 14 people a century ago.

However, most of today's farms, rather than growing food for their neighbors, are producing raw commodities, such as feed corn, cattle, and milk. If not exported, these are largely processed, whether to feed animals, to create consumer goods, or for industrial use. In short, farms mainly grow raw materials, not food items. Less than 1 percent of what farmers sell goes directly to household consumers. Farmers have been told that they hold a competitive advantage when they grow these commodities, and an entire system of supports has been established to encourage them to do so. But net income persistently declines.

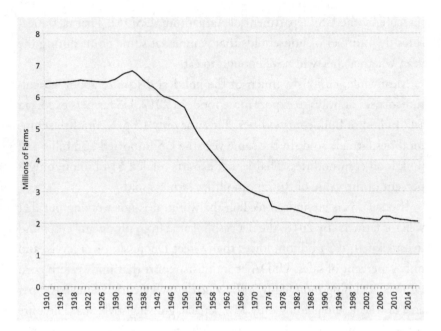

Figure 1.1. Farms in the US, 1910–2017. (USDA National Agricultural Statistics Service)

Net Cash Income for Farmers Erodes

A century ago, when farmers produced food for themselves and for households near their farms, they fared better economically. Figure 1.2 shows farm income and production expenses since that period, compiled by the USDA Economic Research Service.

This chart portrays the dramatic expansion of the farm economy we have experienced, with sales rising 62-fold over the century. Yet production costs rose even faster than cash receipts—a 100-fold increase. Thus there has been no real improvement in net cash income. This now stands at levels similar to 1983 and 1999, two of the most difficult years farmers have ever experienced, and even lower than during the Great Depression (1932). This occurred despite massive improvements in technology, scientific expertise, and productivity.

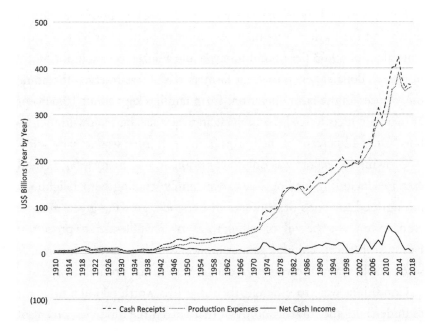

Figure 1.2. Net cash income for US farms, 1910–2018. (USDA Economic Research Service. Farm Income and Wealth Statistics. Current dollars, using the value of the dollar in each year data were reported.)

The era from 1910 to 1914 is still known by agricultural economists as the golden era of US agriculture, when prices were predictable and high for several years running. In those days, many crops were grown to feed or bed horses that labored in the fields, or to nourish livestock raised on the same farm. A wide variety of grasses were cultivated for feed, to build soil fertility, and to reduce weed pressure.

Since the US was one of the world's few large-scale producers, the country could set its own terms for food trade. The net cash income of farming was $2.2 billion (or $56 billion in 2018 dollars). This means that for every dollar of food products farmers sold, they earned 40 cents. Today net income stands at $4 billion. That is only one penny for every dollar sold.

Farmers earned more than they do today because both commodity prices and food prices were high. A pound of butter cost 39 cents, the equivalent of $9.63 per pound today, while a dozen eggs sold for $8.89 in today's dollars. Much of what farmers raised was reserved for home use, or used in the farm operation. Farm families kept about 10 percent of their products to feed themselves, and they also bartered with neighbors. Only 42 percent of the butter farmers churned was actually sold.

Growing for export was only one option among many a farm could exercise, including feeding one's own family; trading with neighbors; raising food for one's draft horses or livestock; growing green manure crops to improve the soil; or selling to a grocer, wholesaler, or processor. Farmers, in short, enjoyed greater choice as well as greater income. It seems likely that this diversity of choice helped fuel profitability.

Conditions were so different then that it is worth taking a moment to understand the rural economy of that era. At the time, 54 percent of the US population lived in rural areas. The average farm size was 138 acres, with a financial value of $6,444 ($159,000 in 2018 dollars). Over 62 percent of the farms were owned by the farm operator. Two of every three of these owned farms were free from mortgage debt, even though the country had gone through waves of recession during the previous 40 years.

The US economy was centered in large part around farming in 1910, but inequalities plagued that post-Reconstruction era. Nearly all (97%) of farm property was owned by Whites, even though people of color ran one of every seven farms (14%). This meant that many skilled farmers lacked wealth. More than 98 percent of the country's Black farm operators lived in the South, and three-fourths of these were tenant farmers. Only 24,000 farm operators were Native American, even fewer were Chinese or Japanese.

Thus the data I highlight in this chapter tell a story that primarily depicts the lives of those privileged enough to own land. Average debt for a farm that was mortgaged was $1,715 ($42,000 in today's currency), 27 percent of the value of a typical farm. Interest rates ran about 6 percent for mortgage loans with 5-year terms, with rates varying from region to region. Often farmers who had the means loaned money to their neighbors. Farmers trusted each other more than they trusted banks, which were often viewed as privileged firms that drew wealth out of their communities.

I should add that when I measure net cash income, I am making a different calculation than the USDA Economic Research Service typically makes. When the agency measures net income, it includes other sources of income, such as the value of stored inventories of crops or livestock. These are important to track, but I get a valuable perspective by examining whether the act of growing commodities actually pays for the costs of farming.

Adjusting for Inflation Reveals Different Patterns

As I hinted earlier, it is also important to adjust these counts for inflation, because the cost of living has eroded the value of the US dollar. In fact, a dollar earned in 1910 would be worth US$25 today. Figure 1.3 shows the same farm income data presented in Figure 1.2, but adjusted for inflation using the US Federal Reserve Bank's consumer price index. Showing data this way offers a picture of how hard farm families had to work over the past century to earn the dollar we use today.

After this adjustment is made, new insights emerge from the same data set. Growth in cash receipts seems farm more muted once dollars are held constant. Net income declines even faster. Most notably, after accounting for inflation, four periods of farm prosperity become visible: (1) the golden era of 1910–1914 described earlier, and followed by sales spurred by World War I through 1920; (2) the period during and immediately after World War II when wartime and recovery-era sales and new technology combined to boost farm income; (3) the OPEC

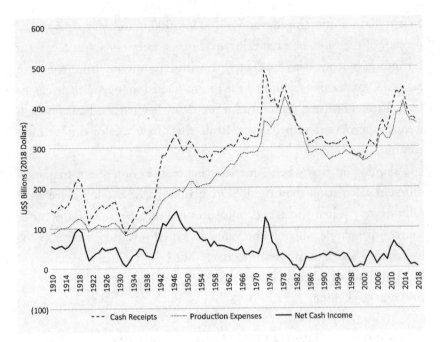

Figure 1.3. Adjusted net cash income for US farms, 1910–2018. (USDA Economic Research Service Farm Income Balance Sheet data. Adjusted for inflation using 2018 dollars.)

oil crisis of 1973–74, when the US sold massive shipments of grain to the USSR in order to retrieve dollars that had been spent purchasing oil at rising prices; and (4) the global housing debt crisis of 2008–11 when speculators' bidding up the price of grains and rising ethanol use conspired to create a commodity price bubble.

This adjusted chart shows that the only truly prosperous periods for US agriculture were due either to global market power (periods 1 and 2), now lost as other nations became competitive producers, or to external shocks (periods 1–4). Each bubble led to decline in the following years, not to lasting prosperity for the farm sector. Given how much these markets have been shaped with federal subsidies, tax incentives, and infrastructure investments that encourage long-distance commodity sales, this is a stark reality. I will say more about that later in this chapter.

Figure 1.3, however, shows only the income that farmers earned from selling crops and livestock. They enjoy several other sources of farm income not shown on this chart. These additional earnings increased from $12 billion in 1910 (adjusted for inflation) to $54 billion in 2018. That is to say, farmers earned 13.5 times more from farm-related income sources than by actually producing crops and livestock (net cash income of $4 billion, as stated earlier).

The main additional sources of farm-related income are (1) the imputed value farm families receive by living in their farm home (in accounting terms, the family essentially earns income by renting its farmhouse to the farm business); (2) insurance payments from commodity losses; (3) renting out land that someone else farms; and (4) doing custom farm work for a neighbor (e.g., harvesting their corn crop for pay). In recent years, the main components of farm-related income were imputed rental income ($19 billion in 2018), and insurance payments ($10 billion).

Off-Farm Income Becomes More Important

Farm families had ample reasons to turn to off-farm jobs. If one or more members of a family took such a job, it helped the entire family stay on the land despite the ups and downs of farming. First of all, with net income declining, it made sense to diversify. Having work off the farm helped offset the need for cash in the spring and the seasonality of farm harvests, and it served as a hedge against unpredictable weather conditions. Second, one or members of a farm family often sought employment to ensure that the family was covered with health insurance. And as mechanization advanced, many farmers could more easily schedule field chores around off-farm work shifts. Often, off-farm jobs simply paid better.

Farm-family incomes often surpass those of the average US household, but primarily this is due to their earning income off the farm, not by producing commodities. Figure 1.4 shows off-farm income per household for the years 1960 to 2017, the only years available. Household income from nonfarm sources rose to $90,000 per household per year, while income from farming is about $20,000, just a tad higher now than it was in the 1960s. From 1979 to 2011 farm income generally fell below 1960 levels. It increased in later years primarily because of the speculative bubble described earlier.

Productivity Doubles, But Brings Little Advantage

However, greater efficiency has not translated into more profitability. Ironically, although farms became phenomenally more productive, net income held steady at best. Figure 1.5 shows this for the postwar years. Productivity more than doubled from 1948 to 2004, as farmers

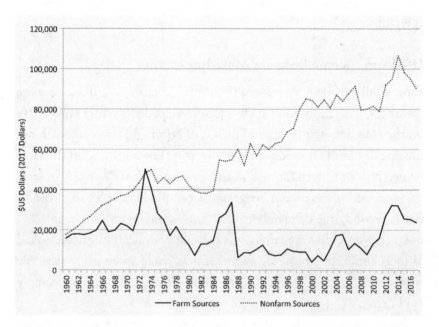

Figure 1.4. Adjusted income per household for US farms, 1960–2017. (USDA ERS Farm Household Income and Characteristics. Adjusted for inflation using 2017 dollars. Note that these figures represent average incomes per household.)

adopted more powerful farm machinery, relied more on manufactured fertilizers and pesticides, embraced more intensive practices, and gained greater scientific knowledge. By 2009, however, this innovation began to taper off, with the exception of a single year, 2013. This suggests that in the future, farm families are likely to seek ways for farming to become more *rewarding*, and pay less attention to boosting *productivity*.

One strong reason for farmers to consider shifting their priorities is that boosting productivity often means taking on new debt, since one of the most reliable ways farm families have had to increase output was to buy more land or purchase new technology—larger equipment, better technical expertise, chemical applications, and the like. Loans, while adding considerable opportunity, also compound the risks that are endemic to farming.

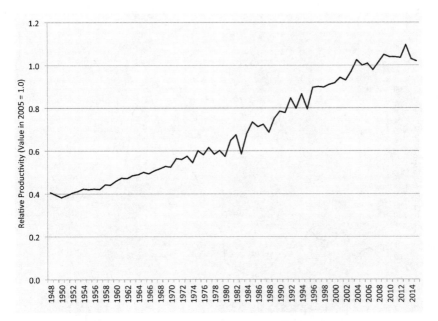

Figure 1.5. Total factor productivity for US farms, 1948–2015. (USDA Economic Research Service, Farm Productivity Series. Table 1. Indices of farm output, input, and total factor productivity for the United States, 1948–2015. The year 2005 is set to a value of 1, with other years compared to that year.)

Farm Debt Is a Potent Indicator of Farm Conditions

Figure 1.6 shows farm debt levels over the past century. Farm debt increased slightly during the so-called golden era, but it decreased during the World War II boom, then massively increased during the OPEC energy crisis, and rose again during the speculative bubble that began in 2008. Indeed, farmers I interviewed in 1978 told wistful stories about the post-WWII days when they had launched their farms and it was possible to earn enough money for a down payment to buy land simply by farming for a year. These same farmers predicted trouble when they saw their neighbors taking on new debts beyond their means in the late 1970s. They saw the farm credit crisis of the 1980s brewing long before anyone else I knew.

Even prosperity can have a shadow side. The high commodity prices of the golden age, followed by strong sales during and after World War I,

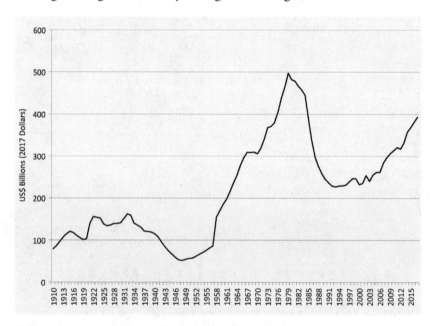

Figure 1.6. Total debt held by US farms, 1910–2017. (USDA Economic Research Service Farm Income Balance Sheet data. Adjusted for inflation using 2017 dollars.)

contributed to a production glut. After Europe restored its own agriculture following the war, US farm prices collapsed and credit dried up. Protectionism caused further economic trauma. These were significant causes of the Great Depression globally, though often overlooked by scholars who focused on the stock market. The prosperity bubble of the 1973–1974 OPEC energy crisis, combined with Secretary of Agriculture Earl Butz's exhortations to "plant fence row to fence row" in order to satisfy "permanent markets abroad" that he promised to find, led to a new phase of massive overproduction, a collapse in grain prices, and the farm credit crisis. It is too early to fully understand the overall impacts of the speculative bubble that began in 2008, but Figure 1.6 shows that this bubble, once again, encouraged farmers to take on additional debt—not to pay off their loans.

This suggests that whether total farm debt increases or decreases is a potent indicator for understanding farm-sector finance. Indeed, successful farmers have often been cautious about taking on debt, both because they felt it would draw money out of their rural community and because one of the key causes of losing a farm is holding debt that is not repaid.

Who Holds Farm Debt?

There is also a deeper level to the story of debt. Not only was farm debt far lower in 1910 than it is today, it was largely held by individuals. Many aspiring middle-class investors turned to farms as one part of their portfolio, often working through a local agent who would aggregate loans on their behalf. Many of these farmer interest payments nonetheless cycled back to households, including city-dwellers who lived close to farms.

In other settings, especially in the South, individual merchants typically offered loans to farmers. This could easily become an exploitive relationship. Farmers would inevitably borrow to cover seed and input costs, as well as family living expenses, during the growing season. But if the harvest was meager or if prices fell, they could not repay the loans. Their families still needed to buy life essentials, but this meant taking on even more debt from the same merchant. Distressing cycles of debt and dependency were created, plaguing sharecroppers and tenants especially.

Banks were a relatively unimportant source of farm debt. Indeed, in some communities, farmers with financial means invested in shares of bank stock but refused to borrow from those same banks. Studies in Minnesota and Illinois found that farmers who borrowed mortgage funds from a neighboring farmer could often simply extend the loan without penalty if they fell behind. Farmer-lenders, it seems, understood the uncertainties of farming. These direct loans also expressed farmers' preference for keeping money inside the community, because a bank might invest elsewhere.

Following the global Depression, influential policy makers recommended rationalizing farm lending by directing it to commercial banks. Economists reasoned that farmers would have greater access to capital if they financed through a banking system, and the lending would in theory be more professional.

However, as farms became increasingly dependent on technology that was sourced outside of their communities, on selling commodities globally, and on lenders that were owned by outside parties, farm interest payments no longer recycled into further economic opportunity for local farms and businesses. Rather, they were siphoned off into what economists often consider "higher uses," essentially metropolitan economies.

Potent insights into the shift toward external sources of credit are given in Figure 1.7, showing which entities held farm debt. This chart shows that in 1910, nearly 80 percent of all farm debt was held by individuals, whereas only 10 percent is held by individuals today. While individual lending has maintained a solid niche, hovering around $35 billion each year, this is far less than the $60 billion of farm debt (in 2017 dollars) that individual lenders held in 1910. And total farm debt, as Figure 1.6 shows, has quadrupled (in adjusted dollars).

Commercial lenders, on the other hand, have been ascendant, expanding from extending 13 percent of farm debt in 1910 to holding 41 percent today. Most commercial farm lenders in 1910 were community based, so interest payments were likely to return to serve as investments in the rural community itself. Today, many small-town banks are merely outposts of larger firms controlled from a distant office. Even a federally initiated credit source, the Farm Credit System, which began as a farmer-run cooperative, has shifted to become a "government-sponsored enterprise" now accounting for another 43 percent of all farm debt.

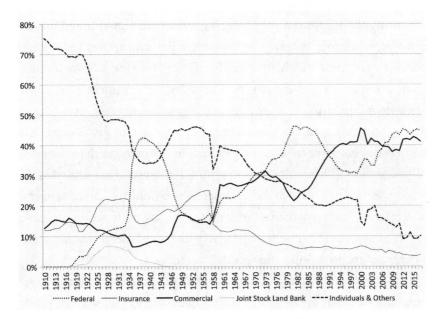

Figure 1.7. US farm debt by source, 1910–2017. (USDA Economic Research Service Farm Income Balance Sheet data. Adjusted for inflation using 2017 dollars.)

Figure 1.7 also helps illuminate the same four periods of farm prosperity identified in Figure 1.3 and discussed earlier. Individual loans declined slightly in importance during the golden era but remained the vastly preferred form of credit. After the turmoil of the Great Depression, and with White farmers who owned land helping to write more effective farm policy during the New Deal, the federal government stepped into lending. The impact was to *restore the strength of individual lending*. When the OPEC energy crisis hit in 1973, federal loans once again emerged as an important intervention into the farm economy. However, in this era the impact of federal loans was *to encourage greater reliance on commercial lending*. By 1988, when the Farm Credit System was converted from a federal loan program to a quasi-private entity, this shift became complete. Now commercial loans, including loans that were once made by the Farm Credit System as a federal institution, became the predominant source of farm debt.

During the Depression, the federal government also assumed for the first time a key role in providing support to the farm sector. Three basic policies were enacted, which were effective because the US was a dominant producer in global markets. The federal government established price floors, held prices steady by creating grain reserves, and loaned money to farmers on favorable terms. These programs guaranteed that farmers did not have to sell their products at prices lower than the costs of production. These supports were not expensive, since the government was assuring that private transactions would be fair to farmers, not offering cash payments. Moreover, the costs of storing reserve stocks of grain at the time were relatively low. The federal treasury actually earned income, and rural wealth was retained.

Conditions have changed dramatically since the New Deal era. As international trade agreements lowered trade barriers on selected products, multinational grain companies began to hedge against both farmers' power to set prices and weather disruption by investing in production abroad, notably in Brazil and Argentina. Essentially, investors used profits earned by trading grain at prices well below the farmers' costs of production for the purpose of creating more competition for those very farmers, ensuring that grain prices remained low over the long term. Emerging grain producers in other countries, carrying lower costs, placed even more downward pressure on prices by increasing grain supplies relative to demand. Later, China entered the market in a forceful way, both as a consumer of US grains and livestock and as a producer of foods that are now imported into the US.

Thus the very foundation of New Deal policy—the assumption that the US could set its own price levels as the dominant producer—is no longer in effect. Global markets hold prices low, since production is expanding. US farms are among the higher-cost producers, so they are no longer favored. Grain storage facilities have become more expensive to maintain. So the thrust of farm policy shifted from supporting fair market mechanisms to offering individual farms some compensation for the reality that markets are unfair. This ultimately meant supporting farmers to produce at a loss, and created economic structures that ensured these losses became a permanent feature of the landscape.

Federal Policy Once Promoted Community Capacity

Farm debt, of course, requires farmers to pay interest on loans, so I consider interest payments next. Figure 1.8 shows total interest payments made by US farmers since 1910. During most eras, as this chart shows, farmers pay a relatively steady amount of money to cover interest charges, even when total debt increases. The big exception was the OPEC energy crisis bubble, when farmers shouldered new loans during a brief period of prosperity but could not repay them once prices returned to normal levels. The massive peak of $57 billion in interest payments in 1982, after the Soviet Union stopped purchasing grain, was the primary cause of the farm crisis of the mid-1980s. The crisis was alleviated after considerable turmoil—including bankruptcies, fore-closures, and national protests—when lenders and farmers worked together to write down farm debt to sustainable levels.

The same patterns hold with interest payments as with overall farm debt, of course. From 1910 to the mid-1960s, farmer interest payments were more likely to cycle back into the community where the farm was located. After that time, interest payments increasingly fled to external owners, leaving rural communities considerably weakened.

Farmers Subsidize the Broader Economy

By producing at a loss, farmers gave significant subsidies to the overall economy. Figure 1.9 shows the payments that federal programs have returned to the farm sector since 1910 (once again in inflation-adjusted

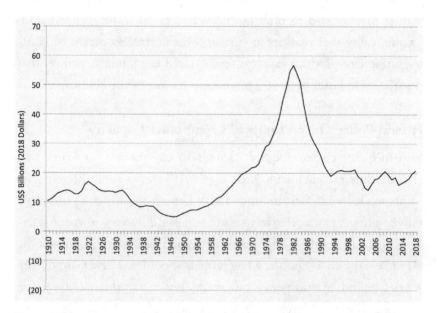

Figure 1.8. Interest payments by US farmers, 1910–2018. (USDA Economic Research Service Farm Income Balance Sheet data. Adjusted for inflation using 2018 dollars.)

dollars). First launched in 1933, federal programs contributed as much as $37 billion (in 2018 dollars) to the farm sector per year during the farm credit crisis. Figure 1.9 vividly shows that subsidies varied widely, depending on the ever-changing provisions of the US farm bill, buffeted back and forth as markets shifted and different parties took power in Congress. From the standpoint of the farmer, this is a critical, but quite fickle, support net. From the standpoint of policy makers and taxpayers, farm programs that once paid for themselves now have become far more complex and expensive. They have required at least a $10 billion allocation every single year for the past three decades—and grew considerably larger once the pandemic hit.

How effectively did federal payments compensate the farm sector as farmers increasingly paid interest to institutions outside their communities? The answer, unfortunately, is not very well. They did not even

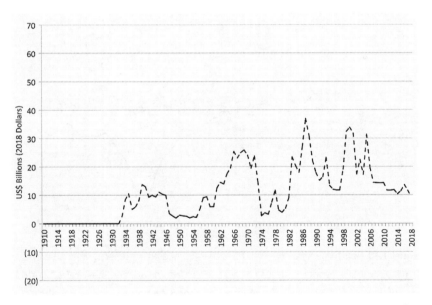

Figure 1.9. Government payments to US farmers, 1910–2018. (USDA Economic Research Service Farm Income Balance Sheet data. Adjusted for inflation using 2018 dollars.)

begin to compensate for the money farmers had spent paying interest on loans. To illustrate this, I combine the data from Figures 1.8 and 1.9 into a single chart, Figure 1.10. Here I place the value of interest payments as negative numbers, since money flowed *from* the farm sector. Government payments are shown as positive numbers because they flowed *to* the farm sector.

I make two simplifications in doing this. First, I assume that all interest payments flowed away from the farm sector, even though I understand that there was considerable recycling of interest payments back to farmers before the 1960s. Offsetting this, some interest payments were made to exploitive local lenders, which were unlikely to

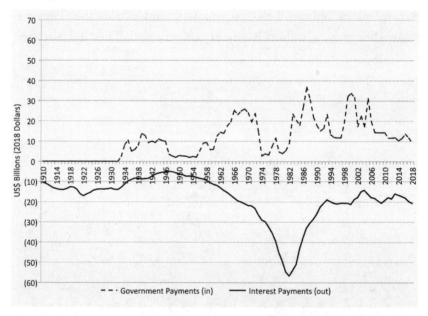

Figure 1.10. Government payments to US farmers compared to farmer interest payments, 1910–2018. (USDA Economic Research Service Farm Income Balance Sheet data. Adjusted for inflation using 2018 dollars. Government payments are treated as flows into the farm sector nationally (positive numbers above the x-axis), while interest payments are treated as flows away from the farm sector (negative numbers below the x-axis).

reinvest in communities. These cannot be measured precisely, but I assume both are small enough to be overlooked for my purposes. Next, I assume that all government payments to the farm sector are channeled to the communities where farmers farm, even though some farm payments are directed to landowners who do not reinvest those funds into their farms. In addition, many farmland owners now live in distant cities. These nuances appear to be small enough to overlook for this discussion.

Furthermore, farmer interest payments are only one channel through which rural communities lose potential wealth. An even more forceful erosion of wealth, I suspect, involves tax payments. But tax data are kept private, impossible to analyze except by government officials or their agents. The analysis spelled out here, while distressing, is only the tip of the iceberg. It is a massive tip.

Money Flows Away from Farms

When the money farmers spent paying interest on loans is subtracted from the money they gained through subsidies, it is clear that farmers suffered an overall loss. The largest outflow occurred between 1974 and 1986. This is portrayed in Figure 1.11.

Figure 1.11 shows that in 1922, before federal subsidies were instituted, interest payments peaked briefly. Borrowing by urban industrialists made capital scarce in both rural and urban areas. Net outflows hovered around $15 billion per year. When federal programs were introduced in 1933, and for the next four decades, net outflows were reduced to near zero. Beginning in 1973, however, as farmers were pressured to "get big or get out of agriculture," an immense sea change swept over the farm sector. Farmers took on massive new debts. Interest payments far overshadowed federal payments, creating immense outflows that became a permanent presence in the economy. Once debts were written down in 1985–86, a

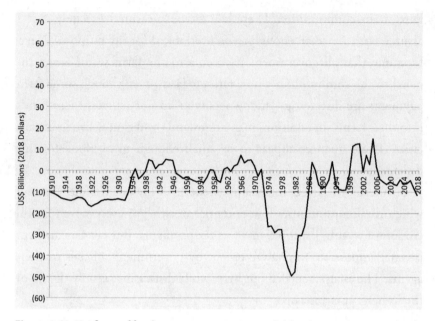

Figure 1.11. Net flows of funds: government payments (in) less interest payments (out) for US farms, 1910–2018. (USDA Economic Research Service Farm Income Balance Sheet data. Adjusted for inflation using 2018 dollars.)

semblance of balance was restored, but with considerable upheaval year to year as markets and policies shifted. After 2007, outflows once again became the norm.

Federal Policy Once Created a Sense of Balance

For two periods, then, government policy held net outflows to low levels, creating a sense of balance in rural communities. This included the first four decades of federal intervention, from 1933 to 1973, and the period after debts were written down, from 1987 to 2006. However, as mentioned earlier, money flowed massively outward from 1974 to 1986.

To show how these outward flows accumulated over time, I present the data from Figure 1.11 as cumulative flows in Figure 1.12. This shows remarkable losses. Before federal farm programs kicked in starting in

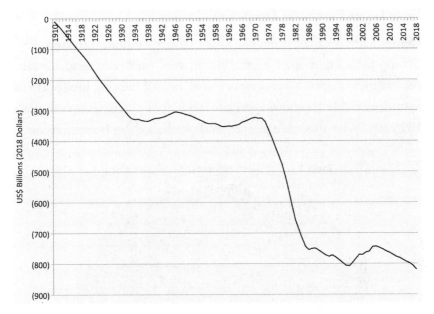

Figure 1.12. Cumulative balance of government payments less interest paid by US farmers, 1910–2018. (USDA Economic Research Service Farm Income Balance Sheet data. Adjusted for inflation using 2018 dollars.)

1933, $300 billion of interest payments left the farm sector. Then, with the birth of New Deal farm programs, interest payments were so closely balanced by federal subsidies that it appears policy makers understood the need to replace farmer interest payments if farmers were to keep farming—and thus continue to purchase farm inputs.

In 1973, however, the bipartisan consensus for balance broke down. A massive increase in interest payments instigated a $450-billion extraction of money from the farm sector in little more than a decade. By 2018, more than $800 billion had flowed away from the farm sector. That is 3 percent of the aggregate value of $30 trillion of crops and livestock (in 2018 dollars) which US farmers sold over that time span. That may not appear to be a large flow from the standpoint of the national economy, but it was a staggering blow to rural communities.

Farm Input Purchases Deepen the Losses

Despite suffering these economic losses, farmers continued to farm. Purchasing farm inputs such as machinery, seed, fuel, and fertilizer each year, farmers helped other sectors thrive, even if farming itself was not rewarding. Table 1.1 shows aggregate farm input purchases over the past 109 years. With this table, deeper levels of the iceberg become visible.

Table 1.1. Cumulative production expenses paid by
US farmers, 1910–2018 (in 2018 dollars)

	$ billions
Feed	3,926
Livestock & poultry	2,019
Seed	820
Pesticides	651
Fertilizer, lime, & soil conditioners	1,463
Fuel & oils	1,092
Electricity	270
Cash labor	2,494
Capital consumption (w/o dwellings)	2,854

SOURCE: USDA ECONOMIC RESEARCH SERVICE. PRODUCTION EXPENSE SERIES.

The same patterns that held with interest payments apply to farm input purchases: inputs that at one time were raised on each farm for its own use became purchases made from a neighboring farm, and then increasingly morphed to become procurements drawing on more distant sources, global farm input corporations.

To take only one example from Table 1.1, farmers spent $3.9 trillion (in 2018 dollars) buying feed over the past century, above any feed they raised for their own use. Some was purchased from neighboring farms, but increasingly farmers turned to vendors offering proprietary and customized rations. Similarly, farmers shifted to purchasing young animals bred with specific genetic attributes. While seed production was once a very localized industry, corporate sourcing is now far more typical. Labor is still relatively localized, with the predominance of workers living on or near the farm. Yet, as immigrant labor becomes the norm, much of this income is recycled to the workers' home countries to help family members left behind. Capital consumption (the depreciated value of land, buildings, machinery, and other capital stock) can denote significant local value, but also invokes federal tax breaks that are hidden subsidies, visible only on tax forms. As machinery gets larger, farmers find that mechanics have become more specialized, and replacement parts must be purchased from a national warehouse.

All told, given these trends, farmers spent $24.5 trillion purchasing inputs over these 109 years, increasingly buying distant items that rural communities once produced for themselves. (Only selected costs are included in Table 1.1, listing farmers' cumulative purchases from 1910 to 2018.) I know of no accurate measure showing how many of these dollars flowed into or out of farming communities, so to illustrate the losses, I focus on three critical inputs—pesticides, fertilizers, and fossil fuels— that are produced almost entirely outside of the farm sector. These cost farmers $3.2 trillion (2018 dollars) over the past century. When added to the $800-billion loss in interest payments, at minimum, $4 trillion has left the US farm sector since 1910. This amounts to 13 percent of cash receipts. It is a conservative estimate. Several equally essential items, such as farm machinery, building materials, or purchased seeds, are not included. Most likely, far more has drained away.

I should add that farmers received tangible goods for each of these purchases. It is not that all of this money simply vanished into thin air. However, the convenience of consuming these inputs did involve tradeoffs. By spending money for things that could have been produced close to their farms, each rural community ended up abandoning its own capacities to grow or make its own life essentials. This is a smart tradeoff when one thinks that other regions are better at producing, say, machinery, and farmers can offer them corn, soybeans, or meat in exchange. However, when rural communities produce farm commodities at a loss, they hold no true competitive advantage. They are undermining their own ability to produce for themselves, and they lose their choice to sell only their surplus. They are participating in the erosion of their own economy.

To sum up, each expansion in cash receipts has sown the seeds of further decline. In three of the four eras of farm prosperity the US has experienced over the past century, resources were extracted from rural communities. The additional money farmers earned during a few years of promise encouraged them to take on new debts, and also prompted input dealers to raise their prices. Potent economic structures have been built to draw money away from rural America. This is not caused by the shortcomings of individual farm families. It is a failure of public policy.

Crop Returns Are Disappointing

Deepening this historic extraction are low margins that farm producers continue to endure. Consider the past 20 years of crop production by US farmers, shown in Figure 1.13. Four crops—corn, soybeans, wheat, and rice—represent a critical component of the commodity economy, and perhaps even more importantly, the US fantasy of feeding the world. All are valuable export crops. Corn and soy are paramount animal feeds. Soy is a major oil crop. All four are processed into manufactured food items.

Figure 1.13 presents net returns earned after paying the full costs of producing each of these crops, including the overall costs of purchasing and running a farm operation. This includes the costs of production, as well as the overhead costs of running a farm, such as buying land and replacing barns or farm machinery. While many farmers overlook these longer-term expenses as long as the farm covers its bills year by year, all come due at some point down the road.

Certain farmers really have few worries about covering full costs. A young farmer may have inherited land that was paid for several generations ago, or may be able to repair machinery for herself, so operating a farm may be more profitable than these data suggest. On the other hand, another farmer down the road may have recently purchased land at a price bid up by suburban development to levels that are difficult for a young farmer to sustain. He may have to purchase an array of new equipment because he is venturing into farming without parents or grandparents to help. His costs would likely exceed these averages. Costs of farming also vary region by region. Figure 1.13 merely shows

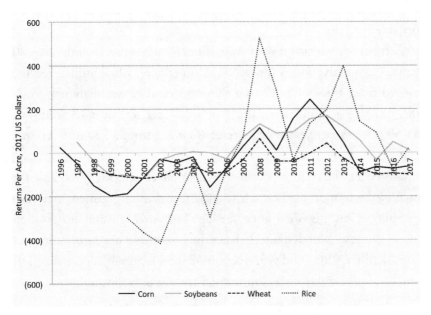

Figure 1.13. Returns per acre for four key US crops, 1996–2017. (USDA Economic Research Service Commodity Costs and Returns data. This shows return per acre when all operational costs are taken into account. Many farmers have higher or lower cost structures, or defer certain of these costs, so these data do not predict returns for a given farm.)

average values for revenues and costs, calculated per acre, for the nation. As before, these data are adjusted for inflation.

The results are rather striking. For corn, the premier cash crop, farmers have made a profit, on average, in only 8 of the past 22 years when full costs are taken into account. In 14 other years, farmers spent more raising their crops than they earned by selling them. Raising corn resulted in an aggregate *loss* of $524 per acre. Annually, returns ranged from a stark loss of $197 per acre to a promising gain of $244.

Soybean returns ran somewhat better, with 13 years of positive returns out of the 21 for which data are available. Yet results still varied widely, from a loss of $118 per acre to a gain of $170. The cumulative return was significantly better than the loss suffered by growing corn: a gain of $544 per acre. Thus, if a farmer strictly rotated equal acreage of corn and soybeans, the result would be a net gain of $20 per acre, or $1 per acre per year.

Returns for wheat growers were dismal, with gains in only 2 of 20 years. Cumulative losses totaled $1,236 per acre, while annual returns ranged from a loss of $117 to a gain of $64. Rice was extremely volatile, bringing a cumulative gain of only $27 per acre over 18 years—or $1.50 per acre per year—while returns ranged from a loss of $416 to a gain of $525 per acre.

Moreover, the chart shows that returns are exceptionally variable for each of the four crops. Left adrift on global markets, farmers may reap exceptional rewards when prices are high but suffer crushing losses when prices are low. Nor is there balance in how these net returns impact farm families. One good year does not make a farm self-supporting, but one bad year can knock a competent farm out of business.

Why Have Some Farms Thrived?

Having grown commodities for questionable returns, and having spent trillions of dollars purchasing inputs, it is difficult to imagine how any farm families could have thrived. Clearly, however, some have. Some farms have purchased all of the land in their township and more. Some farmers now drive immense planters and combines and use drones to monitor their fields. We celebrate hundreds of Century Farms, where a single family has worked the same land for over 100 years, riding through the crests and downfalls shown on these charts. We still see effective farmers serving as pillars of their communities.

It would seem that these model farms share at least one of three attributes. These may be families who purchased land before the farm credit crisis, and held on to their land. They may be farmers who have taken full advantage of tax breaks to write off the expenses of expanding. Or they may be farmers who earned money in a different industry and used those savings to launch a new farm. Without such support, it is nearly impossible for a newcomer to start a farm, so the entire farm sector is at risk.

Farm Assets Vary Greatly

To fill out this picture, it is useful to consider the assets held by the entire farm sector, as Figure 1.14 does. Total assets owned by US farmers are currently valued at about $3 trillion—75 percent of the $4 trillion of financial losses this analysis has traced from the farm sector. While this is double the asset value that farms held in 1960, Figure 1.14 shows considerable upheaval over the past six decades. Significantly, farm assets were valued at $3 trillion in 1979, just as the farm credit crisis was brewing. During that crisis, however, farmers learned that their assets were overvalued. After the bubble burst, farm asset values returned to their former levels of 1986. They remained there until 2002. Then the value of farm assets rose again, in concert with a speculative bubble, to another peak of $3 trillion in 2014. Over the past 3 years, they held steady.

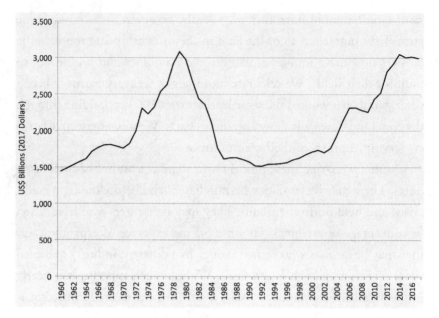

Figure 1.14. US farm sector total assets, 1960–2017. (USDA Economic Research Service Farm Income Balance Sheet data. Adjusted for inflation using 2017 dollars.)

Keep in mind also that Figure 1.14 does not show the value of the farms that went out of business because of dismal economic conditions. It shows the value of the farms that remain in farming. There is no way of knowing today what value these former farms might have added to the sector. Nor can we know how valuable farm assets might be today if there had not been systemic extraction of resources, or policy and price upheaval in the farm sector.

Farmers No Longer Feed Themselves

In perhaps the final irony, farmers' focus on increasing productivity, taking on new debt, and exporting grains globally took them away from actually feeding themselves. In a remarkable development, the value of food that farm families have kept for their own consumption has deteriorated from $21 billion in 1910 (in 2018 dollars) to only $100 million in 2001, as Figure 1.15 shows. After 2003, when the community foods movement began to engage more farmers, and as food prices rose, the value of home consumption has slowly crept up to $300 million, triple its low point. This is not an insignificant share of total farm product sales, at 8 percent, but that ratio is more a matter of the declining income for farmers than a sign of rural independence.

Farm families who sacrificed their ability to feed themselves and their neighbors in order to feed the world might have found this was a trade-off worth making if the expanded commodity trade had consistently built new wealth. As this chapter has shown, however, the expansion of commodity agriculture created competitive conditions that threatened rural community cohesion. Farm families and policy makers chased

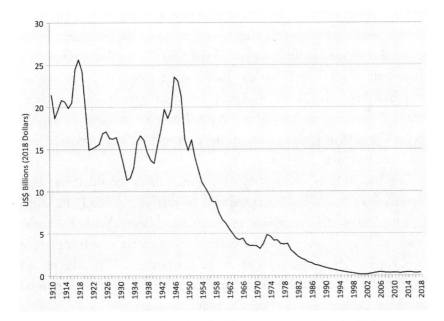

Figure 1.15. Adjusted value of food reserved for home consumption by US farmers, 1910–2018. (USDA Economic Research Service Farm Income Balance Sheet data. Adjusted for inflation using 2018 dollars.)

illusions of feeding the world, strove for individual achievement, and welcomed new technology, only to discover they were running on a treadmill, as the founder of the field of agricultural economics, Willard Cochrane, pointed out.

Deep Dilemmas

Deep dilemmas pervade the prevailing food system in the United States. In a country that claims to feed the world, people go hungry, and food imports are rising. Even as the population expanded, and spent more on food, farmers switched from growing food for people to raising raw materials for industry. Net farm income eroded steadily, in part because of the separation of farmers from the people who purchased the foods they grew. Farm families who once enjoyed a wealth of options in managing their lands and lives learned to conform to the logic of a global market system in which they held little power to negotiate a fair deal. Over a century of trading through extractive economic structures, farmers subsidized metropolitan regions to the tune of $4 trillion, more than the worth of all their farms combined. Brief moments of prosperity erupted when crises loomed abroad, followed by systematic decline. This led rural regions into deeper dependency. By focusing on outside forces rather than looking inward, the potential for independence and resilience was lost.

The trajectory of one farmer's life encapsulates the dilemmas that farm families face. When he started to farm after World War II, he imagined turning an efficient operation over to his children. With their assistance, he became one of the most successful farmers in a competitive farm county. His children all chose different careers. When he retired I asked him about his vision for the future. He held out hope that he could sell the land to a developer to build a nest egg.

Over time, the thrust of farm policy shifted from supporting market mechanisms to compensating farmers for the fact that markets were fundamentally unfair. In 2017–18, the USDA allocated $27 billion of "emergency" relief to farmers. This supposedly compensates for new tariffs imposed in the recent trade wars, but it only delays the day of reckoning. Allocations for 2020 rose to more than $40 billion. More pernicious, these cash payments offer simplistic responses to problems that are inherently complex. Political discourse focuses on short-term election cycles, and has extreme difficulty addressing root causes or managing long-term change.

The silver lining is that the extractive economy was created by public policy. This means it can be reversed. Since trillions have already been sucked out of rural America, however, it will take concerted policy attention and sustained investment to create resilient rural communities.

In the absence of the political will to act, community initiatives such as the ones featured in this book have arisen against great odds. To return to the question posed at the opening of this chapter: Why is this so difficult to do, in a prosperous country that arguably has the most advanced agriculture on the planet? It is because farmers and consumers trade through extractive economic structures that are the tragic legacy of land theft, slavery, and the denial of human rights endemic to the founding of the US. This book shows that even White farmers and landowners have been harmed by these structures. The losses detailed in this chapter create the need for community foods initiatives. They also limit their growth.

With visionary leadership, even disastrous years can spawn creative change. During the Farm Credit Crisis of the 1980s, cogent Montana leaders convened small groups of rural neighbors to devise solutions to eroding soil and financial hardship. As chapter 2 shows, they began to construct community food systems.

CHAPTER 2

Co-learning Is Contagious

Amid the farm credit crisis of the 1980s described in chapter 1, a small cluster of Montana farmers realized that the markets they had depended on were broken, their soil was depleted, and their souls were hungry. Tilling remote fields far from political power centers, they were unsure of how to move forward. They approached AERO (Alternative Energy Resources Organization, based in Helena, Montana), an alternative energy initiative they belonged to, asking what it could do for farmers. The growers made the case that farming, because it harnessed solar energy, would fit the organization's mission. AERO very wisely responded by saying they did not have an answer. But AERO agreed to convene small groups of farmers and researchers who could experiment in their own ways, exploring new crops, new markets, and better ways of building soil health. To foster this work, AERO raised funds to provide small grants to these grassroots experiments. This evolved into a statewide network of collaborative learning clubs that engaged in more than 200 research projects initiated by hundreds of rural Montanans. By inserting more pulses (edible legumes) into crop rotations, farmers nourished their soils and tapped new global markets. Innovative ways of controlling pests were devised and tested. New food businesses formed. This in turn sparked national change. Montana became one of the first groups to help expand a Buy Fresh Buy Local initiative that had been launched from Pennsylvania. The national FoodCorps program was born in Montana. The very term "community-based food system" was also invented by one insightful Montana leader. Building on this foundation, a food-processing center located in Ronan, a town of 2,000, fostered new regional collaborations and also became a national leader.

On the drive north from Missoula toward Glacier National Park, a breathtaking view of the Mission Mountain range emerges—a broad, sheer rock face glistening with snow. At the tribal town of St. Ignatius, the road curls to the north, running parallel with the peaks toward Flathead Lake. Small farms tend scattered fields of vegetables, forage, and wheat, interlaced with pastures where cattle and sheep graze with extraordinary mountain views.

Twelve miles south of Flathead Lake is the town of Ronan. With a population of less than 2,000, the town might easily be overlooked by a driver racing past the metal arch that demarks downtown Ronan, or the campus of the Salish-Kootenai Tribal College in Pablo, to get to the Lake. However, anyone interested in community foods should pause to take a tour of the Mission Mountain Food Enterprise Center (MMFEC), a project of the Lake County Community Development Corporation (LCCDC). On a one-quarter-acre plot on Main Street, MMFEC's sprawling campus hosts a $5 million business that serves scores of farmers and dozens of businesses ranging from Spokane to Missoula. Here, over two decades, a core of dedicated leaders has persistently built one of the most cogent and creative food processing facilities I have seen. In this space, raw crops are converted into value-added foods, such as frozen cherries, lentil burgers, cubed squash, herbal tea, and habanero jam. In the course of welcoming each year's harvest, transforming it into storable food items, and effectively marketing those products, the nonprofit also cultivates strong social and commercial networks. These relationships hold great promise for ensuring that the Flathead region remains resilient.

MMFEC's growth into a strong regional center depended on a wealth of prior work that took place across Montana over decades. Those efforts created a climate favorable enough to persuade consumers to place a priority on purchasing food items grown in their own state, while farmers gained supportive infrastructure to help them meet that demand.

The fact that this food-processing center has survived in such a remote part of the US is a crucial element of its genius. Because residents live too far from major metropolitan areas to be chronically distracted by urban amenities, they focus closely on the people who live near them. Falling back on a homesteading history in which remote settlers pulled together because it was the only way to survive, farmers and food leaders have partnered with economic developers, wholesalers, and household consumers to generate tens of millions of dollars of food trade.

This food trade has been built in fits and starts, constrained by the region's sparse financial resources. Yet, by collaborating openly, maintaining great patience, and reaching out to investors at critical junctures, food leaders have marshaled a forceful combination of earned income with public and private grants to create sustainable businesses. They have also helped form strong statewide networks that provide a political presence.

MMFEC's success was built by persistently responding to diverse constituents, including commercial cherry farmers, emerging vegetable growers, pastured livestock farmers, school food service directors, marketing specialists, and truckers. Jan Tusick, MMFEC's director and sheep farmer with her husband Will, has emerged as a pragmatic businesswoman, savvy farm leader, and trusted partner.

AERO: The Roots of Montana's Community Foods Work

Tusick traces the birth of the Center back to the 1980s, when Montana's Alternative Energy Resources Organization (AERO), based in Helena, began bringing farmers and ranchers together to explore more sustainable practices. AERO, a 1974 outgrowth of the Northern Plains Resource Council, had formerly focused primarily on renewable energy sources. Al Kurki, who became AERO's executive director in 1986, recalled that AERO had launched the New Western Energy Show, featuring a dozen young people, mostly artists and actors, who spread out across the 559-mile-wide state, staging entertaining educational shows community by community. The shows demonstrated renewable energy technologies such as solar ovens and solar panels. Kurki said these early educational efforts were "statewide in the best sense of the word. They had to have been effective. One rancher, who later became AERO's board chair, came up to me many years later to tell me that his first encounter with AERO was watching these traveling artists 'baking cookies in a farmer's field in Northeastern Montana.'" To the rancher, this signaled that AERO was willing to creatively tackle broader change as well, so he got involved. Kurki added that AERO's approach, of moving beyond complaining to creating alternatives, caught him off guard when he first began to work at AERO, but it set a tone that lasted through generations of leadership changes at AERO. "We tended to draw people who wanted to find a way forward."

However, AERO's attention to renewable energy was caught short by a lack of support from Washington, DC, as well as a brewing farm crisis. At the time that AERO was born, Montana farmers, like those in other wheat-producing states, had enjoyed bountiful profits by exporting grain to the Soviet Union. However, when the Soviets precipitously stopped buying, global markets collapsed. As sales fell, legions of farmers could not repay their loans. Waves of trauma spread through rural Montana. By the mid-1980s scores of farms had been foreclosed or had declared bankruptcy; one of every three Montana farms went under during the crisis. This compounded a devastating loss of soil. One-quarter of the state's topsoil had been lost since the 1930s.

Energy and farming came together when AERO hosted a statewide workshop on ethanol. Kurki recalled, "That meeting drew a lot of attention. Farmers were interested in alternative energy, but there was another undercurrent too. Some asked, 'How long can I sell $3 wheat before I lose my farm? And we're burning up the organic matter in our soil. There's got to be a better way to approach farming.'" They asked AERO staff to help them out. Kurki added, "The farmers argued that sustainable agriculture was a better use of sunlight, just like solar panels, so moving in this direction was totally consistent with AERO's mission of promoting renewable energy use."

As a newcomer to the farming discussion, AERO decided it needed to learn more about what its farmer-members were experiencing. It established an agricultural task force to develop a strategy. Over the winter of 1987–88, Nancy Matheson, who left a position at the Montana Department of Agriculture in the mid-1980s to serve as AERO's sustainable agriculture program manager, sent a survey to farmers across the state, whether they were AERO members or not. She posed a forward-looking set of questions. Matheson wanted to learn which sustainable practices farmers were already pursuing. She also hoped to identify which topics farmers would like to know more about, which practices were most economically sustainable, and what types of research would be most useful to the farmers. A total of 188 farms responded.

More than half of the farmers who replied had been pursuing sustainable practices for more than 21 years. They were more dependent on farm income than the average US farmer. They raised a more diverse range of crops and livestock than average, and sought to diversify even more. Among their fellow farmers and ranchers they were exceptionally dedicated to protecting soil and water resources, and to building the health of their soils. They had devised multiple ways of building soil and ecological health, and they reported that all these strategies contributed to achieving their goals; no single approach was effective on its own.

Critically, farmers also complained that their ability to reach markets was severely limited. Yet they were reaching out to their colleagues: they drew most of their information about how to farm from other farmers. This discovery led AERO to engage farmers in learning even more from each other.

Farm and Ranch Improvement Clubs: Adapting a Tested Model to New Challenges

When the survey results first came back, Matheson discussed her findings with supportive researchers at the University of Montana and Montana State University. These experts cautioned that their institutions had only a limited ability to respond to these farmers' needs. They also agreed that the most innovative research projects were based on farms. Drawing upon these discussions, the AERO task force decided to support research that farmers decided was useful. Jonda Crosby, who would serve as AERO's executive director from 2002 to 2011, emphasized that such an approach could only work in an organization that could animate its members to act. "The foundation of all this work was the AERO membership. We told them, 'We don't know how to do this.' The members did, but they needed resources."

Taking cues from Pete Peterson, a retired Cooperative Extension Service officer and eastern Montana farmer, who had enjoyed collaborative farm groups convened in the 1940s by Extension in partnership with the Farm Bureau, AERO encouraged their members to form Farm and Ranch Improvement Clubs (FRICs). By 1990, AERO had raised a small amount of money to allocate to these grassroots groups of growers who wrote specific plans to improve their own farming practices.

Among the first clubs AERO funded were several groups that wanted to expand their efforts to incorporate new crop rotations to build soil fertility and health. Another cluster of vegetable producers sought to market their products collaboratively. In later years a ranchers' club collaborated to convert to grass-fed beef production. One FRIC developed seed varieties acclimated to their saline soils. Another explored ways to incorporate agritourism. Over time, Western Montana would launch a mobile processing unit for slaughtering chickens on the farm.

Each club could apply for funding a maximum of three times, and Matheson noticed that the work deepened with each cycle of funding. Since the clubs were widely scattered across the state, their work addressed distinct climate and soil zones with varied access to markets. In the first 5 years, 27 clubs formed, engaging more than 200 Montanans.

Infrastructure Promotes Co-learning

AERO was able to fund each FRIC with minimal allocations of $200 to $800 per project to cover out-of-pocket costs. In her design, Matheson specified that each FRIC had to enroll at least four members, one of whom had to be a researcher or Extension agent. Each club that applied for funding had to define a specific research question their club would address—something that would potentially reduce soil erosion, promote sustainable agricultural practices, or reduce fossil fuel or other input use. The club had to be willing to introduce some new farming practice at a scale sufficient to address the research topic they selected. The researcher or Extension agent would help lend rigor to the research, and added administrative support for each project. They were engaged for one additional strategic reason, Pam Mavrolas, AERO's executive director from 1994 to 1998, added: "Most importantly, their presence helped influence the larger research establishment about the value of sustainable practices and farmer-driven research." Finally, each club had to promise to make a presentation about what its members had learned to the FRIC network at its annual gathering. To make the process as friendly as possible to busy farmers, Matheson devised an application form that was simple and tightly structured.

AERO staff facilitated the FRICs' gatherings, and an independent consultant, Barbara Rusmore, worked closely with Matheson to evaluate the results of the process. Rusmore told me that although it was critical for each club to generate solid data, the coordinators did not want to make it a purely academic exercise. "We wanted to avoid having the scientists take over the process. We knew farmers were already experimenting. By working together, with technical assistance from scientists, we believed they could do valid research and demonstrations that helped answer the questions they had posed."

Rusmore explained that the FRICs sparked two complementary impacts: the clubs created new knowledge, while agricultural agencies learned to reach out more effectively to farmers and to embrace sustainable practices. All those involved learned from each other, with no one codified as the "expert." By *fostering co-learning*, rather than *offering instruction*, leaders forged a more dynamic process.

How the Clubs Promoted Innovation

To illustrate these impacts, consider one FRIC project that Rusmore highlighted in her research. One group of farmers became concerned about a pesticide that the Bureau of Indian Affairs (BIA) had used on Fort Belknap property to control an invasive weed, leafy spurge. Because the weed spreads rapidly, the agency felt it had to act quickly, by spraying to contain it. But this group of farmers knew that sheep would eat the spurge, so they worked with the BIA and researchers at Montana State University to intensively graze 1,500 sheep on 7,000 acres of tribal lands in 1992. The results were so positive that in the next year, the BIA dedicated some of its pesticide budget to building fencing for tribal members, who were not members of the original co-op, to graze sheep on their own lands. The agency also cut back its herbicide applications. The FRIC, meanwhile, expanded its herd and began to collaborate in selling their lambs.

Kurki mused that with innovations such as this, the FRIC process was "well ahead of the funding world," so it was difficult to raise money at first. "It took them 2–3 years to catch up. We started out with a $20,000 budget. There was a stretch where individual board members would put a check on the table on a quarterly basis, to keep us going. It wasn't until 1987 that the Northwest Area Foundation gave us real money." The budget later blossomed to $320,000 with support of the W. K. Kellogg Foundation.

Mavrolas emphasized that without this external support from funders such as these and the Noyes Foundation, far less would have been accomplished. She added that this funding also helped expand the impact of the FRICs. The Kellogg Foundation, in particular, helped introduce the Montana network to other partners across the US.

One of the most vocal members of the FRICs was Bob Quinn, a farmer in Big Sandy, Montana. Quinn was already innovating in a variety of ways. Over the next three decades, he would be the person responsible for bringing an ancient Mesopotamian grain into commercial production as Kamut® Brand Khorasan. He also began to press oil from his own crops to make cooking oil that he sold to local restaurants— and then reclaimed to filter for use as fuel for his tractors. "Bob is an amazing idea-generator and experimenter. He showed people what is possible," Mavrolas added.

AERO's membership also included another group of profound innovators who had been championing pulse crops (edible legumes such as peas or lentils) for several years, following recommendations by Dr. Jim Sims at the University of Montana. In contrast to most commodity crops, legumes add nitrogen to the soil by drawing it from the air and attracting bacteria that concentrate the nutrient in a form useful to plants as nodules on the plants' roots. When this foliage is plowed back into the fields at maturity, organic matter is added to the soil regime, helping it retain more moisture after a rainfall. This in turn reduces erosion and sequesters carbon, both of critical importance in the semi-arid region east of the Rockies.

The four innovators—Bud Barta, Jim Barngrover, Tom Hastings, and David Oien—had begun by growing black medic, a legume that fixes lots of nitrogen and reseeds itself, to build the health of their soil. It grew well, but this took land out of production for a growing season, leaving farmers with no harvest to sell. The growers then experimented with other legumes that produced an edible seed, hoping this healing process could contribute to their farms' income.

This in turn meant the farmers had to expand their attention far beyond improving specific farming practices. The four launched a new firm, Timeless Seeds, in 1987. As resources allowed, they added equipment for cleaning and packaging these pioneering pulses. Oien traveled to domestic and international trade conferences looking for buyers. Barngrover led the effort to adopt supportive public policies. The pair reached out to the FRIC network, asking for help in identifying new growers and buyers. These new partners often invested extraordinary volunteer effort to solidify the new firm.

Matheson's surveys showed that farmers who were growing pulses considered them economically viable. Word spread through the FRICs and other farmer networks, and more farmers adopted pulses as part of their rotation. As momentum built, federal crop insurance rules expanded to cover pulses. This had a dramatic long-term impact. Today, Montana is the number one lentil-growing state in the US, accounting for 57 percent of all sales. Lentil sales escalated from $1.9 million in 1998, the first year that the US Department of Agriculture (USDA) began to track lentil production, to $74 million in 2018, down from a peak of $210 million in 2016. Acres planted rose from less than 6,000 in 1987 to 800,000 in 2019, as pulses became an important export crop.

Rusmore added that FRIC groups even gleaned great lessons from reaching dead ends. One group added peas to their crop rotations but found that production was less consistent than they had hoped it would be. When the buyer they had lined up withdrew, saying he had found an ample supply elsewhere, the farmers contacted a local grocer. The store was happy to purchase the peas to sell to its customers.

Learning by trial and error during this chaotic period, AERO leaders discovered that they would need to change the food system itself. Ultimately, real reform would not be possible unless Montana consumers dedicated themselves to purchasing food from nearby farms, and that would require new economic infrastructure. As Matheson said, "We concluded that we could make food a bigger part of the Montana economy if we were intentional about doing that."

Working Together Offsets Farmer Isolation

Rusmore's evaluations further determined that one of the critical outcomes of the FRIC process was the personal interaction farmers gained by collaborating, both with neighboring farms and with their statewide peers. This was a potent antidote to the isolation bred by the prevailing farming system. These new connections fostered lasting engagement among farmers but also ensured that results would be disseminated across the state with some ease.

Overall, Rusmore said, the clubs created an important shift in public perception: "The clubs gave viability and visibility to producers who did not want to pursue energy- and fossil-fuel-intensive agriculture." The data AERO collected demonstrated the economic viability of these farms, she explained. This was critical at a time when courageous innovative farmers suffered derisive comments from their neighbors, whether dismissive words from bankers, outbursts at local cafés, or comments whispered across fence lines.

More broadly, the clubs fostered collaboration among food-system leaders. As Rusmore put it, "The clubs created a network of people who found each other by sharing their common interests in different kinds of agriculture." They created connections among people that were uniquely Montanan, Rusmore added: "Farmers in Montana are probably among the least interested in policy. They tend to say, 'If it needs to be done, then let's just start doing it.' But by doing it, their work made impacts across institutions and throughout the community of producers statewide." Years later, she cycled back to these growers and found that those relationships and friendships had lasted over time.

The social and economic infrastructure that AERO created made visible and supported experimentation in new crops and markets that farmers had tackled in obscurity for decades. One anonymous farmer and AERO member, still quoted on the AERO website, related how, even as a grower, he had learned about healthier eating through the network: "*Abundant Montana* [an annual catalog listing Montana producers] has made me more deliberate in choosing who I buy my food from because now I feel part of something bigger than me." Co-learning, it turned out, was contagious.

The Broader Montana Strategy

Moreover, the FRICs were only one element of a far more comprehensive strategy. AERO hosted farm tours where innovators could share their insights, and convened a soil-building conference in 1988–89 that attracted 200 people. Results of the research projects were disseminated through AERO publications and presented at annual meetings. Rusmore recalled that these meetings were inspiring: "They brought innovative thinkers and doers in both the food and energy fields together for several days. New ideas and relationships formed at these events. This influenced further creative work."

In 2001–02, after several years of building the awareness of the potential for Montana food production, AERO published its first issue of *Abundant Montana*. The booklet also helped strengthen the network of Montanans who cared about food by helping farmers and consumers trade with each other.

As the network's capacity to communicate expanded, new challenges surfaced. Originally, Matheson recalled, the Buy Fresh Buy Local effort had considered anything grown in Montana to be "local" food. But this definition placed AERO leaders in complex conversations. If one lived close to the state line and wanted to purchase something grown on the other side of the boundary in Idaho or North Dakota, why wouldn't that also be local food? Moreover, if one lived in a remote part of northern Montana, something raised in Saskatchewan might be more "local" than a Montana product grown 600 miles away.

Puzzling on these issues, Matheson had an inspiration while meeting with a funder. "What we are really trying to build here are community-based food systems," she found herself saying. The work wasn't just about the distance a food item traveled; it was about forging new sets of relationships that created strong mutual loyalties. In this spontaneous moment, Matheson had invented a term that would become a central theme of food work all over the nation. As Mavrolas noted, Matheson's new concept posed a strategic challenge: "How do we go from a few *innovators* to building a food *system*? Matheson had a resonant answer: "By building an economy around this innovation."

Another idea AERO devised was something we might now call "ride sharing" for locally grown foods. In the late 1980s, long before distributors carried such items, AERO was able to put out the word that they were looking for people who could carry locally raised items from farms to their buyers. At first, Matheson personally called those who routinely traveled to Missoula to see if they had extra space in their vehicle. Then someone wrote software that allowed AERO to match these drivers with food shipments that needed to be conveyed across the state.

What Kind of Food System Would Work for Montana?

Expanding on the enthusiasm the FRICs had generated around sustainable farming practices, AERO broadened its approach. In 2006, Matheson developed a curriculum that partner communities could use to foster still deeper conversations about food. Rusmore devised a companion guide for facilitators. AERO then recruited leaders from across the state and suggested that they convene new discussions about constructing community food systems. AERO proposed a simple first step: to invite community members to a potluck meal. Participants were asked to bring some food they had grown themselves if possible, or something from a farm or processor they knew.

To facilitate each discussion, AERO developed a mapping exercise. It gave each small discussion group a diagram showing the key elements of the Montana food system. Those in the room were asked to draw arrows on the diagram, showing how the *current* food system moved food to their homes. Then they were asked to make a second drawing showing how they *would like* a food system to move food to them. This raised a broader strategic question: What kind of food system would work for Montana?

The Food Flow Map exercise "really worked," Matheson recalled. It sparked deeper awareness of Montana's vulnerability, enough that when Governor Brian Schweitzer convened a statewide Food and Agriculture Summit in 2007, facilitated by Rusmore, the participants collaborated in small groups to produce Food Flow Maps on an even larger scale.

That same year, the legislature passed a state law that made it easier for institutional food services to purchase food items from Montana farms, ranches, and processors, by allowing schools to prioritize local purchasing rather than being forced to accept the lowest bid. This was in part inspired by the new University of Montana Farm-to-College Program, launched by four graduate students and the director of dining services, Mark LoParco, in 2003, and aided by subsequent research documenting the state's $33 million institutional food market. Since then, the university has purchased nearly $8 million of Montana foods. The other major university, Montana State, now purchases 25 percent of its food from 109 Montana vendors and coordinates a statewide farm-to-school network. More than half (57%) of Montana school sites have embarked on farm-to-school activities.

In 2009, Matheson returned to the Montana Department of Agriculture to serve as special projects coordinator. In that position she was able to inform state residents that Montana had produced 68 percent of its own food in the 1940s but now produced less than 10 percent. A once-thriving food-processing industry had waned after the farm crisis took hold, falling from 218 processors in 1954 to 115 in 1987. Processors had been concentrated along US 93, a highway that runs from the Bitterroot Mountains through Missoula to Glacier Park—the same highway that runs through Ronan, site of the Mission Mountain Food Enterprise Center.

Especially lost were meat, cheese, and vegetable processors. Yet the data also offered some hopeful signals. After bottoming out in 1992, the state's food processing sector had rebounded to 171 firms by the year that the Food and Agriculture Summit convened.

By 2010, geographic information system experts had worked with Matheson to produce detailed maps showing the exact location of all of the licensed food processors in the state, and a host of other facilities, such as farms, grocery stores, and convenience stores. Soon, AERO transformed *Abundant Montana* into an interactive website.

Matheson later led in developing a 2015 law, the Montana Food Modernization Act, making it easier for home-based food processors to prepare low-risk food items in home kitchens and sell them directly to consumers. "After that, a number of small businesses started up fairly quickly," Matheson recalled. "Montana is really dependent upon small businesses."

Rusmore holds high praise for Matheson's sustained role: "Nancy Matheson had a leading role in guiding the development of AERO's Agricultural Task Force, the Farm Improvement Clubs, and the trajectory of collaboration and development supporting food systems change. She was a key reason that was successful."

Montana Helps Spark National Action

The important progress made in Montana was not confined to the state level. Instead, this diverse group of Montana leaders stepped into national leadership roles, influencing community foods work in other regions. Montanans were early members of a national Buy Fresh Buy Local campaign, first launched by the Pennsylvania Association for Sustainable Agriculture, which engaged food system leaders in 12 states. After her tenure at AERO, Mavrolas became the external evaluator for this national effort.

Two-way learning also thrived in this national context. In addition to serving as exemplars, Montana's food leaders learned a great deal from participating in these national networks. "That campaign catalyzed a lot of our thinking about what could be done," Rusmore said.

One national program, The FoodCorps, was invented in Montana. The initiative was conceived in 2006 by Crissie McMullan, a graduate student at the University of Montana at the time, and one of the four students mentioned earlier who had helped persuade the university's dining service to offer farm-to-table fare. McMullan told me that after having a great experience in AmeriCorps VISTA, she raised money to hire four VISTA volunteers to help colleges bring Montana-produced foods into their dining halls. Though paid a minimal stipend, these energetic young people often inspired food service workers to venture in new directions to purchase food from Montana farms, even when their kitchens were not quite up to the task. These hardy volunteers also did most of the gritty work that made sourcing food work. "It was about 10 percent ideas, and about 90 percent groundwork," McMullan recalled. "Someone had to call each of the farmers to find out what their actual prices were, and someone had to call each food service director to find out what they wanted." Volunteers often used their own vehicles to bring products directly to the schools.

One day in February, while meeting with her adviser, Neva Hassanein, McMullan discussed the fact that institutional food services needed people who focused their time on animating these logistics. McMullan realized it wouldn't work without them. Hassanein had been approached by a funder seeking practical ways to expand farm-to-school work nationally. In a flash of inspiration, McMullan envisioned a "FoodCorps" that would adapt the AmeriCorps model to focus specifically on food services at public K–12 schools as well as colleges. The funder donated $50,000 to get things rolling. The program, initially sponsored by the National Center for Appropriate Technology (NCAT), headquartered in Montana, opened in July 2006.

What made it work? McMullan said there were three main reasons. "We developed a very concrete sense of how local food could happen at a larger scale than it had before. Secondly, launching a statewide program meant that nine schools could work together to share information and resources. It felt like the whole state of Montana was working on this, and the ideas didn't come from Bozeman or Billings. Third, the passionate college grads captured people's attention. It wasn't long before the Departments of Agriculture and Commerce began to recognize this was important work."

Since Montanans had worked closely with food leaders in other states, the idea also caught fire nationally. Five colleagues in other states—Ian

Chaney, Curt Ellis, Jerusha Klemperer, and Cecily Upton in New York, along with Deb Eschmeyer in Ohio—had been thinking along similar lines. They adapted McMullan's model, incorporating elements from similar models that had emerged in a handful of other locations, to create a nationwide program. Encouraging them to take the national reins, and joining their board to provide a grassroots voice, McMullan opted to stay in Montana.

Bringing New Insights Back Home

Exposure to national discussions also helped Montana food leaders understand more about the unique qualities their state held. Matheson recalled one conversation with a national expert who struggled to persuade AERO to focus on raising more produce in Montana, because national leaders had set this priority. "But AERO members grew beef, wheat, barley, and oilseed crops," Matheson told me. The work in Montana, she explained, had to begin with an understanding of that reality.

Mavrolas and Rusmore added that one of the things which made their efforts so successful was that food leaders were not asking people to move to a strange, unknown world; often the thrust of their work was to return to practices family farmers had used in the past. People in remote communities had worked together to solve production problems before, so the concept of convening FRICs was a return to previous ways. Planting crops to build soil health was once common practice. Growing food for one's neighbors was habitual for Montana farmers historically. Many rural towns once had food processors, which often purchased from nearby farms. "This is part of us," Mavrolas said. Further, she added, farmers and businesspeople held enough resources to act on their own initiative, if only in the first stages. "One reason this [campaign] happened was that the people had the ability to make decisions for themselves, and had the power to make the changes."

Despite the fierce independence of Montana farmers, the work ultimately required support from the state government. Ron de Yong, who served as the Montana director of agriculture from 2007 to 2016, was able to make sure that the state's Agriculture Development Council opened opportunities for funding community foods projects. "Local foods really exploded, and we didn't have enough money to support them" until this funding opened up, de Yong said. "When I became director, this movement was growing by itself, but I knew it could grow faster with a push. It required leadership. If you don't have leadership from the state government it doesn't get done. Even small pots of money make a bigger impact than you would think."

Jonda Crosby, who led AERO from 2002 to 2011, added that AERO's ability to collaborate with policy makers was eased by the close-knit culture of the state: "There are only one million people living in Montana. You can walk up to a governor or legislator and have a conversation."

An earlier commissioner of agriculture, Ralph Peck (serving 1994–2004), was especially helpful in offering practical advice in these early stages, Crosby said. "He knew how the political system worked, and he'd tell us why some of our ideas would or wouldn't play." She added that party affiliations mattered less in Montana at the time than personal trust. AERO leaders were "fiscally conservative, primarily rural-based risk takers," as Crosby put it. "They were entrepreneurial and concerned about environmental and social justice issues." Anticipating there might be resistance from mainstream legislators who recoiled at spending public resources, AERO leaders made sure that agriculturally savvy, respected moderate legislators were key sponsors of all their bills. Crosby recalled, "We decided we should always be writing bills where *everyone* would say, 'That makes sense.' And we wrote one for every single legislative session which was either passed outright or assigned to an interim committee for further review." With its statewide membership base, AERO could also place pressure on legislators to work for a common cause—or get voted out.

The emergent food network got a further boost from Montana Public Radio, which offered AERO a regular 5-minute broadcast to spread news of its campaigns statewide. By 2000, the FRIC network had grown to 600 farmers and ranchers, organized into 55 local clubs across the state. Holding farm tours and field days, these clubs disseminated news to their neighbors about what they had accomplished. AERO held annual and quarterly statewide "club gatherings" so people could get better acquainted and build trust with each other.

Crosby noted that traditional plot research was also an essential component that validated the Farm Club member ideas and efforts. Montana State University (MSU) researchers played a critical role in advancing the legume cropping system as a viable soil-building and water-retention method for the semiarid plains. MSU's Alison Harmon opened online courses where Montana residents could gain university credit by taking courses covering food, agriculture, and energy. Professor Neva Hassanein at the University of Montana created opportunities for her graduate students to perform research that advanced food work in Montana communities.

The Deeper Challenge of Feeding Montanans

It was difficult enough to bring an ancient grain into modern-day commerce, inject pulses into crop rotations, or prove the efficacy of weed-reduction strategies. At each turn these innovations in production were hampered by the lack of infrastructure to convey Montana-grown foods to Montana consumers. Moreover, metropolitan consumers globally had more money to spend, and long-distance supply networks were easy to find, so it was often easier to sell to Guangzhou than to Glendive. In 1998, leaders of the Western Montana Farm and Ranch Improvement Club shouldered the challenge of building regional infrastructure in the very corridor that had once served as Montana's leading food-processing center. Members of this FRIC were deeply interested in creating value-added products from their farms' produce. Jan Tusick set out to form a shared-use kitchen where this could happen.

The group obtained USDA funding to write a marketing plan, asking the Lake County Community Development Corporation to serve as a sponsor. As Jan Tusick recalls, she met with Billie Lee, director of LCCDC, and said, "You need to be working with us." Lee's response was direct. "What do you want to do?" Tusick told her she was going to try to build a community food system, starting with the processing center. Lee readily agreed. "LCCDC became the first economic development organization in Montana to look at agriculture as an economic vehicle," Tusick recalled. "That gave us an organizational base to work with, and allowed us to really move forward. It also helped us focus. They are brilliant at doing community projects." The new Mission Mountain Food Enterprise Center ultimately emerged as the backbone of a community-based regional food system that is still being assembled.

Next, the concept required a physical facility. The Confederated Salish and Kootenai Tribes Housing Program in Pablo, Montana, stepped forward with an offer. The tribe had purchased an empty pizza restaurant on the main street in Ronan, aiming to refurbish it as a low-income housing facility. Those plans had not yet moved forward, so the tribe agreed to let this fledgling group rent the space. "We started out with a tiny little kitchen," Tusick explained. "We gutted the building and fixed it up. We opened our shop with two kettles, an oven, and some baking equipment."

Five years later, as the priorities of the tribe shifted further from the housing concept, tribal leaders approached MMFEC to see if they might want to buy the building. The tribe showed exceptional patience, inviting the Center to take as many as 5 years to accumulate the capital. In that span, Montana became one of 10 federally funded food and agriculture innovation centers in the US. The next year, a $1 million grant from the US Economic Development Administration allowed the Ronan center to upgrade the building and its processing equipment and to construct an office building holding meeting and conference space. By 2009 MMFEC was designated as western Montana's food and agriculture center, part of the Montana Department of Agriculture's Food and Agriculture Development Network.

The Center's impact was heightened by the fact that it was growing in concert with a number of sister organizations and businesses. Indeed, Tusick herself has played a central role in fostering these partners, knowing that the Food Enterprise Center could not exist without a supportive network of supporters and clients.

A Cluster of Independent Firms

Will and Jan Tusick also joined an emerging farmers' cooperative, dedicated to conveying food from their farms to regional buyers. The spark-plug of this initiative was the late Jane Kile, a farmer near Dixon who had formed the first CSA (community-supported agriculture) program in Montana. In 2000, the Lake County Community Development Corporation procured a seed grant from USDA's Community Foods Projects to organize the new farmers' co-op. This was matched by local donors, including a philanthropist from Arlee who has stayed close to the Western Montana food movement, investing at strategic times. Indeed, the co-op was launched out of the Common Ground farm in Arlee, owned by this philanthropist.

Representing 9 farmers in its first year of operation, 2003, the Western Montana Growers Cooperative (WMGC) sold $200,000 of food; today 34 co-op members and 41 associated smaller farms sell $4 million per year, including sales through a 425-member CSA they formed in 2008. While organic products are the mainstay, many of these sales are made under a "Homegrown" label created by farmers who were frustrated with the USDA organic program but wanted to assure customers that their farms met ecological and fairness standards. Shared management decisions are clearly critical to the strength of the co-op as a collaborative business, and the integrity of their collaboration in turn offers assurance to its customers.

Under the guidance of Neva Hassanein, graduate students carried out a multidimensional case study of the cooperative. They found that many growers felt reassured by the co-op's connections to buyers, and this helped them clarify their businesses as well as increase sales. Most of the founding members told the researchers that a key benefit of belonging was the collective sense of shared values and experiences. She added, "Reciprocal relationships with other food system actors— including nonprofit organizations, other businesses, government, and more—have been essential." Indeed, the co-op was formed at the same time as the University of Montana dining service's farm-to-table program, so the two grew in concert.

While this growth was fueled by the strength of the state network of food leaders, Tusick had to intervene with co-op managers several times to help the firm grow to its next stage. She needed the co-op to be strong, because viable farms create a better business climate for MMFEC. Even though the co-op sold only about $33,000 of food for processing through Mission Mountain in 2018, Tusick treasures the investment of time she made. MMFEC offered food safety training to the growers, and the two businesses formed a technical assistance partnership covering institutional sales. Now MMFEC performs research and development to create and develop new products (for example, a lentil burger); processes fresh foods on behalf of the co-op and markets these products; and manufactures frozen products for winter use.

Over its 15 years, the co-op has grown steadily, Hassanein said. In 2015 the co-op expanded its warehouse by moving to a more central location near Missoula. It has weathered some internal struggles that arose because founding farmers enjoyed better access to markets than newcomers, and large farms received more favorable terms than the small. Such issues were resolved through compromise, Tusick added.

Responding to Consumers and Constituents

Tusick is quick to point out that this interplay between Mission Mountain and its partners is what makes the work so successful. "We're growing based on the market trends that food businesses respond to," Tusick added. "You need to pay attention to your consumer base. If that is disappearing you need to reevaluate. We try to be flexible enough that we can shift in any direction [our partners take us]." Tusick continued that it has been a real advantage to be part of a nonprofit, tax-exempt organization, so MMFEC can launch new ventures with grants. She also emphasized the need to think broadly about each grant to have the maximum impact across the system. "If we get even one pot of money, we ask ourselves, how can we leverage this with another grant?" The measure of success is often the strength of the partnerships that new funding can help forge, and the multiple benefits that can emerge from a single investment.

Recognizing the importance of her contributions, MMFEC hired Tusick in 2005 to serve as the director of the food center. She was able to take MMFEC "back to our roots. . . . We were created to be a research and development arm for a growers' co-op, to help them explore value-added opportunities." To do that, MMFEC needed grant funds. The priority once again became "to bring in our food partners to have discussions on the front end. Otherwise, we are not sustainable."

Hence, although Lake County is the top cherry-producing county in Montana, nearby cherry growers did not immediately connect to MMFEC. At first, "their priority was to market fresh product," Tusick recalled. This attitude changed when MMFEC purchased a pitter and a freezer, inducing several organic growers to move toward a frozen, vacuum-wrapped product that was more shelf stable. This lengthened the marketing season, which, in turn, led a distributor to carry cherries from this region to a wider market area.

This mutual flexibility also created new products. In late 2011, WMGC contacted Tusick to tell her that they had harvested tons of butternut squash they had not been able to sell. Could MMFEC do something with it? During this slow season, the Center had surplus capacity. Staff peeled and diced the squash, then parboiled the cubes and vacuum-wrapped them for freezing. This cubed squash was directly tailored to schools' needs in preparing school lunches, since they wished to have something the cooking staff could heat in a chafing dish. With this product stocked in the MMFEC freezer, FoodCorps staff contacted school food services. Several purchased the squash. By shaping production closely to each other's needs, this collaboration created a new product that simultaneously benefited the farmers, MMFEC, the FoodCorps, and the schools.

WMGC still sells squash to schools in Kalispell, Ronan, St. Ignatius, and Polson, along with four other products: cut carrots and wedged apples for snacks, and frozen wedged apples and frozen pitted cherries for breakfasts and lunches. The raw produce is typically second-quality produce from WMGC farms, full of nutrition but not likely to sell at premium prices on the private market. A critical element in developing these products, Tusick pointed out, was engaging schools, farmers, and MMFEC staff directly in the planning so that all parties would be well served.

Taking advantage of its broad network of support once again, MMFEC worked with school food services to make use of the legumes that Montana farmers had begun to grow in order to build soil health. Now that Montana was a national leader, MMFEC could count on a steady supply of lentils. Collaborating with the Oregon State University

Food Innovation Center, MMFEC devised a lentil burger that would pass the tough test of taste for Montana students. As a frozen, shelf-stable product, it can easily be shipped anywhere in the state. Now MMFEC offers five lentil burger products.

In spite of this success, Tusick is also humbled by the difficulty of keeping these sales alive. These tailor-made products require additional attention from food service management. Those who are involved in the first stages tend to freely offer that attention, whereas newcomers are less likely. "I have watched as changes in the leadership at different schools totally affected the sustainability of the markets the farmers in the co-op had built," Tusick lamented. Further, unless parents stay involved to apply pressure, good initiatives often erode in silence.

After the latest round of Economic Development Administration investment (a half-million dollar grant that allowed MMFEC to upgrade its equipment once again), Tusick recalled, "Our specialty food businesses started to emerge." Now MMFEC works with some 20 such businesses, offering services that range from business planning, branding, processing, and food safety training, to co-packing. MMFEC also serves as the Cooperative Development Center for the western part of the state.

Reflecting on current market conditions, Tusick cautioned that, in order to remain viable as a business, MMFEC accepts work that pays the bills, even when, at times, this runs far afield of their original hopes for feeding residents of western Montana. She mourned that farmland is under attack, and that political support within the state of Montana has been erratic. In 2019, she described the federal government's prevailing international market policy as "painful."

Fostering a Culture of Collaboration

Through innovation, Montana has created a culture of collaboration that appears well poised to endure. Al Kurki recalled that from the very beginning, AERO tried to set an inclusive tone. "This had to be an umbrella that was big enough for everybody." Although some members "wanted to adhere to a purer track," he cautioned that this was a luxury AERO could not afford. Unity was important to their efficacy. "This is a poor state so we can't rely on the state government to pay for this."

Connection to the AERO network of farmers and other partners made this work "joyful," Jonda Crosby said. Although she has now moved to Pennsylvania, she recalled that her 22 years in Montana were the "most expansive years of my life. I wish I had told more AERO members how valued I felt, even when the issues we were working on often felt so slow to progress from one point to another. AERO was, and is, part of my family. People were so open and honest, and so practical. Our relationships were so rewarding. A collaborative organization has so much hope, and so many ideas."

Crosby quickly added the success was due to the overall network, not simply the organization. "In my early days at AERO, we had received a number of large grants with a few core partners. I sought to expand the number of partnerships and at the same time to be sure we were including emerging new leaders and organizations." Crosby wanted to make sure that at every step of the journey, partners were walking alongside AERO. "Change is all about working together, sharing the load, doing what each is most capable of and reaping the benefits together. None of this happens by working alone."

As the Montana native Nancy Matheson looked back on her experience in building food networks, she added that "it takes a certain kind of person to do this work. We know how to build community and trust." In a sparsely populated state, she added, "We can't afford to compete." Matheson is proud of the fact that entry points were made for folks who have access to only a small amount of land. "It's pretty vibrant now. Marketing is so much easier. The work is rolling along on its own."

"Imaginative Pragmatists"

Barbara Rusmore concluded that AERO work was led by "imaginative pragmatists." One of its strengths was that it challenged people to draw first on long-forgotten insights, and then innovate. "Nothing we did was totally new and different." At times, when she asked people how they got into the work, they would "look over their shoulder" as if to see if a neighbor could hear them, and add in a soft voice but with a strong hint of pride, "This is how my grandfather farmed." Moreover, there were limits to the innovation that people would accept. Rusmore lamented how long it took to gain political support for community foods work from a cross-section of state leaders, ultimately including diverse agencies outside of agriculture.

Ironically, five of the state's key food leaders had moved into Montana from other locations. Perhaps, in fact, this required them to connect more closely with their Montana neighbors to effect change. Crosby said that she, along with Al Kurki, Pam Mavrolas, Barbara Rusmore, and Jan Tusick, had all grown up somewhere else. "When we moved here we could feel this spirit," she said. "We were used to systems working slowly, and we knew that we were fighting *for* something, not *against* something. We were always polite, but we always stuck to our guns."

I often think of these spirited Montana collaborators as I work with groups who consider themselves too remote, or located in such small communities, to make a difference. Montana began with a culture of collaboration and used that to forge an exceptional network of community leaders. People worked collaboratively to create new farming systems, going beyond simplistic answers. They knew the limits of their own resources, used them strategically, and invited others to join in. These leaders enticed farmers to move forward toward a more sustainable future by encouraging them to learn from their grandparents' practices. Disciplined, moving forward carefully based on research that took complexity into account, and ensuring that farmers commanded the process for themselves, they prompted strong innovation and achievement.

Holding a vision as steadfast as the Mission Mountain range, and blending that with a radical responsiveness to the needs of the people near them, these outsiders set deep taproots in Montana. Taking thoughtful risks, sharing information and insights openly, they helped transform Montana's landscape, agriculture, food systems, and sense of hope. All this was seeded by farmers who worked quietly on their own lands to improve the health of their soil and the safety of their water. Making remote communities, such as Conrad, Fort Belknap, or Ronan better, they also held a profound influence on the national food movement.

When farmers approached AERO in the throes of the farm credit crisis, no one could have predicted the outcome. But farmers desperately needed new options and were willing to take new risks. AERO, for its part, was cogent enough to realize that it would be better, rather than issuing mandates, to inject resources into farmer experimentation, so small groups of neighbors could devise their own solutions. Far from being a narrow research project, this was an effort to create a social movement centered on collaboration. Extending small grants to farmer groups that included researchers or Extension agents serving equally as co-learners, rather than as experts, AERO helped more pragmatic solutions emerge. This created a broad spirit innovation that blossomed into a statewide network of inspired animators.

Collaborative learning is also a core element of the community foods work in Hawai'i, thousands of miles away across a vast ocean. As chapter 3 describes, Hawaiians are working to address the Islands' extreme dependency on imported food, and concurrent decline in health, by drawing on ancient cultural taproots.

CHAPTER 3

Invoking Traditional Wisdom to Recover from Plantation Agriculture

The imposition of the plantation system in Hawai'i disrupted ancient food systems that had protected precious water and ecological health for centuries, but also transformed a society that had effectively fed itself into a state that is deeply dependent on food imported from thousands of miles away. This created immense disparities of wealth that would not have been tolerated in traditional society, fueling social isolation and ill health. Then the plantation system itself collapsed, victim to its own dependence on fickle global markets. The last remaining plantation ceased operations at the end of 2016. As contemporary Hawaiian leaders addressed the consequences of this imposition, they discovered that traditional cultural insights helped bring society back into balance. Health care centers, food banks, and researchers now foster traditional ways of building mutual trust, centered upon farming, gardening, cooking, eating, and cultural celebration in ways that rekindle a spirit of 'āina (respect for the land) and healthy lifestyles. Traditional farms have been brought back into production as the core of both public health initiatives and formal degree programs. A health center serves traditional foods at its cafeteria. Subsidized food shares convey fresh fruit and vegetables directly to low-income residents, and traditional

crops have been brought into commercial production. Food and health pro-
fessionals encourage SNAP (Supplemental Nutrition Assistance Program)
enrollment because of the critical contribution these funds make to the state
economy. Health workers and professors collaborate to bring new youth into
farming. Food system leaders collaborate through statewide action networks
that span the archipelago, advocating for state policies that promote food
production by family farms for Hawai'i residents living at all income levels.

Tina Tamai was the first person to meet me after I settled in Honolulu.
She took me on a tour through the city's skyscrapers that challenged
every concept I had ever held of the island paradise. Amid the office
towers and condominiums, largely owned by Japanese investors, and
the throngs of international tourists who flocked to shops and beaches
in their shadows, long-term residents strolled despairing streets. Working closely with those who have been marginalized, dogged food leaders
were returning to traditional values to spark a cultural rebirth.

At the time, Tamai, a state Department of Health official, had allocated part of her budget so my colleague Megan Phillips Goldenberg
and I could perform a food system assessment of the islands. As the
director for SNAP (Supplemental Nutrition Assistance Program) education for the state, Tamai had traveled the state extensively, becoming
intimately aware of the poverty plaguing the islands. It was precisely
the intense tourist development, and Hawai'i's position as an escape
for the wealthy, that perpetuated divisions endemic to the plantation
system that had been imposed on Native Hawaiians a century ago. The
plantations, in turn, were succumbing to housing development. Still,
the social chasms persisted.

These islands were once self-sufficient for food. Carefully pursuing
effective and integrated practices that protected soil, water, and people,
Hawaiians fed a population of more than 800,000, nearly the population

that now lives on the islands. All were amply fed using hand tools and manual labor. Each person worked, but chores were limited to 4 or 5 hours per day, and Hawaiians took advantage of considerable leisure time. Land was understood to belong to the immortal gods and, as a result, could not be owned. People took care of the *ahupua'a* where they lived. An ahupua'a is a division of land similar to a watershed, often wedge-shaped, extending from narrow waterways in the highest hills to the spreading expanses of ocean. But it was also more than a geographic place; the land defined a spiritual center and cultural entity, self-managed by those who lived within its boundaries. The islands have been apportioned into 1,825 of these subdivisions that are still recognized today.

As plantations focused on exporting sugar and pineapple, however, the inhabitants were forced to import the food they ate. Thousands of miles from the mainland, Hawai'i residents became both dependent and vulnerable. With the incursion of foreign investment and prosperous tourists, Hawai'i is now one of the most expensive places to live in the US. Food costs are 61 percent higher than average, while workers' wages are among the lowest. The state imports about 85 percent of the food its residents eat.

Tamai and her colleagues dedicated themselves to showing me how this pinch affected the people she knew. Feeding America, the national food-bank clearinghouse, estimates that one of every seven Hawaiians— 200,000 people—is food insecure. That is to say, at some point during the year, they were unsure where their next meal might come from. This gap is partially filled by federal programs, such as SNAP benefits (once known as food stamps). Distressingly, only about 80 percent of the residents who qualified were actually receiving SNAP benefits. The median income of SNAP recipients ($32,383) was less than half of the state's median income ($74,913). Ironically connected to the plantation legacy, food stamp use was highest on the very islands that enjoyed the most farmland.

These lower-income residents held a curious importance to the state economy because they attracted federal funds. Total SNAP benefits received by Hawaiian residents amounted to $487 million. Meanwhile, the state's 7,000 farms were collectively *losing* about $200 million each year, largely growing commodities for export. This meant that low-income families were bringing more money into the state economy than farming was.

Hawaiian political leaders do understand the extreme vulnerability they face, living on islands separated from the mainland by 2,500 miles. They recognize that their state is grotesquely dependent on fossil fuels, as shipping barges and airplanes convey staple foods to their constituents. As a result, they offer more heartfelt appeals for reducing food imports than any state where I have worked.

I had researched Hawai'i's dependence on imported foods 13 years earlier, and challenged the state to do more in a plenary speech at the Hawai'i Agricultural Summit in 2003. Returning in 2016, I was impressed by how advanced the discussion of local food had become. Yet a plantation mentality still persisted, and farms were struggling. Curiously, one of the most prevalent answers was that Hawai'i should import new food factories owned by mainland corporations. More critically, the prevailing discourse scarcely recognized the realities of poverty.

Tina Tamai wanted me to experience this shadow side for myself. She drove me to a park where thousands of homeless people had set up makeshift shelters, only to be forced out by city officials who did not like the optics of a homeless camp. She introduced me to Micronesians who had migrated to Hawai'i in search of better opportunity, without realizing how expensive life would be in their new homeland. Nor had these newcomers reckoned how difficult it would be to ply their traditional food-gathering skills in this new setting. Tamai introduced me to the largest food pantry on O'ahu, located in the business district of Honolulu. It had lost its lease, even though it supported a dedicated community of Chinese American elders. The director speculated that the building's owner had evicted the pantry after being pressured by property owners nearby. They did not seem to want poor people walking the sidewalks near their office towers.

This turmoil highlighted mounting difficulties on the islands. Hawai'i has the second-highest homelessness rate in the country, after Washington, DC, with 553 homeless people for every 100,000 residents. Moreover, that rate is rising. Nearly half of the homeless population are children, even though two-thirds of their families have lived in the state more than 12 years.

Now retired, Tamai had built a legacy of tackling such issues head on. Yet her approach was indirect, since her official role empowered her on the one hand, and limited her voice on the other. Working quietly, often below the radar, she had learned about those who did the most to address poverty, and she helped them connect with each other. She learned that dozens of incredible projects were under way across the islands to foster health among low-income Hawaiians. Tamai understood that they would benefit by gaining more visibility and becoming better coordinated.

She was in a perfect position to help forge these relationships. Visiting worksite after worksite to learn what people hoped to accomplish, and what obstacles fell in their path, she was often able to connect them with resources—experts, money, or simply another colleague who could reinforce their work—while also staying abreast of minute nuances in each initiative. Over time, connection by connection, she wove a solid web of relationships. As that network began to coalesce, and then mature, she saw that her colleagues became more effective as the network grew stronger.

Most bureaucrats do not view themselves as web weavers; many are content to narrowly follow procedures their agency has established and look no further. Others who are more dedicated might go the extra mile to help individual clients obtain benefits they were due. What made

Tamai even more effective was her willingness to assert a public vision at a time when civil authorities denied the realities she faced. At times she became creative with funding. She allocated funds to make sure that the Food Basket, a food bank for the island of Hawai'i, could send staff to remote areas where homeless people had set up shacks on volcanic rock—to make sure they knew how to obtain food assistance. Tamai was among the first nationally to devote SNAP Education funds to performing a food system assessment (the one that my colleague Megan and I wrote). That has now become a common practice. She used her limited budgets to inject resources into statewide activity, building stronger networks of collaboration that promoted health. Since the work encompassed seven islands, much of it had to be decentralized, which made her role as connector even more valuable. By 2019, the network had launched a statewide "Hawai'i Food for All" campaign, expanding on her legacy.

Expanding Beyond Feeding Programs

As they realized the depth of hunger and homelessness, Hawaiians' initial response was to feed people. Carol Ignacio, a member of a deeply rooted family from Pa'auilo on the Big Island, took stronger action than many. In 1989, she founded a food bank in Hilo and called it The Food Basket. It now ranks as one of the most innovative food banks in the US.

However, even as the food bank gave more and more food away, hunger grew. Reflecting on her career in food banking Ignacio told me, "We were part of the problem." By handing out food for free, she said, food banks were failing to foster survival skills. Multiple agencies began to work in low-income communities but failed to empower residents. "We would give money away, but not ask for anything back."

Nor were food donations, by themselves, the solution. "You can always give SNAP benefits to people, but that won't mean they eat the best food," Ignacio said. "There are families that have been poor for generations, and they are accustomed to eating a certain way." Often they seek comfort more than nutrition.

So The Food Basket continued to innovate, expanding the services it provided. It formed two "super pantries," which, instead of simply handing out food, placed a focus on fostering personal development. Each location was open 4 hours per day for 6 continuous weeks, allowing specialists to join forces to help clients address the broad range of issues they face: domestic violence, anger management, and communications skills. To encourage participation, customers were given a stipend for the fuel they needed to drive to the site. Childcare was provided so parents could focus on themselves. Ignacio recalled, "Julia Zee offered cooking demonstrations and nutrition lessons. We would eat together so people would find fellowship with each other. People really enjoyed building more of a sense of power. The evaluations were outstanding. We experienced real empowerment in most of the women's lives." All but one of the 40 participants graduated from the program. "To this day I meet women who share that this was a game-changer in their lives."

These successes, in turn, led The Food Basket staff to place a higher priority on addressing the root causes of hunger. To accomplish that, Ignacio said, "We have to impact the system in which people live." Offering free food now became only the first step in a larger effort: to create a *culture* in low-income communities that fostered empowerment. Ignacio said that growing food in each community is critical to that quest. Now, she continued, "We are moving to a point where food sustainability and food access become part of our culture."

In 2014, Ignacio tackled a new position as the Government and Community Affairs manager for the Blue Zones Project on Hawai'i Island. This is part of a national effort to encourage communities to eat better, exercise more, and foster healthy lifestyles. "We see our role as beginning to mobilize both energy and power collectively," Ignacio said. Blue Zones has formed partnerships with food businesses that pledge to purchase food from nearby farms and promote healthier lifestyles in a more holistic manner. The first business on Hawai'i Island to become certified as a Blue Zone business was KTA Grocery in Hilo. As an independent grocery, it had concentrated on sourcing food from nearby farms. It had also consistently dedicated itself to collaborating with The Food Basket.

The food bank itself further evolved over time. Two successive directors, En Young and Kristin Frost Albrecht, have launched amazingly bold innovations that helped create new economic opportunity for island residents. Both helped construct a more responsive food system on the island, sharing Ignacio's zeal for overturning the root causes of hunger. They also faced new challenges, due to the changing dynamics in the food bank industry itself. In their earliest years, food banks existed in large part to help food manufacturers divert surplus food items to productive use. Donating to food banks created tax breaks for the donors, and secondarily, in many cases, channeled this surplus food to low-income recipients. Over time, as manufacturing processes moved toward "just-in-time" delivery, those surpluses faded away. Food banks had to find other sources.

For The Food Basket and dozens of other food banks across the country, the obvious next step was to purchase food from nearby farms. Each purchase advanced the food bank's mission in two ways. Since many farmers earned marginal incomes, these purchases helped stave off poverty, while channeling fresh foods to recipients. More significantly, over the long term it created new economic exchange that kept money in each community. Purchasing directly from farms also gave food bank leaders greater choice. Rather than waiting to see which foods might be donated, staff could plan for specific crops that farmers near them were growing. When I visited in 2016, the food bank was purchasing from 11 farms on the island. It buys Grade A produce and pays market price for it because The Food Basket competes with local stores like KTA and Safeway, as well as hotels on the island, who buy from the same farms.

To address this competition, The Food Basket tries to build loyalty into its partnerships. The Food Basket asks farms to donate their second-quality produce—less attractive but still nutritious produce that wouldn't command a high price in the market—as an investment in deepening the relationship.

Nonetheless, some of these donor farms were themselves floundering. One banana farm that had been a reliable donor decided it could make more money raising marijuana, so its donations ceased. Other smaller farms constantly rode a razor's edge amid uncertain markets. So the Food Basket stepped up to build better livelihoods for farmers. Thus it took leadership in building a community food system.

The Food Basket's leaders learned that there was a traditional crop, breadfruit (*'ulu*), that grows easily in Hawai'i and provides an ideal food for folks whose diets are challenged. 'Ulu, a starch, is both nutrient dense and low in fat. It is also rich in calcium, magnesium, amino acids, and several essential vitamins. Yet this traditional food had been overlooked as Hawai'i adopted Western diets full of processed foods.

Moreover, growing 'ulu helps build soil health, since it is a perennial tree requiring no tillage. It is fast growing: each tree begins to produce fruit in just a few years. It was an obvious choice for bringing traditional foods back, but in ways that suited contemporary life. So The Food Basket helped a cluster of growers form a cooperative to raise breadfruit. The food bank also dedicated its food-handling expertise and garnered the financial help of the 'Ulupono Foundation to develop a processing operation that peels, steams, and freezes the flesh of the breadfruit the farmers raise to give it lasting shelf life.

Currently, the co-op sells fresh and frozen packages of two varieties of 'ulu—Hawaiian and Ma'afala (one of many Samoan varieties) in

1-pound bags. It sells steamed pulp of the breadfruit for baking, and offers frozen cubes and French fry 'ulu strips. The co-op further developed more products that blended contemporary convenience and flavor from traditional foods. Hummus is fashioned from mature 'ulu, while a mousse is prepared using ripe 'ulu combined with organic, fair-trade dark chocolate. The Food Basket devotes its own trucks to delivering the co-op's products to island customers several days each week, saving the farmers time. It also partners with several distribution firms to deliver to commercial accounts, including Armstrong Produce, Adaptations Inc., Cal-Kona Produce, ChefZone, HFM FoodService, VIP Foodservice, and Y. Hata & Co.

Now the co-op is expanding to grow several other tropical crops, including bananas, papayas, sweet potatoes, and kabocha squash. It has grown from an initial group of 13 farms scattered in different microclimates across the islands, to a core of 70 farms. None of this pioneering work distracts The Food Basket from its original mission of delivering food. Rather, food distribution has become the first step in reaching out to its constituents to engage each one more fully.

Many of the food-donation efforts focus on schools, since many low-income children obtain balanced meals only at school. To provide for these children over weekends at home, The Food Basket offers *keiki* (children's) backpacks each Friday, prefilled with enough food for each child to eat six meals over the weekend. The students are asked to return these backpacks empty the following week.

The Food Basket also launched several relief initiatives branded with names that evoke island culture. The "Da Box" CSA (community-supported agriculture) program offers a box including seasonal selections among 47 varieties of fresh produce provided by 55 nearby farms. SNAP recipients can use their benefits to purchase these boxes at a preferential rate, whereas those who can afford a higher rate can sign up for workplace delivery. The farmers earned $142,640 of income through this program in 2015. The new "Da Bux" program leverages fresh produce purchases that SNAP recipients make, doubling the value of each purchase, so that if someone buys $10 of fresh produce, they receive $20 worth. A third program, "Da Bus," is a mobile market that delivers fresh food items to remote locations.

On these volcanic islands that are so vulnerable, The Food Basket may be called on to provide disaster relief, often with no warning. When category 4 Hurricane Iselle decimated the Puna district in 2014 with sustained winds that hit a maximum of 140 mph, The Food Basket coordinated with a group of local residents who called themselves the Bodacious Ladies. Together, these partners organized sophisticated relief, evacuation, and medical care systems for residents who were trapped due to downed trees and powerlines blocking roads and highways in the aftermath of the storm. When the Kilauea Volcano erupted in June 2018, cutting off several neighborhoods, The Food Basket was again immersed in relief efforts. As always, however, these emergency efforts were only the starting point. In each case, local partners used the crisis as a stepping stone for performing more sustained planning to address future calamities.

Remarkably, given the intense needs of lower-income residents living on the island of Hawai'i, Albrecht devotes a considerable share of her time to making sure the efforts of The Food Basket are reliably networked with sister initiatives across the islands. She views this as an essential strategy in solving the root conditions that lead to hunger.

Integrating Research and Policy Work

One of the food bank's regular partners in Hawai'i Food for All is The Kohala Center. This independent, community-based center for research, conservation, and education was founded in 2000. It aims to "translate research and knowledge into action" in areas of food and energy self-reliance, ecosystem health, and watershed protection. Nicole Milne, vice president of the center's food and agricultural initiatives, told me that the Kohala Center views its role in food-system development as primarily one of assisting those who are building commercial food trade in community contexts.

Several years ago, the Kohala Center launched the Hawai'i Island School Garden Network, aiming to increase the number of learning gardens in island schools. Leaders hoped this would also instill an appreciation and desire for fresh fruits and vegetables among schoolchildren, and advocate for local farm to school procurement programs. Now more than 50 school gardens operate on the Island.

The Kohala Center is also part of a statewide Farm to School–School Garden *hui* (a Hawaiian word that can be translated as "collaborative") that helps to coordinate this work. Through this partnership, parents have been able to persuade school food services to adopt menus featuring island-grown products, and have incorporated cooking classes and science education into school curricula. When gaps in supply networks become visible, this collaboration also helps ensure that deliveries and policies are coordinated. So far, the work of this network has been embraced more readily by charter schools, since they have more flexibility in funding. Nonetheless, public schools are always encouraged to join.

Technical support for farms and food businesses is also offered by the Kohala Center. This includes grant writing and loan application assistance, business planning services, legal support, low-interest microloans, seed-saving coordination, and beginning farmer education programs. The Kohala Center has found that many budding entrepreneurs require close personal attention before they are ready to take on loans. Milne added, "We are not convinced that people who are going into commercial production always have a broad appreciation for what all is involved." As a result the center offers wraparound technical assistance services that embrace the full person and that focus on the uniqueness of each person's talents. Such community building proves essential to developing successful new food systems.

New infrastructure and policy are also critical, so the Kohala Center has helped develop new models for powering farm and processing equipment with solar energy, as well as designs for innovative on-farm storage.

A Health Center Connects with Its Constituents

A third key partner in the Hawai'i Food for All collaboration is the Kōkua Kalihi Valley (KKV) Health Center in Honolulu. A Native Hawaiian-run clinic grounded in a low-income community, KKV has addressed issues of culture and poverty in remarkably creative and comprehensive ways.

Founded in 1972, KKV serves Kalihi, one of the lowest-income neighborhoods on O'ahu. This community is 93 percent Asian, Native Hawaiian, or Pacific Islander in ancestry. Historically, the Kalihi valley was a self-standing ahupua'a. Further, it was a pilgrimage site, with its highest mountain peak, Kilohana, serving as the cosmological home of Papahānaumoku, the traditional ancestor to all Hawaiian people. Today, however, the valley cradles exceptional inequalities of wealth. Kalihi stands as the third-least food secure community on the island of O'ahu, with 28 percent of residents living in food-insecure households.

The neighborhood hosts four large public-housing projects, so it has become the first home for the majority of new immigrants to Hawai'i. In 2011, 37 percent of Kalihi Valley residents were foreign born, compared to 18 percent statewide and 13 percent nationally. As a health clinic, KKV is charged with guiding these newcomers, and other lower-income residents, to better health. KKV patients are largely Filipino (31%), Micronesian (24%), Samoan (21%) and Native Hawaiian (7%). KKV staff emphasized that half of the patients it treats are best served in some language other than English.

One-fourth of KKV patients suffer from chronic diseases, including cardiovascular disease, obesity, diabetes, asthma, cancer, hypertension, heart disease, and renal disease. This is particularly true for Native Hawaiians and Pacific Islanders. Tuberculosis and sexually transmitted diseases are the most prevalent of the infectious diseases. About 20 percent of KKV adult patients were given diabetes as their primary diagnosis in 2012, compared to 10.9 percent statewide and 11.9 percent nationally.

These facts and figures are all the more startling when one considers Kalihi's past. KKV staff see these inequalities as the result of economic structures that transformed the valley from a self-reliant paradise, managed by its occupants, into one that became subservient to plantation farming and then commercial expansion. As KKV staff held detailed conversations with residents, they heard deep concern about disconnection from the land and sources of nutritious food. Those who are recent migrants feel doubly dislocated by the inequalities they experience.

Bringing the community to health, KKV argued, requires the rediscovery of traditional culture and practices that nourished people for centuries in this valley. Central to that work is understanding what residents can do, rather than treating them as victims. As KKV's Community Food Systems strategist, Kasha Hoʻokili Ho, emphasized, "Our community is inundated with indicators of deficiency—stories told through health and income indicators that name Kalihi as poor. The wealth of our community resides not in dollars, but in knowledge, in culture, in practice, and in love. Many of us still know how to grow our own food; many of us remember the stories connecting us to the land; we still hold our ancestors' voices, recipes, and daily practices of taking care of the earth and each other; and many more of us are learning."

Ho continued, "We have learned that the most valuable opportunities for fostering abundance within Kalihi Valley lie within a return to cultural knowledge, pairing traditional practices and modes of exchange with new pathways being forged between neighbors and markets within the community."

Thus KKV staff foster health by connecting deeply with their clients and encouraging them to connect with each other. They emphasize four kinds of connections:

Connection to place—to have a kinship with ʻāina (land)
Connection to others—to love and be loved; to understand and be understood
Connection to past and future—to have *kuleana* (a purpose in the world)
Connection to your better self—to find and know yourself

KKV staff have found it works best to bring parents and children together, instilling beneficial behaviors and cultural practices that sustain through several generations, to establish a strong foundation of health within both ʻohana (family) and community structures. Staff have created several essential gathering points inside the clinic, including the Roots Café, where neighborhood residents and staff can eat nourishing food, and the Farmacy, a farm stand where anyone can buy fresh produce. They also send out a mobile market that "brings cultural produce directly to the exam rooms of clinic patients, the exercise rooms of our senior centers, and support groups for diabetes patients."

To renew Kalihi Valley's rich cultural heritage, KKV staff have launched an intricate set of initiatives. First, they train new growers at their farm in the upper reaches of the watershed. These growers raise produce for Kalihi residents. KKV also offers a wide range of culinary training and communal cooking activities, as well as opportunities to share knowledge and strengthen networks of reciprocal exchange. Staff work diligently to encourage their constituents to make use of SNAP and other benefits. Budding entrepreneurs can find coaching and technical assistance here as well.

Drawing on Kalihi Valley's tradition of self-sufficiency, KKV works to "decolonize" residents' diets, hampered by stringent work hours that foster a quest for ease. As Roots Café chef Jesse Lipman said, "We found we had difficulty navigating in the middle of a larger food culture." Although the staff encouraged Kalihi residents to eat more vegetables, they found that "no matter how much kale we produced, people wanted to eat breadfruit, poi, and chicken—foods that had been part of that historical lifestyle." So the clinic engaged residents in a series of gatherings where they discussed how US political control had inflicted harmful eating habits, distorting the use of even traditional food items as people sought comfort after long work shifts. New recipes were developed that blended the advantages of culturally resonant foods with fresh fruits and vegetables that could be grown in the valley. These insights were communicated to residents in multiple ways, drawing on cultural nuances among the 15 diverse ethnic groups now living in the valley.

One particularly poignant moment came when staff attempted to encourage their charges to get more exercise. This term held no meaning to several of their clients. "The Micronesian language had no word for 'exercise,'" KKV director Kaiulani Odom recalled, "but people understood gardening." So KKV launched community gardening efforts rather than forcing Western concepts of "working out." Staff noted that they were learning as much, or more, than their patients, in part because decolonizing their language also reduced power imbalances and allowed traditional expertise to emerge.

In further discussions with their constituents, KKV staff came to realize that from an indigenous standpoint, food is medicine. This became one of the many reasons KKV created the Roots Café at their Wellness Center. Open on a limited basis only on Tuesdays and Thursdays, it serves both staff and community members. "We make the meals as organic, sustainable, and local as possible," Odom said. "We work with 18 local farms, including our own Hoʻoulu ʻĀina, to produce quality meals that cost $8 per plate. Staff chefs even crafted an alternative to Spam that has a similar taste, uses local pork, and has no chemical additives." To make sure all felt welcome, Odum added, "We found it is also very important to serve Polynesian carbohydrates such as taro, sweet potato, breadfruit, and tapioca."

KKV's Ho'oulu 'Āina farm embodies all of these insights. Over a decade ago, KKV had an opportunity to take ownership of a 100-acre parcel of land in the uplands of the valley. Historically this property had been a farming center; it was blessed with cleared fields and ample water. KKV began to restore traditional agricultural practices on the land. The farm raises *kalo* (upland taro), 'ulu (breadfruit), traditional medicines, and vegetables. Through their manual labor and studies here, youth learn several important lessons: the culture and knowledge of their ancestors, practical farming skills, and a stronger ability to speak out on behalf of their own vision for the future.

In short, 'āina was important to health in multiple ways. "A lot of things happen through work," Odom said. Growing, preparing, and eating food together were the connecting forces. These create connections to the land, to the past and future, to one's better self, and to others. "We continuously make plants available to our community," she added, hoping to foster still deeper connections.

Yet, in a broader culture that is based on markets, growing food and medicine through traditional practices is not always economically sustainable today. Odom added, "It takes effort to keep this work going while holding on to cultural values. Daily, we balance our work to make food available and affordable, to support local farmers and sustainable agriculture, to integrate health and to honor the ancestral wisdom of our *kupuna* [elders]." KKV relies heavily on foundation support. Although Odom acknowledges that there may come a day when KKV can no longer obtain grants, the work is sustained in part by as much as $750,000 to $1 million of donations each year.

KKV also swims upstream against bureaucratic forces. "This is hard to do under a federally qualified health system," Odom added, under medical rules that have been imposed from Washington. Seldom are these regulations responsive to proven traditional practices. Government officials often press KKV to engage in more behavioral change work. "We don't do a lot of that," one evaluator for KKV said. She finds herself measuring progress in terms of "cultural shifts." Often this is tracked through stories, the medium of cultural exchange that resonates across— and helps build—community networks.

People I interviewed were forceful in reminding me that KKV has set in motion a critical transformation in the Kalihi Valley. It has forged a community, scientific, and professional consensus that supports a culture of health among Kalihi Valley residents. What fosters this culture most effectively, they have found, is working together on the land in a sustainable manner.

This in turn creates broader ripples. At The Towers of Kuhio Park housing project not far from KKV, the social services director, Anni Peterson, described the difficulties that arise when a migrant population is disconnected from land and culture. Although she can encourage the largely Micronesian residents of the project to eat traditional foods for health, "Even these are too expensive at the store." As a result, such insights are often overlooked in daily life. "Traditional foods used to be cheap at the store," Peterson added, but "grocers, recognizing the demand, have raised the price." This is why the project launched community garden and "edible landscape" initiatives. To date, she said, 15 food-bearing trees, such as 'ulu, mountain apple, mango, lemon, and lime, have been planted around the property for residents to harvest. They aim to plant more.

Building a Statewide Network

The leaders of these diverse initiatives also realize that accomplishing all of these extraordinary achievements is insufficient in itself. Each initiative is vulnerable unless all are closely connected to a statewide effort where people can advance their skills and gain important visibility. So, in their "spare" time, Tina Tamai, Kristin Frost Albrecht, Kohala's Betsy Cole, and Kaiulani Odom formed the Hawai'i Food Alliance (HIFA) to provide a forum where these grassroots food initiatives can convene. This is essentially a "network of networks" that fosters greater impact.

One of HIFA's first initiatives was to persuade the Hawai'i Department of Health to pay more attention to enrolling SNAP-eligible residents. Enrollment had lagged in the state, in part due to an antiquated computer platform used by the state government, and also because of the burgeoning demand for benefits. HIFA calculations showed that increasing enrollment could bring as much as $100 million of additional federal payments to the state. If this money were dedicated to purchasing food from Hawai'i farms, that action alone would increase farm cash receipts by as much as 14 percent. Alternatively, it would offset many of the losses currently incurred by state farmers in producing crops and livestock. Thus it could have a profound impact on both eating habits and farm income.

Reclaiming West O'ahu

An extraordinary network of collaboration is concurrently being fashioned in West O'ahu, home of the largest population of Native Hawaiians in the world. Far from the Honolulu skyscrapers, this coastal area is deeply challenged by the inequities of investment. Jobs are sparse, so many people drive 2 hours each way to commute to the metro area. Many of those jobs do not pay well, however, so 85 percent of the area's children qualify for free or reduced lunch at school. That count in itself is a rough approximation of the poverty rate.

Underlying this reality is the history of plantation agriculture on the leeward side of the island. Members of the population that lives here today inherited a legacy of working long hours for little pay and having little command over their daily lives. One of the biggest impacts has been a lack of health. In response, visionary leaders of the state's largest Federally Qualified Health Center, the Waiʻanae Coast Comprehensive Health Center (WCCHC), are working to foster health among their constituents. As with KKV, the health center in Kalihi mentioned earlier, this includes helping to construct a better food system for the community.

It is difficult for Alicia Higa, WCCHC's director of health promotion, to conceal her enthusiasm for tackling this challenge. Having grown up in Waiʻanae, she has experienced these conditions viscerally. "Ours is one of the most vulnerable populations in Hawaiʻi," she said. "We're located on a very secluded section of the island, which was historically home to many plantation workers." In terms of food, people had so little time, and were so hungry, they sought food that was cheap and easily available. "They got used to eating canned food, such as Spam and *saimin*" (an egg-noodle soup similar to ramen), she added. These shelf-stable foods could be stored without refrigeration and consumed quickly. With such limited food choices, people have become accustomed to eating commodity foods. Transitioning to healthier options is not easy.

Moreover, the long commute to Honolulu replicates some of the same issues that plantation life had wrought—the same shortage of time, and a similar need for comfort. "Due to the high cost of living, people are working several jobs to make ends meet," Higa noted. "Their food options take a hit at the end of the month and oftentimes children living in Waiʻanae are left to prepare their own meals using shelf-stable ingredients because their parents come home late. As a result, their best meals may be those they get in school."

After a dozen years of addressing issues such as these, Higa called in reinforcements, creating a position for a community food systems manager within her department. She hired Moulika Anna Hitchens, who moved to West Oʻahu after working with low-income communities in Philadelphia. She is happy to be working now with a "unique health center that is providing more than just a clinic."

One of the early steps the health center took in expanding beyond its primary care services was to open a farmers' market in 2008 so residents would have a place to buy fresh fruits and vegetables. Today the Mākeke Farmers' Markets are open three days each week, attracting 1,600 visitors weekly. Higa is proud of the fact that this has already become the market that redeems more electronic SNAP benefits than any other in the state, with $158,000 accepted in 2018 and expanding rapidly. Of this total, $90,000 in sales were due to a "double-bucks" program where SNAP recipients' purchases are doubled in value. While this leverage has been funded through private donations so far, the health center is now positioned to receive partial federal government funding as part of the statewide Hawaiʻi Good Food Alliance.

Higa pointed out that residents' food options are limited because there are only three grocery stores operating in the community. "The produce sections are very limited and offer mostly imported food." Their offerings are not only meager but also high priced, she added.

The health center also features monthly community wellness workshops at its dining hall, where residents can come to enjoy a meal prepared with the same ingredients that are available at the farmers' markets, and to learn how to prepare them at home. This magnifies the impact of the market itself by bringing residents together to insert these foods into their diet. Higa said that health center staff have tackled the challenge of improving diets by preparing meals that incorporate the comfort foods people are used to, but introducing a new twist. One example is to cook fresh greens with small slices of Spam to ensure that its familiar flavors are present in a healthier meal.

The health center has also launched several food relief programs, recognizing that if they do not convey food directly to people where they live, few will have time to pick up these donations. Setting another precedent, WCCHC became the first organization in Hawai'i to offer a children's produce prescription program. Under it, pediatricians write a "prescription" that allows recipients to redeem $72 of coupons to pay for fresh produce over the next 3 months. In its pilot period, the program delivered prescriptions to 300 keiki (children). Next the program will expand to include a research component in partnership with the University of Hawaii at Mānoa, seeking to discover the best ways to increase produce consumption. The research also aims to encourage health insurance companies to see the value in prevention programs like produce prescriptions and to cover their costs. A similar program for kupuna (elders) is also being planned.

Acting in partnership as a remote outpost of the Hawai'i Foodbank in Honolulu, WCCHC also distributes 'Ohana Boxes (family boxes) of shelf-stable food and fresh produce to families quarterly at the center's 'Ohana Night events. These gatherings also include food demonstrations, community dinners, and information covering health resources. The health center has also opened food pantries in six schools, and plans to add two more school pantries soon. These school pantries were opened because school administrators reported that many of their students were coming to school early in the mornings without having eaten sufficient dinner, or any dinner at all, the night before. They reached out to the food bank asking for snacks. The food bank agreed to supply the snacks, but, due to regulations, the food bank needed a nonprofit community partner (WCCHC) to operate the school pantry. A total of 213,351 pounds of food were delivered through these various initiatives in 2019.

Further, since many children do not eat well during the summer months when school meals are not available, the health center partnered with the Department of Education's 'Āina Pono program to launch a Summer Mobile Meal Program that conveyed nearly 11,000 meals to students in 2019.

Taking on broader concerns meant that WCCHC had to staff up. As community food systems programs expanded, Hitchens was brought on board to coordinate local food activity. Hitchens told me that her role is "to put the pieces together," essentially connecting groups so they can effectively coordinate with each other, and finding additional resources that magnify their efforts. Given the health center's prior accomplishments, Hitchens added, "We know what people's needs are. Our programs have been incredibly successful because Alicia has built strong relationships with our residents and our partners."

As she converses with colleagues working on food systems in their own communities, Hitchens emphasizes that Waiʻanae is isolated geographically: "We're in a constant state of emergency here [in West Oʻahu]. We have to have a plan. It is not enough to simply store MREs [Meals, Ready-to-Eat] in a warehouse. It is important to have a plan for the community to have food today but also prepare for the future, including disasters. Ensuring that fresh foods are part of the response is also important, since people's health is so challenged," she continued.

Higa eagerly shared the news that the health center has now attracted the attention of state officials who are considering grants that would allow WCCHC to acquire land to create a Food Systems Campus. "We currently do all of our food systems work from a 1,200-square-foot building," she lamented. "As we expand to meet the needs of the community, we will need larger facilities." Her first priority is to build emergency food storage so the health center can supply residents when conditions break down. Next most important is to build a community demonstration kitchen where the health center can hold classes with greater ease. Eventually, she hopes the campus will also feature edible landscaping and a sheltered meeting space for hosting workshops. Through the Traditional Hawaiian Healing Center at WCCHC, *lomi lomi* (massage), *hoʻoponopono* (forgiveness and conflict resolution), and *lā ʻau lapaʻau* (traditional plant medicine) practices are offered as part of holistic care.

By introducing healthier and indigenous foods to children and providing opportunities to connect with their own culture and land, the children become advocates within their families. Hitchens added, "If the kids try these foods, the parents are more willing to try them. They start talking about what to buy, and they go to the farmers' market together." This even cycles back to feed the clinic staff in new ways. "We learned so much from our pilot food prescription program. We learned that the caregivers are starting to change their own diets, making sure they are eating healthily themselves."

Connecting a Farm and a University

As children grow up, they will seek job opportunities. So the health center is closely networked with a nearby training farm, MA'O Organic Farms. They work in such harmony that when I first met the farm's founders, Gary and Kukui Maunakea-Forth, we met in the clinic's board room. The couple opened the farm in 2000 as the primary program of the Wai'anae Community Redevelopment Corporation (WCRC). A social enterprise, WCRC earns more than $700,000 of revenue by selling fruits and vegetables raised on the farm, and it combines the sales income with grants to support personal and professional development by West O'ahu youth. This includes training to become leaders in building a more sustainable future for the communities where they live.

MA'O is an acronym for Mala (garden) 'Ai (food) 'Opio (youth), or "youth food garden." It was founded in the hope that by reconnecting youth to the land and restoring mutually nurturing personal relationships through this engagement, the entire West O'ahu region will be strengthened. WCRC seeks to reclaim a heritage of 'auwai, the historical organizing principle that fostered a love of the land ('āina) among Native Hawaiians through their daily practice of fishing and farming in closed-loop community food systems.

It is no coincidence that MAʻO Organic Farms sells produce at the Mākeke Farmers' Markets; these nutritional efforts grew up in concert. The 281-acre farm also supplies food to buyers in Honolulu raised on about 35 acres that is currently under cultivation, where youth learn how to grow food by drawing on traditional practices as well as contemporary science.

WCRC offers scholarships to young people who have worked least 20 hours per week for more than one season on the farm. This work experience qualifies them to continue working on the farm for at least 20 hours per week while they study, in exchange for tuition that can be dedicated to either a 2-year degree at Leeward Community College in Waiʻanae or a 4-year degree at the University of Hawaiʻi.

Assistant Professor Albie Miles has developed a sustainable agriculture degree program at the university in close partnership with both MAʻO Organic Farms and Kamehameha Schools, a statewide private school district focused on educating Native Hawaiians. The program focuses on cultivating critical thinking and leadership skills through study that revolves around the deeply pragmatic work of farming. "I believe we have to train the students to solve real-world problems," Miles told me.

Although each student has agreed to devote 20 hours per week, Miles said, each is likely to actually invest 30 to 40 hours each week on the farm in addition to their studies. To ensure that this is a solid experience for the youth, WCRC adds wraparound services for the students, including several types of counseling. Miles said he meets with MAʻO Farms staff at least once each week and works closely with each student to help each one thrive.

Another service WCRC hopes to offer is shelter. As funds are raised, it will build permanent housing for farm interns on some of the farm's uplands. This will become increasingly important now that the program has begun to attract students from the mainland.

Miles explained that the education program seeks to develop the intellectual infrastructure required for Hawai'i to cultivate its own, more equitable and resilient food system. After the university asked Miles to advise the effort in its early stages, Miles was hired to manage the program. As the only tenured faculty for the program, he jokes that he feels sorry for the program's students, who find that he is the professor for nearly every course they take. Through courses in economics, ethics, and political economy, he said, students graduate with finely honed skills in critical thinking. The US Department of Agriculture offers the students small grants to support research projects. They can use these to engage with larger research efforts as resources become available.

Despite the practical nature of the degree program, Miles said, "We're not really doing farmer training." Many of the graduates move on to jobs that pay better than farming does. Rather, Miles is focused on ensuring that the students enter their careers with solid critical-thinking skills. "We need to think more critically about the food system we have," Miles explained. "We have to address the externalities it produces. We have to ask, what does society really need, rather than just adapt to the systems society gives us. We have to determine what is optimal in a social, cultivation, and economic sense." To advance that purpose, Miles also builds connections with other scholars across the state and globally. He added that an Office of Indigenous Innovation had just been established inside the state government, as a way of ensuring that Native Hawaiian traditions would have a strong voice in future planning for the state.

Leadership in State Government

Although Tina Tamai retired from the Department of Health, she remains active in coordinating the work of the Hawai'i Food Alliance. The current SNAP Education coordinator for the state of Hawai'i, Tammy Chase-Brunelle, traces her work back to the visionary ground that Tamai first broke.

As a result of this prior innovation, "Hawai'i is unique in SNAP-Ed," Chase-Brunelle said. "I don't know of any other states that have taken such a broad approach." She noted that the state had taken national leadership in defining who is eligible for SNAP benefits, as well as in its systemic approach to food systems. Whereas Tamai once worked below the radar to connect individuals who often felt isolated, and fostered a new vision for food systems, Chase-Brunelle is now charged with institutionalizing that approach into the state government on a variety of levels. Overall, her priority is to "create a broader food systems coalition." Her work involves educational efforts to illuminate "how the Hawai'i food system works *as a whole*, and remind everyone how they can make a difference" in shaping it. This food systems thread encompasses constituents from early childhood education all the way to state offices. Many of the individual trainings and educational outreach efforts that Tamai launched have now been relegated to other organizations or agencies.

Chase-Brunelle added that the individual islands which make up the state of Hawai'i have distinct histories and cultures, so this food system work has to be grounded in the unique qualities of each place. SNAP Education funds now pay for three local food systems coordinators in three counties—Hawai'i, Kaua'i, and Maui—and she hopes to extend this to Molokai as well as the O'ahu locales of Wai'anae (home of WCRC and WCCC), and Kalihi (home of KKV). On two of the islands, this coordination is performed directly by county staff. On the third, Kaua'i, the nonprofit Mālama Kaua'i plays host. "Each community is very different," Chase-Brunelle added. "We want each local group to create a work plan based on the needs in their own community." This means that while work on the Big Island focuses on gardening, gleaning, and establishing a food council, Maui partners with the Maui food bank to promote healthy eating among youth, and Kaua'i focuses on farm-to-school efforts.

As just one example, Kaua'i fosters systemic change by bringing key stakeholders into direct negotiation with each other, Chase-Brunelle emphasized: "Every single public school on Kaua'i now has a farm-to-school program. Farmers are at the table discussing what they can supply, and teachers are learning how to incorporate these foods into lesson plans."

This community-centered work is echoed by related initiatives at the state level. The local coordinators convene once each month to discuss common concerns, and to harmonize statewide activity. This might include the county groups forming collaborations with each other. Chase-Brunelle herself then assists the state Department of Education as it trains teachers to expand farm-to-school efforts, such as incorporating gardening activities into any type of course offerings, including health, science, and history.

Chase-Brunelle also works with a state government Food Access Transportation Committee that brings multiple state entities together, including planning, transportation, and environmental officials, to consider how each of their activities impacts food. "We are now starting to see the built environment as part of what we're doing," she explained. In Honolulu, she works with rapid transit officials to explore ways to make healthy foods available at rail stops.

"We're in the middle of a movement," Chase-Brunelle continued. Her work increasingly focuses on how institutions can purchase food from farms in nearby communities, and not just from some source in Hawai'i, to ensure that smaller homegrown farms are not overlooked as the state courts outside agribusiness firms. Still, she recognizes that this is difficult because farmers are few, land prices are high, and imported foods are still less expensive to buy. Incentives such as double-bucks programs are critical to expand, she added.

Having staff in place allows the network building to move forward with far more efficacy because someone prioritizes coordination. Just as critically, this funding allows a new generation of food-system leaders to enter professional life while the elder pioneers are still very active. New verve can be blended with seasoned expertise.

Reclaiming Culture

At the end of the plantation era, Hawai'i's 7,328 farms were spending $800 million per year to raise crops and livestock they sold for only $626 million. Several excellent, pioneering farmers were quitting their produce farms out of despair over a lack of public support. The last parcels of sugar plantation were being rededicated to raising and processing food for those who live on the islands.

But the cultural habits bred by the plantation system still echoed across the watersheds and mountains of the islands. Countering these patterns, diverse groups in the Hawai'i Food for All network strive to forge new ways of stewarding the land in a contemporary context. Some coach individual constituents as they bring them food assistance, helping them to address the multiple issues they face. New jobs and new systems of trade have been created. Scholars train youth in critical-thinking skills.

As in Montana, building a statewide network was critical to expanding the impact of the food systems work. The critical element in Hawai'i was to reclaim ancient cultural practices and adapt them for this new setting. Chapter 4 reports on a stellar initiative launched by a food bank dedicated to fostering social advocacy among low-income residents of Tucson—where wide expanses of sand, not valleys with resonant waterfalls, are the norm.

CHAPTER 4

Building the Capacities and Voice of Low-Income Residents

As the US strove to "feed the world," SNAP (Supplemental Nutrition Assistance Program) benefit allocations soared sevenfold, from $7 billion to $64 billion (all figures in 2017 dollars) over the past 50 years. America has essentially exchanged solid farm income for widespread poverty. Food-relief sector workers know that short-term food donations are critical for people's survival and health as long as inequalities exist. Still, food banks are increasingly using food donations as only the first step in building a more empowering relationship with their constituents. In Tucson, Arizona, a nationally respected food bank focuses on building economic opportunity for its constituents and breaking down the isolation low-income people experience. As this work has matured, food bank officials increasingly engage low-income constituents in the planning and management of food bank programs. Gaining new voice and visibility, some have been inspired to launch new businesses, to strengthen student success and neighborhood support networks through gardening, and to run for office to change municipal policies.

Our bus rolled down Interstate 19 toward the US–Mexico border at Nogales. As we passed checkpoints where border patrol officers were checking credentials, drones soared overhead, scanning the Sonoran Desert for unusual activity. Semitrailer trucks loaded with Central American goods roared north in the opposite lane. When we reached the outskirts of Nogales, massive warehouses became visible on the frontage road. Soon we saw the border itself—scarred by a series of 20-foot-tall, rust-brown metal posts, embedded in the ground in snug formations and scaling hillsides at precarious angles. Daylight streamed through the gaps between the posts, offering glimpses of the Mexican countryside. The ominous line resembled a mammoth set of sutures, and "itched" in the same manner: I felt eager to have them removed.

The nearly three hundred produce warehouses, typically built out of rudimentary cement blocks, also seemed out of place, scattered as they were among desert brush. But they belonged, a physical testament to the fact that Nogales is the largest produce shipping port in the world—$3 billion of produce moves through in a year, including 94 percent of the fresh produce imported from Mexico. Overall, in 2017 Nogales accounted for 86 percent of the goods the US exports to Mexico, and 87 percent of the goods the US imports from Mexico.

Nogales itself, divided into two cities with the same name on either side of the border, creates another huge flow of pedestrian traffic, with 10,000 people per day entering the northern town. Mostly they shop at superstores on the US side, but many also head across to go to work or visit relatives who have been separated by the fence. The Mexican Nogales has a population of 212,000, while the Arizona Nogales has 20,000. Yet the best stores and opportunities are found on the Arizona side. These stores thrive in large part because of Mexican consumers, who have no comparable choices south of the border. Certainly it is not because of a free-spending clientele. Roughly two of every three Nogales, Arizona, residents live below the 185 percent of poverty line, a rough measure of a livable wage. Poverty rates are even higher in the Mexican town.

Crossing Borders

I was brought to Nogales by a food bank. On this particular day, I was part of a contingent of food leaders attending a national conference of food banks in Tucson, hosted by the Community Food Bank (CFB) of Southern Arizona. At the conference I learned about strategies food banks are testing to expand their role beyond donating food to low-income people, and to assist their constituents to take more power over their own lives. This field trip was centered around the CFB food pantry in the town; the irony of Nogaleños living on either side of the border having difficulty eating an adequate diet while tons of produce flows past their doors was not lost on our hosts. Nor was the fact that the US town depends mightily on customers living in Mexico. The economic development director, in fact, had told me in 2011 that his main development strategy was to attract Mexican visitors.

The food bank itself depends heavily on Mexican produce, importing 7–10 million pounds from Mexico each year: about one-third of its total produce donations. One owner, Phil Ostrom, CEO of Patagonia Orchards, told me he sells tons of "second-quality" organic produce items to the food bank. These look less attractive than the premier-quality items but are still fresh and nutritious.

When I interviewed him in 2011, Ostrom pointed out that "a lot of Mexico is ahead of the US [in organics]. Many of the farms are owned by Mexican entrepreneurs. They are ahead in growing technology, with greenhouses and irrigation, and ahead in packing technology. Every farm is third-party audited."

Instead of serving rural Mexican consumers, however, that massive infrastructure was dedicated to shipping food to metro areas of the US, where consumers hold considerable spending power. Meanwhile, Arizona had great difficulty supporting its own farmers who wish to raise food for local residents. And groups like CFB cope with structural inequalities, while trying to get food to as many mouths as possible. In

2018, CFB gave 71 million pounds of food through five locations to more than 200,000 people in their five-county service area. That is one of every six residents. CFB counts 140 nonprofit partners in its five-county service area, and it distributes food at 400 locations. Its annual revenue tops $125 million.

CFB does this food relief work very well, but it won national recognition for something else—its innovations in assisting its clients to advocate for themselves. Feeding America, the food bank umbrella group, named CFB the best food bank in the US for 2018. This award signified a tectonic shift within the national organization, which in the past has evaluated food banks primarily on the basis of "pounds in/ pounds out": how many pounds of food they collected, and how many pounds they gave away. Recognition from this national body revealed that the food bank industry more generally is questioning its own model, and looking to food banks like Tucson's for inspiration. This is also a step toward a larger understanding that the prevailing food system is itself creating poverty.

My studies for CFB estimated that Southern Arizona spends more than $3 billion buying food each year that was grown elsewhere. These desert valleys hold only a limited tradition of family farming, because pioneer livestock ranches and the large plantations that once surrounded Tucson were geared to shipping food in mass quantities to northern climates. In its way, CFB has shouldered one part of the task of constructing a food system that could bring income to southern Arizona families and help reduce poverty.

Chief Program Officer Robert Ojeda told me that CFB has consistently strived to be responsive to its clients, paying close attention to them as human beings and listening to what they say they need. When constituents pointed out that it was difficult for them to afford much of the produce sold at farmers' markets, CFB launched the Santa Cruz River Farmers' Market that offers subsidized produce. To supply this downtown farmers' market, the food bank either purchases produce or accepts donations from growers, and then it resells these food items at affordable prices.

When it became clear that many food recipients did not know how to grow food for themselves, and that very few farms were able to supply produce to Tucson markets, CFB launched a network of community gardeners. Their weekly meetings, where 25–40 gardeners routinely convene, led to advocacy for new garden plots. Now the CFB network boasts 1,120 community gardens—and these gardeners are encouraged to give back to the community by donating thousands of pounds of produce to food pantries.

When the group of new gardeners tried to sell herbs and spices to local restaurants, they discovered that city ordinances prohibited these sales. So CFB worked with a local celebrity chef, Janos Wilder, to change city policies. As momentum built for growing food, it further became clear that some residents would want to farm at a commercial scale, so the food bank opened a training farm inside the city. When I visited this farm in 2011, I saw lush green plants springing out of desert soil, with no artificial chemical use. Fertility was built by composting organic scraps—through an effort organized by the food bank.

Several recipients wanted to launch food businesses as a way of boosting their income, so the food bank opened the Caridad Kitchen, a certified processing space for community use. Caridad provided 328,290 meals and engaged 270 volunteers in the process. Perhaps more impressively, CFB hired 35 "interns" from among low-income ranks to help manage the kitchen, creating rudimentary employment for people who collect food relief from the food bank.

Fostering Entrepreneurs

Having such a facility is empowering in its own way, but the food bank further recognized that some recipients would benefit from training if they wanted to move into commercial production. So CFB launched an entrepreneurship program to give them a boost. One of the success stories is La Tauna Tortillas, which opened in 2011. Diana Teran and her husband, Francisco, developed the business concept after their son Jonathan had been ill for several years. Through considerable trial and error, they discovered that a diet which included whole grains and no preservatives was an important part of his cure.

Diana began making tortillas by hand, adapting an old family recipe to create vegan tortillas using natural grains and without lard. The food bank coached her on opening the business; the first place she began to sell them was the CFB farmers' market. Four months later, the tortillas were offered at the Food Conspiracy Co-op, and in every Sprouts grocery store. Only 8 months later, Diana and Francisco were selling through private labels and direct to stores across both Arizona and New Mexico.

At this point, CFB "did an awesome thing for me and I'll never forget it," Teran recalled. "They actually worked with a TV station that would be interested in our story." The food bank also encouraged a local newspaper to carry a story about the tortillas. Sales increased 30 percent. During this expansion, the Terans made contact with San Xavier Farm, a Native American farm located on the grounds of a former mission, which grew heirloom non-GMO corn for them. In turn, the farm was featured by La Tauna. The couple then opened a small café to showcase their tortillas as part of healthy meals.

Gradually, the La Tauna firm made its way into all of the Whole Foods stores, and the entire All Natural chain, in Tucson. They began to focus on the wholesale trade and eventually closed the café so they could focus on this specialty.

Teran regrets that in this phase they outgrew San Xavier Farm's ability to supply them. Moreover, the firm's expansion took a difficult turn when the partnership they had formed to reach wider wholesale markets fell apart. Teran views it as an important learning experience. "I'm in this business because it is my passion. If you have such a passion for a business and don't understand there will be problems, then you are misleading yourself. [Having a crisis like this] just makes you stronger."

The couple emerged from the breakup of the business partnership with a strong desire to return to their roots in Tucson. "It made me appreciate my community all the more. Now we are trying to get back to our neighbors in Tucson." The firm will open a retail store right at the tortilla factory, and they hope to move to a new location near the University of Arizona campus.

The couple also made one important change in their branding. As Diana recalled, "After being 5 years in the market, we noticed that even natives from Mexico were not familiar with the meaning of our brand name La Tauna [stone mill]. Most couldn't even enunciate it. Therefore we decided to change our name to something easier to remember and that would relate to our products. This is how we became Natural Grains Tortillas."

When I spoke with Diana in late 2019, she told me she had just returned to the food bank farmers' market to sell tortillas, part of her effort to return to the community that had helped them launch. The couple also reconnected to a CSA (community-supported agriculture) farm to provide fresh tortillas offered as part of the farm share. She was soon heading to a middle school to show students how to make tortillas from scratch for themselves. "It's not that big a deal to make them yourself," she said. She plans to appear on a national Hispanic TV network to help Latinos learn more about eating healthier foods, including how to cook several traditional dishes with better ingredients. She has just contracted with a Brazilian firm to provide organic corn.

While Diana has long outgrown a need for the food bank's technical assistance, Natural Grains does cater meals for them from time to time. She added that they could be very useful in helping her reconnect to the Tucson community. "I love what the food bank does for the community," she beamed.

While not all business start-ups are this successful, the Terans' experience shows that entrepreneurship can thrive under the proper conditions. Still, this alone is not enough to complete the circle for the food bank. Drawing on the previous victories in setting new policies, CFB has also begun training constituents in advocacy. They have now formed a leadership academy that is open to low-income residents and others in the community. After graduating scores of people through this leadership training, the CFB hopes to build a core of leaders who can work to make sure public policy supports the needs of Tucson residents over the long haul.

Forging Connections in a School Courtyard

The food bank also responded generously when Moses Thompson, a guidance counselor at the Manzo Elementary School in Tucson, launched an effort in 2006 to grow food at the school on a little-used inner courtyard. He had been transforming the small space into a garden on his own, but it soon became part of his counseling practice. He recalled that when he applied his counseling skills to working with students who were having difficulties, the usual techniques didn't work. "They were just put off. I was still this white man working with kids of color who experienced a lot of trauma in their lives." But they took notice of his work in the garden. "So I started to garden with the kids. We filled it with seedlings and seeds. If they were in trouble, instead of taking them into my office I would suggest we work together in the garden. Working together was more therapeutic than all the techniques I had been trained to offer. Our conversations were better, because we were doing a kinesthetic activity. Their anxiety dropped, and they began to self-regulate, simply by working in the garden. That hooked me."

Thompson added that this had a snowball effect he hadn't anticipated. "The other thing was that the garden activity removed the stigma about going to the counselor's office. So other kids in the school began coming to the garden without being invited." As he got to know these students, his understandings deepened. "Even though most of the students were low in socioeconomic status, their skills became obvious. And they would talk about their parents, who were skilled in trades. They were carpenters, concrete finishers, and plumbers." Thompson invited the parents to participate in the garden project, too, by applying their expertise. "They made it a far better garden, and they felt proud of their contribution."

The ripples spread even wider, as neighbors came to visit the garden. "People would see the plants and remember the gardens they had as children. Or they would remember their grandparents' farm. They would get so excited to have a cultural connection at school." Thompson also offered training to the Manzo teachers to help them learn why gardening was so effective, and how they could engage. This, in turn, created more goodwill across the neighborhood. CFB helped create this buzz, because it had several staff dedicated to promoting community gardens, and it could provide volunteers. CFB helped train both school staff and gardeners and invested in many of the early food-growing facilities at the school. Building this strong support from diverse members of the community would pay off in the future.

In the short term, however, Thompson was exhilarated by the way the culture of the school shifted. "When I started working there, Manzo Elementary had a low enrollment rate. It was viewed as a low-achievement school. Parent involvement was low. My job as counselor was to address all of these issues—and they all improved." Today, he added, "achievement is up and there is a waiting list to get into the school." He attributes that to the culture and community that have been built. Now, "we have both a student population and a neighborhood population that are connected with, and value, food production. I feel like, to some extent, that's why our kids feel comfortable and are excited to come to school. The same goes with the parents."

As enthusiasm swelled, Thompson added a composting operation, an aquaponics operation, a rain irrigation system, and plants that attracted pollinators. Then the students began to raise chickens. As their expertise grew, and more students became involved, Thompson began to show them what farmers do. Moreover, Manzo Elementary also earned enough from selling produce from the garden to pay for the following year's seeds, feed, and operating supplies.

During the 2011–12 school year, however, while Manzo Elementary was still viewed as underachieving, the school district made plans to close the school and consolidate it with another building. "At this point, the garden was just hitting stride," Thompson recalled. "The neighborhood got very vocal about wanting to keep their school." With the broad base of support the garden had cultivated, parents quickly found strong allies. The mayor, the Audubon Society, and two universities spoke out in support of Manzo Elementary. "We were able to get ourselves off the closure list."

This, in turn, attracted the attention of a University of Arizona geography professor, Sally Marsden, who suggested that Thompson should focus more broadly than on one single school. She arranged a position for him, shared by the Tucson United School District and the university, where he could write a curriculum for Tucson schools to use in fostering student skills by raising food, and also teach a school gardening course at the university, where he arranges for university students to gain service credits by working with school gardens across the city. "Now we have 120 students a year working at 11 schools," Thompson added.

Once the curriculum was under way, Thompson opened the Tucson United School District's Green Academy, which has trained over 50 teachers to foster school gardening across Southern Arizona. Thompson added that the Green Academy has been critically important for institutionalizing school gardens: many are launched by an energetic teacher who then changes jobs, or runs out of steam. With the Green Academy in place, more people are available to fill such gaps and keep the work going. And with new college interns every year, there are new energies to welcome: three of Thompson's interns now teach in the school district, one is the garden coordinator at a school, and another is now on the full-time staff at the Green Academy.

But that did not mean that Thompson abandoned Manzo Elementary. In the summer of 2018, when somebody broke into the school building, trashing the greenhouse and destroying the aquaponics operation, the gardeners' network of skilled neighbors came out in force to repair the damage. "One local business donated $5,000 to help us rebuild. A restaurant held a fundraiser that netted $10,000. Now the garden is in better shape than before."

Thompson added that he hopes to continue the work on a "slow, nice trajectory" in the next few years. He said the school system support has been solid, allowing the Green Academy to have a staff of four. "We get a lot of pressure from funders to embrace scaling up and replicability. In school gardens that doesn't work. We have no plans to make gardens in each school. Instead of growing broad, we want to build deep and long-lasting support. Having a stable network is more important to us." He adds that he views his work as community organizing for a very pragmatic reason. "We don't pretend to be apolitical. If we want to see more of these projects, we need strong community support."

He does hope, however, that he can build an endowment for his work at the university so he does not have to spend so much of his time raising money. "With a staff of six at the university, I have to raise $350,000 every year to keep us going." In a sense, this commitment has supplanted CFB's role. CFB has now cut its gardening staff to one, and Thompson says there has been a bit of a separation. "We love the work they do, but we're really not working together now."

The experience that CFB had with partners such as Thompson informed their discovery that they, too, should become more devoted to empowering residents. CFB further realized it had to incorporate the voices of low-income recipients more formally in its corporate decision making. The course for this work was set long before Ojeda arrived at the food bank, expressing the vision of a visionary executive director, Punch Woods, who established the principle that those most closely impacted by a given situation should decide what to do to address the issues involved. That approach was continued by Bill Carnegie as well as the current director, Michael McDonald. As a result, Ojeda reports, the CFB board of directors has remained steadfast in pursuing this vision.

As the food bank committed itself to *changing poverty*, not simply offering food, the vision deepened. CFB commissioned university researchers to perform an ethnographic analysis of its constituents in Cochise County. The scholars were asked to identify the assets that low-income residents held, and to engage them in a deeper conversation about their personal concerns.

"The interviews told a vastly different story than the data sets we had consulted, which often focused on what was going wrong. We learned how vibrant and capable people were," Ojeda recalled. On the other hand, the research also showed that the food bank's constituents "felt really isolated from everything." In a second urban study, researchers found the same sense of isolation among seniors. "It can be paralyzing if you don't feel you have support behind you," Ojeda added. As the CFB staff and board embraced these insights, the organization set a strategic priority of breaking down that isolation.

Now CFB has formed a Community Engagement Team, charged with enhancing the role of the food bank's partner pantries so they could more effectively engage their constituents. Indeed, the pantries are now called resource centers, where recipients can go, not just to obtain food but to learn more about their rights, the services that are available to them, and how to engage with food bank governance. Knowing that language was often a special barrier for its constituents, CFB began to offer engagement training in Spanish as well as English.

Today the food bank offers a Civic Engagement workshop for residents who wish to devote their attention to policy change. Special curricula have been developed for mothers, gardeners, and teachers, reflecting the special strengths of each group. Garden leaders learn about producing more food, and they gain access to the Abundant Harvest Co-op, a network of farmers and gardeners. Teachers connect with other teachers across the region and learn more about mounting effective advocacy at their schools. Mothers launch empowerment efforts for women in the community. All of these groups also receive more general training in understanding the economic structures that keep people poor, clarifying power dynamics in Tucson, and developing a stronger voice as advocates, whether within their families or in more public circles, such as parent-teacher organizations or neighborhood associations. Ojeda estimates that about 300 people have completed these courses, and that about one-third of graduates are low income. From the ranks of these graduates, trainers identify those individuals who have the skill and interest to participate in larger governance structures, whether at CFB or in the broader community.

One graduate worked her way up from learning how to garden to joining a leadership academy to getting elected as chair of her neighborhood association. From that position, she leveraged $300,000 of county funds for neighborhood improvements, such as traffic calming and better illumination, Ojeda added.

Another group of gardeners asked the food bank to support them in forming a producers' co-op. They now grow food to sell to two local hospitals and one school district. The food bank assisted them in marketing and uses its warehouses and trucks to aggregate their produce and deliver it to the buyers.

In a third case, a group of food bank recipients who worked full time for landscaping firms installing water-harvesting systems (that collect sparse rainfall for later use) realized through leadership training discussions that they could create a business opportunity for themselves in this field.

They learned more about soil and water conservation and formed partnerships with the City of Tucson to obtain rebates for landowners who install these systems. Now they collaboratively run their own landscaping business. They earn more than they used to, and they also enjoy taking command of their own enterprise.

"Are We Creating Equity?"

Ojeda emphasized that the general approach the food bank takes is to work in partnership with its constituents, not as an agency to a client. He said that the process of engaging low-income stakeholders has often been a "painful process," but it has led to a fundamental transformation of the food bank's governance. "The question we always ask now is, 'Is what we're doing creating equity?'" This will not mean the food bank abandons its traditional role, but he hopes the percentage of their budget allocated to food relief will shift from 80 percent to 60 percent in the near future.

The food bank also commissions research to help them establish action priorities. One ethnographic study pinpointed that health was a primary concern. Researchers also documented that CFB's constituents suffer from high rates of diabetes and heart disease—and furthermore, that many of the foods the food bank had been dispersing were not promoting health. The CFB board took note of these findings, and after 6 months of considerable deliberation, "looking at the nutritional value of all the foods we distribute," Ojeda said, developed a nutrition policy for the food it donates. A new Health and Nutrition Team was formed to screen the food items the food bank procures, to upgrade the nutrition education it provides, and to engage in broader change to promote healthier lifestyles. This team was tasked with engaging clients in planning "what a healthier food box would look like," understanding that if constituents helped decide what was in the box, they were more likely to use its contents.

This, in turn, led to refined policies for the food bank itself, moving from measuring just the pounds of food donated to a more nuanced approach that balances investments in educational programming, network strengthening, community development, deeper engagement by constituents, and food and health.

Ojeda is quick to point out that none of the work of the food bank could succeed without its community partners. "The solutions for alleviating an ever growing hunger problem lie not only in serving immediate needs but in supporting the creation of robust and resilient local food systems," he told me. None of the advocacy for low-income clients succeeds without trusted partners in nonprofits, or city or state agencies, who can clear away red tape. None of the four CFB farmers' markets would survive without low-income shoppers supporting them. None of the food businesses could thrive without technical assistance partners drawn from the community.

To strengthen this broader network, CFB staff also coordinate a broader effort, Somos La Semilla (we are the seed), a cross-border network of native and community food leaders who strive to build sustainable food systems across the Sonoran Desert region shared by those who live in the northern parts of the Chihuahua and Sonora states of Mexico, or in Southern Arizona. The Nogales branch of CFB has been a key partner in this endeavor, along with Avalon Organic Gardens, the Mariposa Community Health Center, and Nogales (AZ) Community Development. One major focus of the network, Ojeda said, has been to renew threatened food traditions, and to promote broader cultural renewal, in ways that connect residents on both sides of the borders.

Breaking Barriers

The curtain that slashes through the Nogales countryside is not simply an ugly scar. It is also a severing of families, of individual and collective liberty, and of ecosystems. The wall, along with the policies that sur-round it, makes it difficult for struggling immigrants to attend public meetings across the US, where they might find new ways to establish themselves. It creates health and hunger problems. That is why CFB wanted us to experience the border firsthand—and to learn how the food bank itself is breaking down some of the internal walls that once divided its managers from its constituents.

The issues that low-income people face are complex and intertwined. On a personal level, a person might confront hunger, health concerns, gaps in skills, the threat of incarceration, domestic violence, and a lack of spending money, all in a single day. The most effective approaches I know of embrace these complex issues one by one, staying connected to people with multiple traumas, and backing them up as they address these issues. The wisdom of the Tucson approach is to take this work even further, into the realms of business development, neighborhood organizing, and elective office—as well as bringing low-income con-stituents into defining the food bank's needs, analyzing the food bank's approach, and helping the food bank better serve the community. This creates more inclusive collaborations to build a better food system in the Tucson region—one that serves all people well, and engages limited-income residents as active stakeholders in building the system.

Poverty also erupted as a concern for economic developers in North-east Indiana, serving a vastly different population and climate, as chapter 5 shows. In this case, however, the starting point was an effort to bring large food manufacturers into collaboration with highly productive commodity farmers, in the hopes of building a regional food network. When that effort faltered, however, these flexible leaders embraced the insights their constituents brought them. Their discoveries brought the developers close to family farms, low-income residents of Fort Wayne, and immigrants.

CHAPTER 5

Placing Food Business Clusters at the Core of Economic Development

Taking advantage of two regional strengths in Northeast Indiana, economic developers launched a strategy of connecting nationally visible food manufacturers with the commodity farmers near them, hoping to build greater wealth in the region. However, the food processors saw little reason to collaborate regionally, because they focused on national markets and viewed each other as competitors. Looking for new approaches, the Northeast Indiana Regional Partnership asked a team of consultants to assist. When developers viewed our maps showing the support networks that family-based farms had already built to engage household customers in purchasing from their farms—and how effectively these farms had already networked with each other—the developers turned greater attention toward supporting these farms as a cluster of local businesses. Yet the maps also held potent unexpected insights. As strong as the collaborations were among the emerging farmers, most of their food was shipped to distant metro centers, and little was available to lower-income neighborhoods. So the partnership expanded its work to address these issues as well. Through separate channels, the developers also came to realize that the economic growth of their region required new immigrants. They began to market their region as an attractive place to live, largely by ensuring that high-quality, locally raised food was available.

John Sampson's office holds a commanding view of the Allen County Courthouse in downtown Fort Wayne. Springing up from his chair, he greets his visitor with a warm smile and heartfelt handshake. As director of the Northeast Indiana Regional Partnership, Sampson is charged with coordinating the economic development discussion in an 11-county region rich with farms and food manufacturers. His eyes focus intently, conveying a deep interest in listening. I was immediately struck by his candor.

I met with Sampson in 2015 as part of the Partnership's initiative to create a stronger collaboration among farms and factories. I had been brought in by Chris Manheim, a Chicago-based development consultant who wanted food and agricultural expertise to be included in the process. Remarkably, rather than giving me the standard sales pitch about the region, Sampson began by telling me what had gone wrong.

"We have not had real success when it comes to food," he said. Sampson and his development partners had imagined that they could bring the region's farmers and food manufacturers together to build more effective business clusters. With its flat, fertile fields and global customer base, Sampson had hoped that all parties would find common ground to create a new competitive advantage unique to the region.

Yet little progress was made. The farmers were quite willing to talk about selling their raw commodities to local processors. But the manufacturers were much harder to convince. After meeting regularly for 2 years, exploring ways to collaborate, the discussion stalled. Essentially, Sampson said, the manufacturers saw each other as competitors. Each was trying to reach the same markets and saw no benefit from coordinating efforts. He hoped we could suggest a new approach.

Sampson envisioned creating a Northeast Indiana Local Food Network. Manheim had helped the partnership raise US Department of Agriculture funds to create a plan for this network. Sampson provided the backstory. "When I started here, I was a complete neophyte" to economic development work, he recalled. Local business leaders had asked him to fill this job in 2006, because they sought a new voice. At the time, he continued, "things were totally dysfunctional. It was widely accepted that economic development in Indiana was not working. Of course there were winners and losers. But we had become so competitive as communities that people tore each other apart" trying to attract new investment. "We had lost touch."

One investor who had sought to locate a steel mill in the region warned Sampson, "People are so competitive here." That investor went elsewhere. One county official and a hospital executive told him, "We have to create a new model."

"I Did a Lot of Listening"

To develop that new model, as a newcomer to the development field, Sampson told me, "I did a lot of listening." He spoke with mayors, county commissioners, and business leaders, asking about their experiences with economic development. He looked for national models that he could replicate in Northeast Indiana. The common element in success was that people worked collaboratively.

The question Sampson still had was how to make that happen. "You can't force this," he said. Everybody who works with our partnership is a volunteer." They are making decisions daily about whether each meeting is worth their time. In the end, however, he found that he could count on people coming to the conversation with a great deal of honesty. "If we had not started with having a lot of trust from elected officials and business leaders, I don't know how we would have done this."

Meeting one-on-one with county commissioners and economic development staff from each of the counties (only nine were involved at first), Sampson's staff developed a list of agreements that would need to be in force if the collaboration was to survive. "We built greater trust one step at a time. Each time we made a decision, we wrote it down." Then the team went back to the people who had made each decision to wordsmith it until everybody was satisfied, even if that required several meetings. The most important of those decisions became the basis for a code of ethics for economic developers across the entire region. The code, inspired by a similar effort in the Denver region, included provisions that counties would share information and not fight each other to attract specific projects. The Partnership asked each county commission and each local development office to sign this document. Each did. Once this code was in force, several counties began to invest their bond funds collaboratively, even to support projects that were not located within their physical boundaries, for the sake of strengthening the region as a whole.

Next, Sampson convened the county development organizations to establish a common vision for the region. It was called Vision 2020—and has since been updated to Vision 2030. It stated that new investments would be gauged by whether they helped advance specific elements of the agreed vision.

As a result, Sampson said, "We've built the most collaborative region in Indiana." He added, "There was no one secret sauce that made this work." It worked because people found they were doing better by working together. "For us to compete in a global marketplace we need to collaborate." When the State of Indiana offered substantial grants to "regional cities" that devised the most exemplary investment plans for new development, Northeast Indiana won a $42 million grant. Sampson said the region has matched this with $255 million of its own investments, placing projects in 10 of the 11 counties.

One core of the vision is to strengthen business clusters—groups of food businesses that gain synergies by being located near and trading with each other. Sampson imagined manufacturers promising to purchase raw commodities from nearby farms, and these processors saving money by buying essential supplies collaboratively. This would reduce costs and increase the number of dollars circulating in the regional economy. Hopefully, it would also ensure that each of these businesses would become more resilient over time.

Creating an Action Guide for a Local Food Network

At this point Sampson wanted to move forward on a different tack. He showed me 10 previous studies that had already been published covering the potential for boosting local food trade in the region. None of the plans had really taken root. Now he wanted a guide for action. I began by collecting some basic data about the region's farm and food economy. Then I interviewed several of the region's farmers and food leaders, selected in collaboration with the Partnership. I knew several of them from prior work in Indiana.

The interviews fairly quickly illuminated one of the key barriers to moving forward. When I asked my sources how each would like to see the "food network" advance, it became clear that people had wildly diverging notions of what "local food" meant. To some, it meant whatever crops and livestock were grown by farms in the region, even if it were exported abroad. Indeed, a pig farm that was helping Chinese growers develop a pork industry was highlighted as a great example of "local food." Others simply pointed to the farms they felt were managed the best, as if trading in "local food" was primarily a way of featuring the most exemplary farms. Hitting closer to home, several food leaders simply stated that "local food" meant anything grown or processed, and then sold, in the state of Indiana. Yet this definition did not identify anything unique to the region itself. Still others said that local food involved raising food on Northeast Indiana farms for the region's consumers. One leader had a more precise definition: "Local food is when people have an opportunity to know where their food came from, and it is presented thoughtfully in a relational marketing way."

Although each of these definitions held some merit, it was also clear that any discussion about collaboration would be difficult to pursue if some people were talking about exporting food while others were focused on relational marketing to local customers. In my first comments to the Partnership, I spelled out the different definitions I had heard. I said it was the region's choice how to define the term, but they should choose one definition and stick with it for long enough to see what collaborations might be possible under their definition.

The partnership chose the following definition: "Local food is food that was raised on a Northeast Indiana farm and eaten by consumers in Northeast Indiana." This intersected nicely with Sampson's own view: "This project is about getting locally produced food to local consumers. Right now, that happens at the farmers' market, with small entrepreneurs. Our mission as a region is to build quality of place and support entrepreneurship, so this fits in under both counts."

Uncovering Unrecognized Leaders

My interviews with farmers were especially revealing, because they were already collaborating with each other in business clusters of their own invention. But most had not been invited to become involved in the Partnership's effort to build a regional network. The farmers told me that the economic developers did not consider their farms to be businesses: the development discussion seemed to be focused on attracting large employers from outside the area.

My interviews also documented how effectively the farmers already coordinated their efforts. All shared information with each other. All of the pioneering farmers I spoke with were also selling to one restaurant, Joseph Decuis Restaurant in Roanoke. That restaurant served as a vital connection point. One farmer dropped off his CSA shares at the Joseph Decuis Emporium, a retail store down the block from the restaurant. There his customers could pick up their shares and then shop at the store. The owner of the restaurant and store, Pete Eshelman, had previously convened these farmers, along with many others, to introduce legislative proposals. They had also worked more informally to share farming insights and technical advice.

One farm, Seven Sons Farms, was itself a farm business cluster, complementary firms owned by seven brothers of the Hitzfield family. I profile this farm in greater detail in chapter 10: They raise and sell beef, pork, and eggs to some 5,000 household consumers, and have created exceptionally profitable systems. As business manager Blaine Hitzfield described the family's amazing set of innovations, I asked if he would be willing to share the addresses of the farm's drop sites so I could map them out. He readily agreed. Less than an hour after I sent a request by e-mail, he returned a spreadsheet showing all the addresses. I turned these over to Brendan Heberlein, a GIS mapper who produces elegant maps. He plotted the 45 sites, drawing lines that connected each to Seven Sons Farms.

Heberlein also produced similar maps for several other farms and firms. The WOLF Cooperative, formed by a group of 80 Amish farmers, had launched a co-op grain elevator. Surviving a fire that destroyed their property immediately after they opened, they rebounded remarkably quickly, raising sales 10-fold, from $1.6 million to $15 million in just 3 years. They now served 120 growers who supplied organic grain to dairy and poultry farms nearby. Greg Gunthorp raises pastured pigs and turkeys. He had built a small USDA-certified slaughter and processing plant on his farm so he could retain maximum value for his animals. Greg sold mostly to Chicago and Indianapolis markets. A third operation, run by Jeff Hawkins and his son Zach, sent me the addresses of their chicken processor and the restaurants that served their free-range heritage chickens (today they process chickens right on the farm). Mapping each of these firms individually, Heberlein finally constructed a map showing how these farms interacted with each other.

When I showed these maps to the Partnership, there was a noticeable release of energy in the room. In 30 seconds of viewing these gorgeous maps, the developers had been reminded that farmers are businesspeople, too, and that they should be included in developers' planning. The networks each farm had built to support their businesses were precisely the type of networks the Partnership had hoped to strengthen. "We have to work more closely with the farmers," one developer declared.

Yet in the same breath, a second insight also emerged. Most of these farms were focused on selling food to distant metro markets; only one was truly determined to sell to neighbors close to the farm. As one developer exclaimed, "We need to pay more attention to Fort Wayne *consumers* too."

At that point, Jain Young spoke up. Young had patiently been building a collaboration with the Community Harvest Food Bank focused on making sure low-income consumers in Fort Wayne had access to fresh foods. The food bank had recently been given a former catering facility. It had spent $5 million to renovate the building to serve as a produce-processing center. Using the facility's kitchen, the food bank could blanch and freeze fresh produce that had been donated during harvest season, and then keep it secure until it was needed for distribution during the winter months.

As this facility took shape, Young, a long-term food activist, worked with food bank officials to launch a food hub at the site, using its loading docks and storage areas to stage deliveries. Young had already written several major grant proposals to bring this idea to fruition. None had been funded so far. Members of the Partnership now realized that while they were running in circles with food manufacturers whose horizons were global, they had failed to connect with what was already under way in their own town. They immediately invited Young into the office to make sure her efforts would coordinate with theirs. After all, who needs to be engaged in economic development more than low-income residents?

Over time, Young's approach was refined into Plowshares Food Hub, focusing for now on a food delivery program that ships boxes of fresh vegetables to low-income Fort Wayne residents. Each box costs $35, and the boxes are ordered for 15-week seasons. Customers can also order individual items as they wish. Orders are placed using software that was developed in Australia. When I spoke with Young in the summer of 2019, as many as 100 families had ordered deliveries in a single week.

Once again, voluntary collaborations paved the path. Many of the farms supplying Plowshares are Amish. Each box is assembled at Community Harvest's facility in North Fort Wayne, which rents the space at low rates. Young took out a $50,000 personal loan from the Brightpoint Development Fund to seed the business, including covering the costs of purchasing and fixing a used refrigerated box truck. A science fiction bookstore in Indianapolis also assisted financially. Restaurateurs Pete and Alice Eshelman hosted a fundraising dinner at their farm in May 2019. Young relies on her day job at the local Central Labor Council and continues to hunt for grant funding wherever possible.

The Network Matures

The Partnership expanded its local food network discussion immediately after our 2016 report came out. A steering committee was formed, including representatives from three county economic development offices, the regional partnership itself, Purdue extension, and Greater Fort Wayne. Also involved were a farmer, a chef, and local food visionaries Janet Katz and Jain Young. This group developed a mission and specific goals for the Northeast Indiana Local Food Network, which was formed as a nonprofit organization and sponsored by Wells County Economic Development. Ultimately, Janet Katz, who had passionately advocated for local foods for many years, was chosen to coordinate the effort. She held a fresh degree from a midcareer graduate program in sustainable food systems.

Katz told me that she takes no pay, even though she works "from 10 to 100 hours" each week advancing the Network's cause. She added that she can do this because her husband is a physician. Most of the Network's board members have full-time work, she added, "so I am the primary doer." The Network is currently conducting a Founding Donor campaign to hire staff and expand programs. A "local food ambassa-dor" has been designated for one participating county. Over time, Katz hopes to designate such an ambassador in each of the region's other 10 counties.

One of the prominent events on the Local Food Network's calendar is an annual Local Food Forum, held each year in March. This event had initially been launched in 2015 by Purdue Extension, but, Katz contin-ued, "we wanted to take it up a notch, and focus more on building our network." In 2019, 210 people attended, and Katz was pleased to report that an ever-expanding cross-section of people participate. "When we say we are building community, it is really about strengthening rela-tionships. Our [evaluation] surveys show that the networking we do is the most beneficial thing for those who attend."

This is also a network that achieves. "We need to grow the demand for local food, the supply of local food, and meanwhile create a viable organization," Katz said. Two farmers' markets near downtown, founded before the network was organized, attract as many as 5,000 shoppers per day. The Network has now published a detailed local food guide to highlight local farms and restaurants, helping build visibility for the movement. It has dedicated a percentage of the proceeds from the Local Food Forum to support training for emerging farmers. The Network's tagline is "Our Land. Our Tables."

Business leaders in Fort Wayne are also proposing to create a food court in a former General Electric factory. If it reaches fruition, this "Electric Works" may become the permanent indoor location for the farmers' market, as well as the site of a brewery and restaurants. Planners envision this hall creating a gathering space south of downtown that resembles Cleveland's West Side Market. Whether this becomes a key facility in structuring the local food network, or primarily serves as an amenity for tourists and office workers, seems to remain an open ques-tion. In either case, the food hall will serve as a potent symbol of Fort Wayne's interest in food.

Immigrants Will Be Essential

The past several years have proved to be a potent educational process for John Sampson. When I interviewed him a second time in 2019, he insisted on patching Janet Katz onto the call. He told me, "The Local Food Network has become far more important than I once thought it would be." The Partnership's tour of a food hub in Greenville, South Carolina, where they were hosted by the Hispanic Chamber of Commerce, helped Sampson cement his belief that "we have to become far more sophisticated in what we grow in Northeast Indiana." Further, he added, "We're going to have to rely on an immigrant population to get where we need to be."

Although the "quality of life" conversation that drove the Partnership to look at food as a concern was once viewed primarily as an amenity that would attract young professionals to Fort Wayne, Sampson is now taking a far broader view that encompasses immigrant workers. "Economic development is strongly attached to talents and skills. Moreover, the decision a family makes to locate somewhere is a very personal decision. If we cannot grow our population from within, we have to attract newcomers through our quality of place. If we don't they will search somewhere else for economic opportunity. We have to welcome them as a good place to live, to work, and to play."

Reflecting on the first decade of the Partnership, Sampson concluded that its initial vision had been mostly focused on building any form of collaboration that might take hold. He said that the next vision was far more focused on measurable outcomes. Under Vision 2030, the Partnership has set bold goals. For years, per capita income has declined. Now the Partnership wants to increase per capita income to 90 percent of the national average. Further, it wants to increase educational attainment to a 65 percent rate. Finally, it seeks to increase the population of the region to 1 million.

To do this, Sampson added, "we need to be a welcoming community. We need to be seen as a community where immigrants are welcome, and encouraged to live here. For a long time, we've protected what we have, instead of planning for what we're going to be."

Economic developers in Northeast Indiana were brave enough to listen to their constituents and change course. To establish a firm foundation for change, they carefully forged collaboration agreements and adopted them formally. Each of the 11 local development offices agreed to share information openly and to refuse to compete with each other in attracting new businesses. When their first attempt to bring manufacturers and commodity farmers fell short of their hopes, they were able to draw on this spirit of openness to change course.

In one of the stunning reversals, developers realized that they had tended to think of farmers as outsiders, not as businesspeople. When our network maps showed that that these farms had built precisely the kind of commercial networks their initial efforts had sought, there was a huge sigh of discovery. When they realized that grassroots food leaders had already laid plans to include lower-income residents in creating a better food system, the developers also brought that work under their umbrella. Finally, realizing that decades of antagonism toward immigrants had resulted in economic stasis, the Partnership concluded that their future depends on welcoming new immigrants. These new insights took them into uncharted territory they never would have anticipated at the beginning.

Not far away, in Southeastern Ohio, visionary community leaders had fostered adaptive networks for decades, centering economic development on the needs of lower-income residents of their Appalachian region from the beginning. That, in turn, took them down a path they had not foreseen. I will tell that story next, in chapter 6.

CHAPTER 6

The Cradle of
Food Democracy:
Athens (Ohio)

Building community networks was also the core of an economic development approach taken by a cluster of newcomers to Athens, Ohio, who moved into a community together because they viewed it as a place that was open to change. As in Northeast Indiana, these leaders paid close attention to their constituents and learned significant new insights from them. Yet they focused on lower-income residents from the beginning. Now, after nearly 50 years, Athens is (along with the Mission Mountain Food Enterprise Center in Ronan, Montana discussed in Chapter 2) one of the two leading centers in fostering food-business development in lower-income areas. The Athens cohort began by launching worker-managed food businesses. Two of these still thrive today. As low-income residents expressed their lack of interest in group ownership, however, the original animators redirected their efforts to incubating new entrepreneurs. Leveraging antipoverty grants, they created ACEnet, which runs a food-processing center where aspiring business owners can create new value-added products. Over time, ACEnet expanded its attention to nearby Nelsonville, opening a shared woodworking shop, office space, and warehouse facilities.

I strolled into the Kroger supermarket in Athens, Ohio, to investigate a tip. One community food leader had told me the store carried locally made food products, and I wanted to see how prominently they were displayed. My eyes brightened to see 25 feet of shelf space, up to seven shelves high, stuffed with more than 100 Ohio-made products. Most had been produced right in Athens. The shelves featured dense, moist loaves of bread from Crumb's Bakery downtown. Grains, cereals, dried beans, pasta, chips, and polenta packaged by Shagbark Mill and Seed in attractive paper containers overflowed another section. An assortment of ketchups, salsas, and barbeque sauce stood near tall bottles of Ohio wine. Eye-dropper vials of herbal remedies filled another shelf. Some distance away, huge photos of local farmers loomed over glistening produce displays. Some of the best milk in the US, bottled at Snowville Creamery in nearby Pomeroy, beckoned from the dairy coolers.

In my experience, this was a rare expression of local pride from a national grocery chain. This expansive display made me wonder how all of this came to be. The short answer was that the store manager, Dave Schull, knew the importance of local farms. He had grown up on a farm 40 miles to the northwest, and he hoped to retire to that farm. He drew added inspiration, perhaps, soon after he took the reins of the store in 2001, by discovering that he was about to compete with a Walmart planned for construction next door. When a corporate vice president visited, Schull persuaded him that the best hope Kroger had for competing with the discount chain was to differentiate—by featuring local foods.

Schull was taking only a small risk, because he knew that his community had a wealth of farmers and food entrepreneurs who were dedicated to supplying their neighbors with high-quality foods. When he retired 15 years later, he had built the largest section of local products of any of the Ohio Kroger stores, in a town of 25,000. One local newspaper credited Schull's success to his ability to "coordinate between

Kroger's corporate management and local businesses." His was not an easy path. The store had been remodeled four times since he took over, and only at the final remodeling was the local products section integrated into the new design. In his final days, Schull insisted that keeping the local offerings intact was his number one priority. Department heads, at long last, expressed their appreciation for the way he had built the store's identity to fit the community's: "Yeah, that [section] needs to stay because that is Athens."

Newcomers Foster a Food Identity

Schull, in turn, credited his relationship with ACEnet, the Appalachian Center for Economic Networks, for paving the way. ACEnet had been formed by a dedicated core of leaders who began to settle into the Athens area in 1981. They had chosen to move to the town after meeting each other through the Federation of Ohio River Cooperatives, a six-state collaboration that built a distribution network in the 1970s to supply co-op groceries. June Holley, one of those leaders, recalled that she, along with four others—Pat DeWees, Carol Kuhre, Roger Wilkins, and Marty Zinn—selected Athens as a place to live because it seemed ripe for change.

Holley added that she was so frustrated with the limited possibilities in West Virginia, her previous home, that "I just had to get away from there. *All* the people who wanted it to change left." Since both of her parents had grown up "dirt poor" in Ohio, she could claim some roots there. The newcomers' early experiences in Athens also suggested that something unique was possible in this community. "People were very welcoming. We were warmly received." The town's political structure was responsive to residents. The newcomers discovered they could fill a new niche, as well: "Athens people were innovators, but they did not collaborate." The group decided to intentionally foster networking, creating an economic base for this collaboration by helping new businesses form and linking them together.

The newcomers' vision was not to inflict change on others, but to inspire them to step forward on their own. As a sociology graduate student, Holley had concluded that the social issues low-income residents faced were complex. She also learned that poor people effectively organized their own efforts to solve the issues they faced: "People have the capacity to see what needs to be done, and do it," Holley said. It was a fitting vision for a town named after the cradle of democracy.

Holley and her colleagues set out to create models of what change looked like. With Roger Wilkins and Marty Zinn, Holley helped form a collaboration among skilled people called the Worker Owned Network. Members began to explore how to assist low-income residents in 32 Appalachian counties to start worker-owned businesses, thinking these would in turn hire lower-income neighbors. The trio helped ten worker-owned cooperatives form; two still thrive today as businesses in Athens.

At first it was not immediately clear how best to do this. Holley recalled that a more concrete vision came to her while attending a conference. There, a group from Spokane described their efforts to refurbish a former army base. They had created a business incubator in a vacant building. The story sparked her imagination. "*That* is what we could do," she realized. By purchasing equipment for many to share, and offering below-market rent for office space, the network could cut down the costs of opening a new firm. Their first business incubator opened in 1990.

As Holley pondered her discovery, she thought about the folks who lived in Athens. Her rural neighbors might be struggling financially, but they knew food. That meant Athens needed a very specific kind of incubator. If the network created a licensed community kitchen for shared use, they could respond to farmers, chefs, and low-income residents who wanted to test food business concepts. Organizing as a formal nonprofit corporation, ACEnet would bear the burden of outfitting and managing the facility and obtaining the required licenses. This would reduce costs for emerging firms. It would create one path for people with limited incomes to earn some much-needed money. Simultaneously it would establish a place where experienced chefs could nurture commercially successful products. After 3 years of deliberation, planning, and construction, the 30,000-square-foot Food Ventures Center opened in Athens in October 1996.

Just as the facility opened, ACEnet leaders began to realize that new computer technology was changing business practices tremendously. New efficiencies were being created in handling information, but many Athenians lacked a command of the new technology at the time. Several emerging business owners had limited knowledge of basic computers. Staff organized trainings specifically designed for local business managers so they could master these new approaches to financial accounting, inventory controls, and labeling.

Maintaining a broad vision, the leadership group viewed these initiatives as part of a wider strategy of building flexible manufacturing networks. As word of the network spread, Holley was invited to travel to Italy to see how networked small businesses had made an impact. In the fashion industry, for example, large clothing firms would contract with cottage seamstresses to make component parts, making certain that the income they earned from global sales also penetrated into smaller communities. Indeed, the large firms felt a responsibility to help build a network that would protect small and large firms alike.

An Incubator Requires Supportive Networks

For Athens, similarly, no community kitchen incubator, no matter how cleverly designed, would survive without a supportive network giving it life. Holley and her peers saw ACEnet as the vehicle for forging the required networks. Paying close attention to food production made sense, Holley added, because "the food economy is connected to the rest of the economy."

ACEnet leaders were also aware that the extractive industries which had characterized much of the economic activity in Appalachia, such as agriculture and mining, had allowed many to build wealth but had left those who did the most demanding labor—the long-term residents—disadvantaged. Simply starting new businesses would not be enough; the community also had to create ownership opportunities for residents, build wealth that remained at work in the area, and commit itself to supporting local businesses.

Certain elements of that network were already in place, and of course formed a strong element of what had attracted the group to Athens. An independently owned grocery store, the Farmacy, had opened in 1970, featuring food from local farms when available. Some of the region's more enterprising farmers had begun selling their food on downtown streets, feeding the meter at parking stalls to command a space. By 1972, the City moved to formalize this trade, opening a farmers' market east of town, at the site of a former airport for Ohio University. The market became a vibrant meeting place, as well as an important commercial venue for farmers. It further served as the best place in town for a new farm to announce its presence.

Former market manager (and retired editor of *Cooperative Grocer* magazine) David Gutknecht explained that the farmers' market offered a place for growers to built product recognition without spending a great deal. "It has also been an important venue for folks who develop a product in the community kitchen at ACEnet," he added. After establishing themselves in Athens, many vendors build up their businesses enough to sell in larger metropolitan areas, such as Columbus.

Ominously, conversations at the farmers' market also captured the plight of farmers who were struggling to make ends meet and facing an impending credit crisis. Farmers and food leaders now gravitated to ACEnet's leaders to ask for help. By 1985, ACEnet had opened an office. Later that same year, a worker-owned cooperative restaurant, Casa Nueva, opened nearby. Wilkins and Zinn facilitated the formation of the co-op. This new Mexican restaurant featured produce from local farms. It still thrives today, some three decades later, with management decisions made by consensus of all the workers. The following year, another worker cooperative, Crumb's Bakery, opened. This firm also passed the test of time.

The Incubator Opens

It took another decade for the incubator to take shape. By 1996, ACEnet had amassed the equipment needed to safely prepare a host of food items. With this single investment in shared equipment, dozens of emerging businesses could be served. The kitchen was a facility-in-waiting, open to any entrepreneur who had a promising business idea, the willingness to pursue it, and the ability to pass through the organization's screening process. Knowing that equipment alone would not satisfy their clients' needs, ACEnet surrounded successful applicants with wraparound services: help in refining recipes, creating a business plan, designing a brand and printing labels, accessing capital, making marketing connections, or whatever else it took. This meant that a limited-income entrepreneur with a solid concept could gain the new skills required for a launch.

At times, the most useful assistance ACEnet could offer was to work with budding entrepreneurs to refine their business concepts. As the current executive director, Larry Fisher, told me when I visited in 2012, many people think they have to come up with some new product that has never been made before. Although novel products can be interesting, he added, most successful firms produce something that has already found a place in the market. "If something is on the shelves, that means someone is buying it. If it is not on the shelves, there may well be a good reason no one is making it."

Over time, as more businesses forged through the startup phases, Holley mused, the wisdom of forming collaborative networks became increasingly clear. "The town of Athens is surrounded by conservative communities where no one wants anything to change," she said. A whole system of support was needed for risk takers to endure. That also meant that new food entrepreneurs could not simply hope to tap markets within 30 miles, although many did. They had to reach larger markets outside the Athens region as well. According to Holley, "Building the local economy was based on tapping higher-end markets that helped prime the pump."

The network further self-organized its own expansion. "One salsa maker made it into Kroger, and then he connected other processors to the store," Holley recalled. From simple acts such as these, the city grew what Holley called a "collaborative mindset." ACEnet, for its part, strove to engage as many sectors as possible in each initiative, consciously building whatever linkages people felt naturally inclined to strengthen. "We never wrote grants by ourselves," Holley said. She insisted on engaging as many partners as feasible: "Only when a bunch of organizations work together does the network get built."

The Network Self-Organizes its Expansion

Indeed, ACEnet spawned nonbusiness organizations that themselves strengthened the overall network. While ACEnet sharpened its own focus on business development, Carol Kuhre saw a need to build connections to rural residents. She helped form a mobilization group that is now called Rural Action. Kuhre still serves on its board. The coalition helped organize, and still manages, the Chesterhill Produce Auction, where Amish and other farmers bring their wares to wholesalers. It has also hired scores of AmeriCorps volunteers who applied their youthful energy to building stronger programs that aid rural people.

One further ACEnet spinoff, the Community Food Institute, formed in 1992 and has focused on connecting lower-income residents to community garden plots where they can raise food for themselves—though Ohio University faculty and staff are also welcome. The Institute asks that these gardeners donate 10 percent of what they harvest back to the community. This insistence, of course, also builds a stronger network by engaging new people, who in turn make tangible contributions to others.

Recognizing the need that so many emerging businesses have for credit, ACEnet also created a loan fund specifically geared to microenterprises, such as those that relied on the Food Ventures Center. That fund, ACEnet Ventures, spun off as an independent firm in 1999, then built up enough reserves to qualify as a certified Community Development Finance Institution, eligible to take advantage of federal incentives and financial assistance. This, in turn, allowed small firms in the ACEnet network to extend their reach.

Local markets for local food products also have to be built; they do not spring up spontaneously. It took years for ACEnet to persuade the Athens Kroger store to open its special section of locally produced foods, and that decision was sparked by a crisis when Walmart entered the market. Nonetheless, leaders persisted with the store. Launching a "Food We Love" marketing campaign, ACEnet enlisted several of the town's grocers to boost their local offerings. In harmony with this drive, Kroger expanded its local produce shelves.

Other initiatives focused on creating destinations where visitors could contribute and learn. Targeting Athens area restaurants for a second marketing campaign, "The 30-Mile Meal," ACEnet encouraged chefs to make their local sourcing more visible, and it also nudged tourists to ask where their meals came from. "This was our effort to bundle the tourism experience in a new way so we could make more money for farms and businesses in the region," ACEnet's director of programs, Leslie Schaller, added. As it pursued the campaign, ACEnet once again expanded its network of partners, asking the Athens Tourism Bureau to assume sponsorship of the campaign. The bureau made the campaign an integral part of the fabric of life in Athens. One food writer quoted the head of the tourism bureau in 2011: "From the tourism bureau perspective, culinary tourism is really a major trend right now. We feel like it helps us promote Athens as a destination."

Similarly, two key partners have been Ohio University and Hocking College. Under some persuasion from ACEnet and its partners, each has committed its food services to purchasing more local foods. Once that course was set, many of the farmers in the ACEnet orbit could plant new fields. With assistance from the Ohio Department of Agriculture, ACEnet purchased a cluster of new equipment that helps create value-added products. This includes fresh-cut vegetables, flash-frozen produce, or prepackaged food items especially suited for college food services.

Woodworking and Warehousing

In 2016, ACEnet expanded into Nelsonville, about 15 miles northwest of the original Food Venture Center. The organization purchased a 95,000-square-foot industrial building with 5,000 square feet of office space, part of an effort to engage residents of a smaller community that had more limited resources than Athens itself. It was also an opportunity to create space that larger food processors could use, since the Food Venture Center has essentially been overfilled for years. In particular, ACEnet moved some of its larger equipment, including a $500,000 thermal processing unit, to Nelsonville. The new venue also provides space for a major food manufacturer who sought a larger facility for preparing frozen dinners. Snowville Creamery leases cooler space here.

ACEnet has dedicated 20,000 square feet of this building to support new food enterprises. The extra freezer and storage capacity makes it possible to broaden the distribution reach for ACEnet and several of its partners.

These new partnerships created synergies that fostered viable economic trade over time. Through a combination of spontaneous invention and strategically calculated steps, trade expanded. Schaller helped launch Casa Nueva, a Mexican restaurant (mentioned earlier) featuring food from local farms. This, in turn, provided a regular customer for Shagbark Seed and Mill as it built its business of supplying heirloom corn, beans, and spelt from nearby farms, and processing its own tortilla chips. The restaurant then installed a walk-in freezer and cooler at the ACEnet campus to store these foods until they are ready for plating, and it uses the Food Ventures Center to flash freeze produce for off-season use. Shagbark Seed and Mill, in turn, has expanded its operation twice, first to the original incubator and then to the larger plant at Nelsonville, increasing its capacity to supply restaurants such as Casa Nueva. Further, Marty Zinn, one of ACEnet's cofounders, now directs human relations and serves as bookkeeper for Shagbark Seed and Mill. Money earned in each venture creates spending that stays in the community.

None of this happened by building a wall around Athens County. Although local business leaders focused on meeting local needs first, they also recognized that outside sales could help them earn valuable income, which would help them more consistently supply local markets. Nor was this a success of free enterprise alone. The work has relied on large grants from federal and state agencies. But these precious public dollars have been invested carefully in ways that create lasting capacity for the region, rather than momentary bursts of spending. The network was built by drawing on the wisdom held by Athens County residents, but it also relied on outside inspiration at key points.

As a result, when recession hit in 2008, Athens was a bit more prepared than other towns that had built no such productive capacity. When moderate-income residents were downsized, or took early retirement, during the upheaval, many explored launching a food business. They knew right where to turn.

Schaller estimated that since ACEnet opened its Food Venture Center in 1996, about 400 people have made use of the facility to process food items. Although more than two of every three of these, she added, had started out as low-income residents, some of their firms grew so large that they were able to build their own processing space in other locations. "Our value proposition is to build sustainable livelihoods for rural people," Schaller said. "Often that involves deep dives into the details of launching a business."

One of the biggest challenges ACEnet faces, Schaller added, has been the attitudes of some of the region's civic leaders. "We've enjoyed strong bipartisan support, and we have amassed a lot of political capital. We keep doing the same thing, getting different sectors to work together to cross-pollinate their efforts, and have been so successful that our region has developed a lot of notoriety. But there is still a segment of the population looking to attract some bigger business from outside." And many potential investors can be fickle; "some economic developers are just looking for the 'flavor of the year.' This creates a big disconnect between the social capital we have built, and financial capital. Unless we pay attention to the intellectual and social capital of the individuals who live in our region, our workforce will fall apart." She recommends investments in boosting the capacity of vocational schools and technical colleges.

Still, Schaller sees troubling signs on a daily basis. The opioid crisis has taken a deep toll on rural communities, along with other substance abuse. This further means that many adults have been incarcerated and have trouble getting jobs. Unemployment rates range as high as 33 percent in some sections. The patient network building in Athens has not been enough to alleviate all of these issues, but it does provide a foundation from which people can move forward in the future.

That future is now largely in the hands of much younger members of the network, who reap a harvest that is 50 years in the making. The group who brought this vision of a democratic economy to Athens have taken on more reflective, senior roles. Schaller still occupies the trenches at ACEnet. Marty Zinn, as stated earlier, takes leadership at Shagbark Mill and Seed. Pat DeWees retired from a position at the Voinovich Center for Business at Ohio University. Roger Wilkins directs the Center for the Creation of Cooperation, which he founded a decade ago, to facilitate community renewable energy projects. Holley heads her own national initiative, Network Weavers. From this position she steps back to codify key insights from her decades of practice, and she trains others in how to advance their own network capacities.

As Holley concluded, "It wasn't ACEnet [that made all this happen]. It was the network."

Constructing a resilient network on relationships of trust meant that people could take in new information as conditions changed, and form new insights together. This allowed ACEnet to reposition itself toward connecting more closely with lower-incomer residents. By paying close attention to what their constituents required, and building broad support among the wider community, ACEnet became a national leader. More importantly to its neighbors, ACEnet created new paths to entrepreneurship in a region that has had its share of economic distress.

ACEnet is a prime example of how working strategically to build trust over time, and inviting an ever wider circle of stakeholders into a common approach, allows a community food network to tackle more mature challenges as the work advances. People who were once skeptical or even antagonistic can be engaged as partners. This brings new commitments, new resources, and new energy to the effort. As long as these newcomers pursue a vision consistent with that of the founders, as has happened in Southeast Ohio, the potential for larger impacts multiplies.

Today, some communities are in the very early stages of launching their community foods work. While working in very different settings, they face some of the same issues of establishing a foothold that ACEnet leaders faced. For a prime example of an early-stage effort, chapter 7 turns to Phoenix, Arizona, where community foods leaders are confronted by intense pressures for housing and commercial development that have isolated some of the most effective produce farms in the US.

CHAPTER 7

Metro-Area Farmers Need Supportive Networks

In several communities, efforts to support local farmers are just beginning to take root. One such metro area is Phoenix, Arizona, where development pressures are intense. In 2017, the Maricopa County Food System Coalition asked us to document the networks that their community foods initiative in Phoenix has built over the past few years. They were looking for some way to capture the attention of civic leaders who had not yet grasped the import of community foods efforts. Our interviews documented that the county had several exceptionally accomplished produce farms and a strong heritage of food production. There were ample markets, with residents purchasing $12 billion of food every year. A private food distribution firm had dedicated itself to selling Arizona foods locally, and tried to coordinate farmers' production. But farmers felt isolated, and civic leaders seemed to imagine no future for farming in Maricopa County. Developers owned much of the productive farmland. By showing city officials network maps that portrayed the farmers' isolation, the Coalition evoked a strong response. City officials are now convening with farmers and launching campaigns to encourage more Phoenix residents to eat food grown on Maricopa County farms.

One of the members of the Maricopa County Food System Coalition suggested I go online to review a map showing future land use, published by the Maricopa Association of Governments. What I saw there was staggering. In a county where more than 4 million people dwelled, spending over $12 billion per year buying food, planning officials contemplated reducing the amount of agriculturally zoned land from 4 percent (260,749 acres) of the county land base (5,902,858 acres) to 0.6 percent (37,427 acres) over the next several decades. The largest swath of future farmland to remain would largely be held by one Native tribe that maintained productive farms in the county.

This was stark confirmation that municipal officials had not prioritized planning for the future of food. It was easy to conclude that the interests of those who wanted to build housing and commercial buildings in Maricopa County were closer to the decision-making process than farmers were. For a city that had built itself around the growth of cattle ranches, cotton farms, and vast orange groves, it was a curious denial of the very foundation of the settlement.

Tempering this statistic was the fact that considerable farmland in the outlying areas of Maricopa County does not appear to be subject to zoning at all, so there are vast fields of alfalfa, cotton, and wheat on the outskirts. Of course, these farms do little to feed Phoenix residents, so there was still a planning issue at stake.

Desert Soil Is "Just Filled with Nutrients"

Casting my midwestern eyes over the expansive, flat, sandy fields, I wondered if farming was simply a questionable pursuit in this county. That notion was quickly dispelled when I visited Mark Rhine in the San Tan Valley southeast of the city. Mark had moved from his previous farm after a disagreement with his business partner, so he was less than a year into farming at his new location. He had 30 years' experience in organic farming and ranked among the first farmers in the state to become certified for Good Agricultural Practices (GAP). Rhine sells millions of dollars of produce each year, primarily to grocery chains. As he led me on a rapid walk through his fields, he swept the view with his hands, reminding me this land was in an ancient riverbed, where water had deposited runoff for eons. "This soil is just filled with nutrients," Rhine added. "You put some compost down and the organic matter draws the nutrients up for the plants to use."

Rhine then suggested I visit Erich Schultz at Steadfast Farm, in Queen Creek. More than any place I visited in Maricopa County, Schultz's farm typified the push and pull of agriculture amid expanding suburbs. Shultz told me his business model, for the time being, was to develop his farm so that it could be moved at a moment's notice. He found it was relatively easy for farmers to lease land at a low price from developers because the housing market had cooled since the global recession, leaving developers with idle land. Leasing these fields was attractive to farmers because purchasing land was so expensive at $100,000 per acre—due to development—that no beginning farmer could buy land. Landowners loved to have farmers working their lands, because they qualified for a tax break if the land was kept in agricultural use. The downside was that after a year or so of farming, there was always a risk that the developer would reclaim the land to build houses. So Schultz's business model centered around installing portable hoop houses that could be removed quickly, and building up the soil as best he could until he had to move on. His work station, where interns washed and packed fresh greens and other produce, was installed in a trailer. A second trailer had been carefully insulated and featured a CoolBot for storing produce until it sold.

Farming in a temporary manner reduced Schultz's overhead considerably. Relying on small equipment and hand labor, he said he had purchased only 25 gallons of gas to fuel his machinery in 2016. To increase the value of his produce he devotes considerable attention to detail in packaging and displaying the farm's products beautifully, so "we can charge what it actually costs to produce food."

Located in a prosperous suburb, Steadfast Farm was able to attract restaurants and households that could pay higher prices for produce. Carrying these products to three farmers' markets on Saturdays, and delivering food directly to 15–20 restaurants and 18 CSA (community-supported agriculture) drop sites, as well as selected commercial clients, Schultz told me he could sell $150,000 to $200,000 of produce *per acre* on a 2.25-acre spread. One neighbor suggested that this was a modest estimate. "We do all of the delivery ourselves," Schultz said. "I like the direct connection with the buyer." He added, "This business is primarily built on relationships. This is how I stay abreast of what my customers need." At one point, a distribution firm offered to carry food for him, and he said no.

This makes Schultz one of the more productive produce farmers in the US—well above a farm in Georgia that claimed to raise $100,000 per acre, the best I had encountered before meeting Schultz. Taking full advantage of irrigation and building up organic matter in the soil to retain moisture, he can harvest year-round. He achieves this in a suburban setting with very little supportive policy.

So the fact that Maricopa County planners were not cultivating a future for agriculture was not because there was an absence of farmers or the land was unsuitable for farming. Indeed, a well-established egg farm, Hickman's Family Farm, which started as Hickman's Egg Ranch in 1944, now raises 10 million hens on three farms in Maricopa County and Pinal County, Arizona, as well as in California and Colorado. The T & K Red River Dairy, a 12,000-acre dairy that milks 12,500 cows, was established by a Wisconsin farm family that moved to Arizona in 1962.

But produce was clearly not part of the public calculation, perhaps because the Nogales produce port, the largest inland food port in the world, is only 3 hours south of Phoenix, and the southwestern part of the state, near Yuma, is the largest producer of greens in the US. These offer a seemingly endless supply of fresh produce at lower prices than Maricopa County farmers would need to charge. Implicit in the public calculation was the concept that the county could afford to spend $10 billion or more each year to purchase food grown outside, without losing its power to determine its own future. If this meant that young Phoenicians might have no clue how food was raised, where it came from, how to prepare it well, or how to eat properly, it was a civic toll public officials were willing to embrace.

Does Housing Pay Its Own Way?

A second assumption underlying this train of thought was that there was more value in building homes and commercial properties, hoping the new tax base they generated would cover the costs of City and County governance. This notion persists despite the American Farmland Trust's compelling research showing that the costs of city services (such as fire and police service), at least for residential development, typically exceed the value of any newly generated tax base. Municipal officials, like farmers, appeared to be walking a treadmill of their own, fostering a new tax base that essentially required them to create ever more new tax base to pay for rising public sector costs. This, in turn, forced up the value of farmland as developers rushed to build more housing.

One nationally prominent farm was branching out to distant locations as a hedge against rising land costs and the erosion of farm infrastructure. When I visited Sean Duncan, son of Arnott Duncan, the founder of Duncan Family Farms, he greeted me warmly at the door of the farm's office in Buckeye. He began by apologizing that there was not more to view during the intense heat of August. The farm left its 8,000 acres in Maricopa County fallow this time of year, moving its workers and equipment to California, Oregon, and New York State, where more temperate weather reduced the need for intense irrigation.

The Duncan family holds deep roots in Buckeye. Arnott Duncan was the fourth-generation owner of his family's farm but began raising conventional cotton and alfalfa on a new 50-acre farm in Buckeye in 1985. Arnott served on the board of directors of St. Mary's Food Bank, and the farm donates almost a million pounds of food each year to them. My interviews showed that Arnott's viewpoints are deeply respected by civic leaders.

After several transitions, the family now focuses on raising baby greens, both organically and conventionally. The family first ventured into organic farming after they began to offer farm tours, feeling that, because of the potential health risk, they should avoid applying chemicals to the fields where tour groups visited. As they learned organic techniques, Sean recalled, "we began to see there were benefits agronomically to using organic methods, and we decided to be proactive in making that change."

The family's greens are washed and packed at processing centers run by others in Yuma County, the Salinas Valley, and the East Coast. Distributors in these locations sell the packaged greens to the major firms globally, including in Canada and the United Kingdom. "We're the number two supplier of organic bagged salads," Sean said in a matter-of-fact tone.

The family also sells organic specialty bunched greens (kales and chards), bunched herbs (cilantro, Italian parsley, curly parsley), bunched root crops (red, gold, and Chioggia beets), romaine hearts and Salanova® lettuce for distribution to both institutional food services and retail stores. Over time, the firm has grown from about a dozen employees to more than 200.

The Duncans were attracted to open new fields in New York State because the Wegman's grocery firm collaborated with them to feature locally raised produce. Sean added, "There is not a lot of infrastructure to support large-scale farming here [in Maricopa County]."

Sean said that labor is one of the family's constant concerns. "I don't really have a good solution for this now. We hire local people where possible, but we also rely heavily on contract labor, including the guest worker program." Yet that program is restrictive too: "If we hire a group of workers for the harvest, we cannot ask them to do another job like weed control unless we rewrite the contract." While the family likes to adopt new technologies as they become available, and would like to automate, "that would require infrastructure here," such as mechanics who can repair new equipment.

A Produce Distributor Steps Forward

One firm that tried to create some of the needed infrastructure is Stern Produce, a fourth-generation, family-owned firm that has operated in Phoenix for more than a century. In addition to delivering to commercial customers in the region, it is also part of the national PRO*ACT network, allowing the firm to source produce from anywhere on the continent.

Kristen Osgood, former regenerative strategy manager for the firm, was tasked with creating a program to source food from Arizona farms. When I interviewed her in 2017, after her first year on the job, the trajectory seemed optimistic. "I see myself mostly as a bridge between our buyers and the growers," Osgood told me at the time. When she was first hired in 2016, she added, the firm had sold only 6,500 cases of Arizona-grown food. "We were selling ourselves as a local, family-owned company, but we were not doing the same with selling our local foods." Stern tried to expand that niche under the Arizona Fresh Together brand.

Osgood spent much of that first year traveling to meet farmers at their farms to learn more about their operations and their needs. When I interviewed her in 2017 she had set a target of selling 35,000 cases of Arizona food items, including eggs and milk, and hoped to boost that to 68,000 cases statewide the following year. Interest from farmers and buyers was high, and she surpassed her goals. By the end of 2017, Stern had shipped 96,593 cases of food, purchased from farmers for a total of $1.8 million. A year later, Stern had moved 142,475 cases, representing $2.1 million in purchases from Arizona farms. "We never lost money on product," she recalled, but there had been shrinkage (losses due to spoiling or lack of payment) of about 7,000 cases. At the end of the chapter, I will discuss how this promising initiative floundered. But first I want to describe how it was assembled.

Even Osgood's early meetings with growers had some complexity. When she reached out to meet them, some farmers were skeptical, in part because of their previous experience with the firm. Osgood explained, "I spent my first year on this job convincing people we wanted to work with them. None of the growers would commit to coming in for a meeting at our distribution center. I had to go out to their farms." She traveled to four farms before word got around that she was trustworthy. Then the ice began to melt. Even then, however, communications gaps erupted. "One grower who had agreed to grow for us pulled 400 tomato plants out of his fields and didn't tell us," leaving her in short supply. Others had to negotiate prices with her. "A couple of farms had to lower their price points in order to sell to us," she added.

She acknowledged that a key challenge of her job was to improve the firm's "internal skill set." Under her guidance, Stern dedicated an entire wing of its warehouse to Arizona-grown food offerings, developed SKU product codes for local items to make reporting more accurate, and hired a buyer given a specific charge to source food items locally. The firm also opened new lines of communication to keep buyers abreast of what was available. "We're the only Phoenix firm with a special program dedicated to local foods," Osgood added at the time.

After initial meetings with the growers, Osgood convened 27 farmers who were part of her Arizona Fresh Together program. She told them she was "committed to making local trade work for all parties." Her urgency came from a conviction that "we're going to have supply shocks with global warming." She set out to ensure that the firm could address those changes proactively.

The largest gaps she saw involve "ensuring the consistency of availability," since buyers tend to assume that all products are available year-round, whatever the limitations of climate may be. She also worked with chefs to help them address seasonality as they drew up menus. "People are so far removed from their food," she lamented, that consumers ask for "local" foods that are not in season.

Osgood also noted that the lack of community spirit in Phoenix made her work more difficult. "We have a lot of business relationships, but we don't have partnerships. I am trying to move that." She saw the importance of repositioning the firm through an outreach campaign. "How do you let people know you want to do business in a different way?" she asked. Her answer was, "We're going to do special events with a local focus." These events would feature the foods that Arizona farmers grow, and they would highlight the farmers who raised them.

Special events like these that introduced farmers to consumers had been adopted long ago by the Food System Coalition and echoed the foundational work of Cindy Gentry, a food systems coordinator for the Maricopa County Department of Health. One of the prime networkers in the region, Gentry has helped inspire several others to launch community foods businesses. Gentry said that her supervisors have been exceptionally supportive of her work. Yet as we interviewed key stakeholders in Maricopa County, we gained the impression that political leadership had dedicated few resources to community foods infrastructure or food-systems development.

Mapping Networks

When Gentry and Kate O'Neill of the Maricopa County Food System Coalition contacted me about assisting their efforts, they asked if I had any suggestions for how to harness greater attention from civic leaders.

As we spoke, I asked if it might be useful to simply show them the networks the community foods work had created. They immediately took to the notion. I asked them to identify the farmers and food leaders who were doing the most to create new futures for food, and they worked hard to develop a solid list.

When my colleague Megan and I interviewed each of these people, we asked four central questions. These were selected because previous researchers had identified them as key tests of network strength: (1) Who are your five closest associates in community foods work? (2) Which of these do you share information with? (3) Which do you turn to when you need advice? (4) Which of these do you trade with financially, either through sales or through barter?

We took the answers we were given and coded them into spreadsheets for Paula Ross, a researcher retired from the University of Toledo, to analyze. Ross had developed an extraordinary set of network maps when she was coordinating community foods work in her own region, Northwest Ohio. Now she painstakingly developed a series of persuasive maps showing the connections people had, and had not, made.

The farmers we spoke with expressed deep isolation. Although one beginning farmer noted that a Young Farmers group, sponsored by the Arizona Farm Bureau, had been a great place to gain encouragement, this was not typical. One farmer complained of Phoenix that "City officials won't do anything." Another interviewee agreed, "The City is very difficult to deal with [for farmers]." Some felt it was a waste of time to meet with researchers such as ourselves, and O'Neill had to gently persuade them to lower their guard. What was more remarkable, however, was that several farmers felt mistrustful of each other. One farmer's main source of information about how to farm came from the internet—not from family or fellow farmers. Some farmers were reluctant to have other farmers visit their land.

Our maps bore this out. Very few of the farmers identified any other farmers as a central part of their network. Two weak clusters had formed around two respected farmers, but these two clusters appeared not to make much contact with each other. Even when we included farmer organizations the maps were rife with the same disconnects. When we added food nonprofits to the map, we learned that few of them had helped farmers connect with each other. More troublesome, about a dozen of the food nonprofits did not mention any farmers as one of *their* key partners! The network only gained strength as we mapped out the food buyers, because each farmer did have core partners who purchased from them. Some of the buyers even helped farmers meet each other. Once we added civic agency staff, the overall network appeared quite robust. Yet it still left farmers feeling isolated. Our interviewees suggested that this might be because few City or County civic leaders were even acquainted with any farmers, or held any direct knowledge of agriculture.

Our main recommendation became, then, that civic leaders should make a concerted effort to get to know Maricopa County farmers, have intentional dialogues with them, and engage them in policy discussions. It was the same strategy that Stern Produce and we ourselves had followed: visit farmers at their farms, take strong interest in their lives, and work with them.

First Steps Forward

We filed our report and heard very little for several months. We assumed that the Coalition was digesting our findings. After what seemed like an interminable time, O'Neill called to say that she wanted our findings to be presented at the Arizona Food Summit, to be held in Tucson in January 2019. However, there was a catch: conference organizers had decided that no outside speakers would be brought in; leaders wanted homegrown experts. Fair enough, I said, you can use our slides to convey our findings. A month or so later, she called again with joyful news: the Vitalyst Health Foundation had allocated money for me to make the presentation in person.

When I arrived in Tucson, I was pleased to find that my presentation room was the plenary hall. A large contingent of the delegates, who were mostly nonprofit staff, listened with rapt attention, and enthusiastically welcomed our recommendations. Few farmers attended, however. The state's director of agriculture kept a distance.

Later that night, as Coalition members gathered over dinner at The Hub, Rosanne Albright, the environmental programs coordinator for the City of Phoenix, raced to sit down next to me. When I had interviewed her the previous year, she emphasized that some progress was being made but cautioned that there was little strong interest from policy leaders. Tonight, she wanted to tell me that the network maps had been powerfully persuasive. "They looked at those maps and realized they had better engage with farmers." The City hired an AmeriCorps VISTA volunteer to help coordinate food activity and convened an April 30, 2019, meeting with farmers, the Local First Arizona Foundation Food & Farm Forum. It is now planning a CSA program for City staff and writing a 2025 food action plan.

Kate Radosevic, the Food & Farm Initiatives manager for the Local First Arizona Foundation, pointed out late in 2019 that our report "completely changed the way the Food Systems Coalition does its strategic planning. Rather than simply following whatever is the current hot topic, as we used to do, our decisions are rooted in data and stories we have already collected. It caused a shift in how we talk about issues. We focus far more on connecting with farmers."

Yet, she added, two of the farms most dedicated to growing for Phoenix consumers lost significant access to land, and two more farms went on the market since our report was published. In each case, the landowner wanted to use the land for housing development. A fifth farmer was forced out for a housing development, and the owner would not even wait until crops were harvested to displace the farm. Erich Schultz moved Steadfast Farm to a different site, and changed his business model, focusing on fewer clients who purchased the most, and earning more of his income in consulting. A promising food project in a low-income neighborhood was nudged out by light rail development.

Gaps Emerge in the Marketing of Arizona Produce

When I spoke at the Arizona Food Summit in early January 2019 I had no clue that Stern Produce's prodigious effort to build a strong program of sourcing food from Arizona farms was waning. Later that month, Stern's head of the Arizona Fresh Together program, Kristen Osgood, left her job to take a consulting position at Arizona State University. After 2 years of strong growth, she said that the program was forced to scale back, even though it enjoyed solid support from management, from participating farmers, and from the schools and chefs that purchased from Stern. However, she added, the firm's efforts dissipated.

"We got to the point where orders were falling," Osgood continued. "We were not fulfilling orders accurately. Sometimes we were short of stock. We were not delivering products on time. The warehouse was not always rotating fresh produce forward on the shelves, so the quality declined. We were losing a great deal to shrinkage [products that were spoiled or not paid for]." Although the program had always paid its own way, she saw signs that this would not continue.

When I asked her what should have been done differently, Osgood said, "The senior leadership at Stern Produce had a clear passion for the program. The chefs were excited. Farmers wanted to believe in it." The shortcomings were more in the logistics. "I never understood why this happened," she added. Stern had more than a century of experience in handling fresh produce. It had cold storage areas and trucks of its own. But shifting to feature Arizona farms required extra work, and that met resistance among a staff already stressed by a fast-paced work environment. Overall, it seemed to Osgood that performance eroded because of a "lack of accountability." At times, staff appeared to be confused which bin to pull local products from, or simply did not take the time to select carefully. Training procedures may have fallen short.

Moreover, there had been significant staff turnover. "We had trouble hiring. In the three years I was there, we lost four inventory control managers and three food safety managers, and we had four different transportation managers. And that was just the management. We lost workers when the minimum wage went up, because they could work somewhere else for the same pay with much less stress."

Compounding that was a new software package, launched in December 2018, that promised to integrate internet ordering with warehouse space allocation with fulfillment. "It was supposed to make us more efficient. But in the short term it exacerbated all of the tensions among the staff. It probably came too late. At that point everything cracked and crumbled."

"I think we tried to do too much too soon," she recalled. While the firm's executives tried to foster a shift in culture among employees, this was introduced in a superficial way at a large employee gathering, rather than phased in during working meetings. The new culture aimed to promote a stronger business and "the well-being of our employees and the relationships we weave within our local community." But this seemed to threaten some employees who had been accustomed to doing just enough to get by, she said.

Osgood was also quick to point out that two people worked incredibly hard to make the Arizona Fresh Together program work. One was Ashley Schimke, Arizona's farm to school coordinator. "A lot of our sales came through a Department of Defense program [where military budgets covered the costs of delivering food to schools]." Ashley made sure that was a very robust program. It reached the highest level it had ever been. But when it became clear that growth could not be sustained until logistics improved, she eased her promotion efforts. The second person, Dennis Negrete, did his best to fill the logistical gaps within Stern.

This confusion came to a head during the summer of 2018, when Osgood suffered a "heartbreak" when she had to cancel a new initiative she had launched. "I pulled together a collaboration of the farmers to see if we could sell large quantities of a single product, basil. I was trying to get the growers to work together on this one crop, hoping they would expand the collaboration as it matured. The farmers were so excited, and I was so excited." Osgood cleared the program with an executive, who supported the program and was supposed to engage one of the firm's key produce buyers. The buyer, however, scowled when he came to the meeting with the farmers. Apparently, no one had told him about the initiative. The next day, the buyer announced that he had just contracted with growers in Hawai'i to purchase a large quantity of basil at about the same price the Arizona growers were asking. The buyer offered to allow Osgood to fulfill a matching order. "But this meant that one single farm could supply all that Stern wanted," Osgood lamented. "There was no reason for the farmers to work together to supply that load, so I declined." After that, she said, things deteriorated until she left.

From her new office at Arizona State, Osgood remarked, "I miss the food systems work terribly." As she scans the Phoenix market, she sees that two small firms are growing steadily by working directly with farmers. "Sun Produce has formed a partnership with Pivot Produce in Tucson, so the two firms can supply each other. Pivot's Erik Stanford got funding for a small commercial cooler. Both businesses are growing."

Billions of dollars of produce still flow north through Nogales and Yuma, ensuring that Maricopa County sends billions of dollars to distant places as its own farmers languish. One food distributor's creative efforts to foster local produce trade have faltered. Water shortages still loom. But in halting steps, civic leaders have begun to recognize they need to connect with their neighbors who farm if their desert city is to survive. And consumers continue to seek food from local farms. The Maricopa County Food System Coalition has indeed shifted the conversation by pointing out the need, and the wisdom, of building social and commercial networks of support for farmers who wish to feed Maricopa County residents. They have their work cut out for them in persuading civic officials to invest in that process.

For inspiration, Phoenicians might turn to Brighton, Colorado, a Denver suburb that faced rapid encroachment by housing subdivisions. The community created a new vision after a small group of farmers spoke up, asking for farmland to be protected. Chapter 8 describes how officials of Brighton and the surrounding Adams County heard their concerns and took bold steps to purchase farmland at its development value, far higher than even established farms can afford, and protect the land for farming.

CHAPTER 8

Municipal Officials Collaborate to Protect Metro Farmland

Cities were founded close to farms, so productive lands are deeply threatened as metro areas expand. Not only have millions of acres been taken out of production, land prices have soared to levels far higher than working farmers can pay. The intense pressure for development can polarize communities. When two farmers in Brighton, Colorado, challenged civic officials to protect agricultural lands, both city and county staff rose to the challenge. Collaborating unusually closely, they absorbed considerable public criticism and invited fierce opponents to testify publicly. Individual interviews with landowners holding diverse views also helped identify a strategy to reduce the conflict. A design firm offered innovative options, rather than new restrictive policies. In the end the two municipal governments invested heavily in protecting two key properties, knowing this action would not protect all the farmland but would establish a richer sense of place that would set a new tone for the future.

The City and County purchased two farms at their development value to reserve it for agricultural use. Taking this action eased tensions. Now this rural district is being rebranded according to its agricultural heritage, and developers are invited to respond to that civic vision. None of this could have happened without a network of collaborators embracing a tense situation with great openness to build trust.

My colleague Megan and I had been forewarned that we were walking into a hornet's nest. Public meetings in Brighton, a city in Adams County, Colorado, northeast of Denver, to deliberate about whether and how to protect farmland, had erupted into dissenting factions. Several landowners were staunchly opposed to preserving farmland. Tempers were fierce. Some of the most argumentative residents expressed deep mistrust of both city and county governments. But the resolute public staff stayed serene and insisted that all viewpoints be heard. They hoped that a transparent process would enable the community to come to a decision that would satisfy people over the long haul. The City and County staff further detached themselves by inviting outside consultants to gather input and lead public meetings.

After considerable turmoil, community leaders concluded that tempering the conflict required courageous public investment. To assert their good faith, they purchased farmland at its development value to protect it for agricultural use, knowing that farming income could not support the purchase, and that the future of farming itself was uncertain. The two governments jointly created a new historic district, proudly turning the region's agricultural heritage into a lasting attraction, and potentially the rootstock of an emerging new food system.

When Megan and I first drove along Adams County's expansive vegetable fields one luminous summer day in 2015, I marveled at the strict rows of lush red and green cabbages and onions, spanning hundreds of acres. Dispersed among these productive farms, however, were strip malls, tract housing, and skeletons of warehouses that had encroached as Brighton grew. To the south, across the city's border, stood even vaster expanses of identical new houses, regimented in dense rows like the cabbages. I immediately understood why someone would want to protect these farmlands from a similar fate, and why the courageous souls who advanced this vision were struggling against powerful political forces.

Our interviews confirmed that Adams County featured some of the best floodplain farmland in Colorado, with ample water supplies, including senior water rights from the nearby South Platte River. This was largely thanks to irrigation ditches that had been carved a century earlier. Most of the vegetables we drove past had been planted by Petrocco Farms, owned by an Italian immigrant family who had tilled land here for nearly a century. Nearby stood the headquarters of Sakata Produce, owned by a Japanese American family who had been interned in camps during World War II but later settled in Brighton, where they prospered as farmers. Each farm ran massive packing complexes in the city. Historically, as vegetable growers, they had made more money than many neighboring farmers who raised cattle or wheat. Now, however, these established farm families were feeling pinched by suburbia.

I thought of all the cities where we had worked whose farmers were distraught because they had no farmland left and had lost the intricate skills of raising food for people. Those partners would be stunned to see the opportunity Brighton enjoyed, as part of a metropolitan area where people spent more than $7 billion each year buying food—even if most of that food is currently grown on distant farms.

Brighton's business district, a bit mottled by vacant storefronts, still displayed the remnants of its agricultural heritage. Its downtown storefronts orient themselves to conform to a railroad line that connects Denver with eastern states. First platted in 1881, Brighton's first manufacturing firm was a brickworks. Its second was a vegetable packing plant. A grain elevator looms over the tracks on the northern edge of the historical business district, near a curving street that shadows a rail spur—Cabbage Street. Planners noted that this deeply rooted town with its rural infrastructure promoting agriculture retained much of its original function, even as the integrity of this infrastructure was fragmented by development.

The Birth of the Historic Splendid Valley

Planted in the midst of this mélange is a freshly painted wooden barn, bright red, with hay bales, a white picket fence, and potted flowers beckoning visitors to the front door. This is the farm where the idea of protecting farmland was born: The Berry Patch Farms LLC, where Tim and Claudia Ferrell have raised produce since 1991. Families can take a hay ride here; pick their own berries, cherries, and vegetables; or purchase harvested items at the farm store inside the barn. On this diversified farm of 40 acres, the Ferrells have trained a number of younger people to farm organically. One, a former farm manager, Lora Epps, launched a vegetable farm in Brighton focused on selling to Denver households.

In addition to shouldering the frantic schedules endemic to tending produce fields, the Ferrells are active in civic affairs. They recognize that the future of their farm depends very heavily on the survival of the fields that enclose their land. The Berry Patch Farms might cease to be a quiet respite with open skies if commerce and housing encroach too closely. Yet, to many of their neighboring landowners, development represented an opportunity to sell their property at top dollar.

Years before, Tim and Claudia Ferrell had joined an emotional protest when the City of Brighton sold a farm to a developer. "It was a done deal. That's how it was," Ferrell first concluded. But the incident sparked several residents to suggest ways to avoid any further sales. As Tim Ferrell recalled, "The big thing that helped us was the economic downturn of 2008. Development came to a screeching halt. That gave the City some time to consider: Is this the city that we want to be? Just another metropolitan suburb? Do we want to keep providing for the costs of offering police, fire, roads, and other public works?"

Finally, after months of persistent cajoling, Tim Ferrell was able to persuade city officials to create an agriculture subcommittee to explore farmland protection. Discussing this with Adam Kniss, a former Sakata

Farms operations manager, he discovered that they held strong common ground. Sakata Farms operated its packing shed on the southern edge of the Brighton business district but had stopped raising vegetables inside the city itself because they increasingly felt conflicts with the encroaching suburban lifestyles. The farm had begun ordering its immense tractors and combines off the town's rural roads unless they were first placed on the back of a semitrailer that could keep up with highway traffic. Moreover, the farm sprays its vegetable fields to fertilize the crops and stave off pests, and the Sakatas grew increasingly concerned that families in nearby homes would consider this a health hazard. The Sakata family had hedged by purchasing land farther north, where prices were lower and regulation less stringent. It was cheaper for them to haul produce 30 or more miles from these farms to their packing sheds than to pay higher lease rates on the land, but it was also a hedge against uncertainty. The founder's son had quietly considered moving their packing sheds north, to be closer to their new fields and further reduce operating costs. Because their markets were national, locating so close to Denver was no longer a priority. At the same time, they also felt the pull of their heritage with the land and community of Brighton and preferred to stay.

While not as intimately involved in the land discussions, the Petrocco family had similar experiences. The Petroccos, a second major vegetable farm in the area, were about to celebrate a century of farming in Brighton. They still farmed tens of thousands of acres close to their established packing plant, but they also leased land to the north, in Weld County. Their strategy was in part to hedge against weather incidents, but also to hold open the option of relocating their entire farm if development became too problematic. The family owned fields in Brighton and leased thousands of acres, but they told us they would not buy any more land there. It was too expensive. Their tractors, still driving on rural roadways, often encountered slow commuter traffic or oblivious drivers. In public discussions, they preferred to stay neutral, not wishing to alienate any of their neighbors. They expressed their strong desire to remain in Brighton, but they also supported neighbors who wanted to sell their land at a high price.

A third large farm, the Palizzi Farm, owns considerable land in the city and runs a farm stand on a main east–west route. After farming in Brighton since 1929, the family had sold some of its acreage for a strip mall that includes a regional supermarket. Another important farm vendor, Lulu's Farm, specializes in chili peppers, mostly grown in warmer climes, and also features homegrown produce at its farm stand southwest of town on US 85.

Farmers Cannot Afford Farmland

As commercial buildings and housing developments encroached, land values had soared to levels that none of these farms could afford. Prime farmland was now valued at $30,000 per acre, but one could not farm that land without owning water rights. In this arid climate with sandy soil, little would grow without irrigation. Adding water rights doubled the price of farmland to $60,000 per acre. No farmer could repay that kind of expense by raising vegetables.

The Ferrells and Adam Kniss took leadership in creating a more formal municipal body, the Agriculture Preservation Committee, which became the most visible proponent of protecting farmland in Brighton. Some of their rural neighbors, who might have been expected to cheer them on, grew frustrated with their initiative. Many had farmed in Brighton for decades and saw the prospect of development as their ticket to retirement funds. Many had farmed at exceptionally low margins for decades but had held on, hoping they could one day sell their land to a developer. For these folks, high land values were warmly welcomed. Some had no heirs who wished to farm the land. Others were third-generation descendants with little involvement in agriculture. Getting value from the land was their biggest concern.

Engaging All Points of View in the Design Process

We entered into this ferment. Terry Freeman of Two Forks Collective and Megan Phillips Goldenberg shouldered the task of calling several of these landowners, wanting to make sure their points of view could be incorporated into our planning. Freeman patiently sat with land-owners for hours, hearing their concerns and indulging their complaints, making sure they felt their perspectives had been taken seriously. The three of us had been invited to join the project by Jeremy Call of the design firm Logan Simpson, based in Fort Collins. That firm prided itself on guiding responsible change, and they felt that our expertise in agriculture would play a critical role in making sure that all stakeholders were fully understood. Logan Simpson was preparing Brighton's Comprehensive Plan and had been asked by both the City and the County to determine whether a joint special agricultural district would be beneficial. Both bodies had already voted to protect open space, but there was no effective plan in place for doing so.

Having the two public bodies coordinate their efforts was a highly unusual step. With respect to farming, however, it made perfect sense, since Adams County generally framed policy for agricultural lands outside the city limits, while the City of Brighton held jurisdiction over the farms inside their boundaries. As a suburban county with an expanding tax base, Adams County also had access to considerable resources. Adopting a joint plan for the district as part of their respective Comprehensive Plans, they hoped, would allow the two entities to coordinate more easily.

The Logan Simpson team attempted to calm the situation by meeting with stakeholders one by one, and making it clear that planners were always accessible and would listen. "We made substantial progress after that," Call said. The team strived to maintain a humble presence and avoided imposing their views. Freeman said she felt the design team was "viewed as a neutral party. As outsiders, our presence helped soften people's words a bit."

Yet after listening to long diatribes by several landowners, Megan and I were disheartened. Primarily people were venting their frustrations and seemed to be inflexible in their positions. No discussions seemed possible, because several folks would not consider any evidence that did not fit into their preformed positions.

As Megan and I discussed the situation, we began to understand why some parties were stuck. Certainly, opponents of the agricultural district had good reasons to be concerned about getting maximum value for their land. Yet they were also taking wholly inconsistent positions as they pressed their case. They put themselves into a bind that can be summarized as follows.

On the one hand, some of the most virulent opponents of protecting farmland had originally moved to Brighton to farm, valuing the community because of its working lands, its wide vistas, the rural lifestyle, and a peaceful separation from urban life. They told us it had been a great place to raise kids, and they had enjoyed the independent lifestyle farming provided. If someone suggested that the land be developed, they became irate that this rural way of life would be diminished. Yet at the very same time, these same folks held an entirely contrary position: that as free Americans, they had the right to sell their land for the highest possible price, and that meant to a developer. Several owners felt that agriculture was dead anyway, so there was no reason to protect farmland. When protecting the land was mentioned, these same folks now became incensed that they could not be fully rewarded for the contributions they had made by farming. Thus any and all options that might be suggested ignited fury.

Interlaced with these concerns was a profound recognition of the imbalances of power that farmers faced. Although historically farming had been a source of considerable wealth, the entire farm sector in Adams

County was financially challenged. Our research showed that in 2013, the county's farms earned $91 million less than they had earned in 1969, after adjusting for inflation. Its 841 farms had spent more money producing crops and livestock than they earned by selling their products every year since 1994, and nearly two of every three farmers reported a net loss to census takers in 2012.

This financial wound was compounded by civic processes. While farmers and landowners attended interviews and meetings as volunteers, professionals (including myself) earned money by inviting them to offer input. Moreover, we could come and go, while the landowners dealt with the consequences over the long term. Several of the landowners, now living far from Adams County, felt they lacked representation through local officials. Many residents, in and beyond the farm community, doubted whether any public body could make effective decisions, especially after years of allowing development to encroach. This was despite the fact that the City had already purchased farmland to protect it from development, and was contemplating the creation of a farming heritage center on one historical farm.

With all of these concerns simmering, half of the farms in the district had exercised their "nuclear option," and more threatened to do the same. A landowner could sell the water rights to their land, allowing someone else to divert water for other uses, without actually selling the land. As these rights were sold, the land would never return to the farm—at least for any crop that required water—because all the valuable crops required water. With no future in farming, these properties became an easier target for developers.

Despite these ominous winds in the community, several of our interviewees generously gave us their insights. Freeman had elicited great trust with people on all sides of the issue. In quiet rooms our respondents provided us with a rich sense of Brighton's history and gave us nuanced impressions of the issues involved.

The Momentum Shifts

For me, the discussion turned one day at a meeting of key city and county staff convened at the Adams County Government Center. I tried to adopt as neutral a tone as possible when describing what our research had found. In short, historic farms were being abandoned, water rights had been sold, and regional agricultural infrastructure was fragmenting. The farm families who had thrived growing vegetables in the past had stated clearly that they could not buy any more farmland in Brighton at prevailing prices. Lots of developers were happy to purchase land as it became available, but few, if any, would hold any interest in agriculture. Some rich individual might intervene to purchase farmland, but unless an unusual person came along who wished to spend their fortune to farm at low margins, it was unlikely to be cultivated.

This left the City and the County as the only entities that could potentially purchase land for the purpose of retaining it for agricultural use. It would be a financial stretch to purchase these properties, of course, but the alternative was that the farmland would disappear. At risk were not only the livelihoods and heritage of Adams County farmers but also $22 million of income earned by local farm workers. Further, I suggested, such a purchase might help break the impasse. Suppose the City or County purchased one farm from a dissenting farmer who wanted development value for their land. This would send two signals at once: first, that the City and County were not going to try to condemn the land or squeeze landowners on price, so their retirement options were secure; and second, that these public bodies were committing themselves to a future for agriculture in the area. There was reason, therefore, to keep one's land in farming.

After this was spelled out, Terry Freeman quickly sensed the shift of momentum in the room. She began to outline the next steps for approaching a land purchase, and specific plans were cast. Yet there was still considerable consternation in the community. Opponents, and those who were mistrustful of *any* city action continued to rail against saving farmland. Two families were especially vocal critics.

The Adams County director of regional affairs, Abel Montoya, decided the best way to move forward was to bring everyone together in the same room. City and county staff dedicated themselves to making sure every single family with land interests in the district was invited, even if it took three or four calls to persuade them that it was a sincere gesture. Nearly every family was represented. "Some family members even flew in from out of town," Freeman recalled. "It was a contentious discussion, to say the least." Yet, in the end, "the people in the room kind of convinced each other" that protecting farmland was the best option. A couple of weeks later, in March 2016, the City Council and the County Commission each adopted the plan for the Special District.

A year after the district was approved, the City was able to conclude a purchase of one parcel of land from one of the most vocal opponents of protecting farmland. After several more months, a neighboring farm placed their land in a conservation easement, permanently protecting its agricultural character.

Complex Issues Still Simmer

The impasse may have lifted, but there was still considerable complexity in moving forward. In our report to the City and County, we also noted that purchasing farmland would not be enough in itself. Because farmers and consumers had been so sharply separated from each other, Adams County farmers were losing money exporting commodities to distant markets, while their neighbors spent $1.2 billion each year buying food sourced from outside the county. If the City and County wanted farming to survive, it would also have to shoulder some responsibility for constructing a more localized food system, one that would better reward both farmers and consumers. This meant investing in infrastructure supporting community food trade, and launching marketing campaigns enticing local residents to support neighboring farms with their consumer purchases. Such a journey was one the two public bodies would need to tackle patiently over time.

Some resentment still simmered, but broad agreement had been reached through an exceptionally patient embrace of opposing views by Montoya and the city and county staff, Freeman, and the Logan Simpson team. All collaborated courageously to nurture the process politically. Freeman recalled that the key staff "all were very much on board with protecting farmland. They had good camaraderie with each other. There were no hidden agendas." These resolute staff included the county's Rachel Bacon, Shannon McDowell, Abel Montoya, and Lori Wisner, and the city's Marv Falconberg, Holly Prather, Aja Tibbs, and Gary Wardle.

"All the Stars Aligned"

Jeremy Call, head of the Logan Simpson team, said that this was a rare situation where "all the stars aligned." He credited both the City and the County with mobilizing a planning discussion that would work for all parties over the long term. "It was a huge step of trust for both of them," he added. "It could have gone either way. By deciding to pool resources and confront roiling issues head on, the two public bodies decided not to just play the safe game."

Abel Montoya was the driving force, Call explained. "Abel was the real visionary. He spelled out that we need to create a vision that is so exciting and compelling nobody would want to stand in its way." With a decade of seniority in Adams County government, he was well placed to take this lead. As Call said, "Abel was not a zealot or a disciple of any specific planning method. He simply had an inner conviction that every place should be the best place it can be."

The Logan Simpson design team also set a high goal for themselves under Call's direction: "This would be an outstanding process as well as a plan." He sought to offer opportunities and incentives, rather than prescribing answers from outside. "We wanted to use planning tools to satisfy property owners, while also reaping public benefits." Rather than proposing regulations such as restrictive zoning that limited options, the team told residents, "Here is a menu of tools you can choose to use if you wish." Rather than attempting to save every acre of farmland, protections were very targeted. Priority was placed on protecting the best farmland with adequate water, and relegating future development to other areas, such as properties where water rights had already been sold.

By January 2017, a joint District Plan Commission had been formed to implement the plan, with five county and four city representatives. Over time, the Brighton/Adams vision coalesced around several key concepts. More land would be acquired, and a local food system developed. Staff would be hired. The new district would become a haven for residents as well as a food destination for visitors. Bike trails along the South Fork of the Platte River would weave past farm fields. Restaurants and breweries would feature locally grown foods. "You can't do much of this unless you protect the farmland," said Ag Innovation Specialist Anneli Berube, whose position is jointly funded by the City and County.

Branding the Historic District

Ultimately, one of the first steps toward creating that possibility was to brand the land that had been identified as part of the Special District in a highly appealing manner. A Denver firm, Domoto Brands, was called in to build a stronger identity for the place. As the firm researched the history of the community, with support from the Brighton City Museum, as well as financial assistance from the Colorado Tourism Office and the Brighton Lodging Tax, the branding focused on one historical moment. The man credited with filing the first plat for the town site of Brighton, Daniel Carmichael, had said he "took a fancy to the place and determined there should be a town here that would be a credit to the splendid valley of the Platte."

True to these roots, the district inherited the name Historic Splendid Valley. The City of Brighton has now installed a website posting details about the plan and its activities. The Greater Brighton Chamber of Commerce created an additional site showcasing all of the farms in Brighton. Both have sponsored special events featuring farms and products. In 2019 a local nonprofit, Brighton Shares the Harvest, worked with local farmers to donate to local food pantries. These partners are collaborating with the Platte Valley Medical Center to host a workshop addressing food access in the valley. A partnership with a veterans' farmer-training project has grown on the site of one historic farm, The Bromley/Koizuma-Hishinuma Farm. One new farm has opened. The City now leases conservation-protected property to Petrocco to raise vegetables.

To date, the City of Brighton and Adams County have purchased a total of 288 acres of land. Another 78 acres were placed in a conservation easement. They still hope to purchase another 640 acres of important farmland. Another 500 acres are under private ownership that seems dedicated to continuing agriculture. That makes a total of 1,140 protected acres, out of a total of 1,500 acres in the district that are marked as eligible for protection.

This is only one segment of the entire 5,000-acre district. Clearly, there will be houses built, and commercial properties constructed. Yet, by branding the Historic Splendid Valley and showcasing the farms that raise food there, Brighton and Adams County have set a tone that may help this future development complement, rather than undermine, those farms.

Berube added that both Petrocco and Sakata have kept their Brighton processing plants open, and support from both the City and the

County has held strong. While the tension in the community has not completely ended, some have let go of their anger. Plans have been announced for a new high-end housing subdivision that would include agricultural plots.

Berube also waits to see what will happen when some of the heirs of current farm owners begin to take ownership—especially those who do not wish to farm their parents' land but want to accrue value from the property. Working farms still struggle to find and afford the labor needed to operate their farms. The district's farms are all strapped for resources, including time and money. There are still tensions between tractors and commuters on rural roadways.

Nor has branding the district prevented clashing uses. Tragically, one Brighton landowner leased drilling rights to an oil and gas exploration company, so now an oil fracking rig and distribution depot have been planted in a former farm field, right across the road from The Berry Patch Farms home farm. This means more truck traffic in the neighborhood. Freeman said she sat with the landowners several times, hoping that if she heard their concerns they might soften. Yet they steadfastly refused to sell their land to the City because they harbored a deep mistrust of government. They also would have incurred some steep costs if they continued farming because they are in the Platte floodplain. Despite having declared the area a place for protecting farmland, the City had few policy options, precisely because it had kept the program voluntary and because the state, not local government, regulates oil and gas development. At public meetings, Freeman recalled, it became clear that officials were under "an enormous amount of pressure" from the oil firm.

Tim Ferrell took an even-tempered view. He told me late in 2019 that the rig was far enough away that it was only a minor distraction. "I'm used to it. I can see it from several places on my property, and especially from our fields. But there are no derricks moving, and no noise. It looks benign, but we know what they are doing."

Ferrell continues to run a new organic farm on city-owned land north of The Berry Patch Farms. The Petrocco family began to farm organically on the same property. The main opponent of protecting farmland sold their property to the City and has moved away, Ferrell said. "We don't have to put up with the toxic feelings any more." He is pleased that the City is engaging farmers in monthly discussions about how to create stronger collaborations. These encourage farms to cross-market each other's products, creating synergy among the farmers. The City is trying to raise funds to install signs that would feature each of the farms in the area. Retailers have reached out to purchase food from The Berry Patch Farms. The Brighton Chamber of Commerce held a dinner at the Ferrells' farm, "and a lot of our fellow Chamber members came out. It's living with your neighbors. It's something you just have to do. We're all in the same community, so we often touch each other. The concept of keeping this a strong agricultural community has a strong feeling behind it. It doesn't matter what color you are. It has become a strong selling point that we want to keep farming viable and we want to keep it in the community."

Ferrell is also pragmatic and knows that the situation may change over time. "I wonder if we are always going to have to be on our toes. Political leaders will change. Developers have deep pockets. They might begin to purchase water rights [again], and then we would lose more farms." He also noted that there continue to be traffic conflicts between suburban drivers and farm equipment.

Berube is optimistic. She hopes that Brighton's farms will sport the official logo of Historic Splendid Valley and wants to create a passport for visitors to stamp each time they visit one of the farms. She aims to get Brighton businesses to engage in the effort, and intends to build signage so that everyone who enters the valley knows its identity. She is creating a toolkit for local schools to use in purchasing from nearby farms.

So far, she added, there has been no pushback from developers, but many already had entitled land before the district was created, and the new district took nothing away from them. One developer even rebranded itself with an agricultural theme. She added that it is too early to tell whether the Historic Splendid Valley designation has raised property values.

Nonetheless, on multiple levels, the stars aligned in Brighton. Few municipal governments are as visionary and courageous as those in Adams County and the City of Brighton. They brought people together to work through conflict, allowing hope and innovation to flourish. Success grew out of open, transparent discussion that engaged diverse viewpoints. City and county staff, landowners, designers, and civic leaders confronted immense issues honestly. This set a course for a better future, embracing a new identity that evokes the long-standing rural heritage. Protecting a small number of acres provided the symbolic gesture that defined this vision.

Similar collaborations were constructed patiently, below the radar and with far less conflict, in a suburban county in Minnesota that also faces exceptional development pressure, as chapter 9 shows. Over decades, one savvy county official built solid community support for protecting green space, water, and wildlife habitat at first, to construct a network of greenways that also became welcomed by developers as an amenity. Now Dakota County is expanding this initiative to embrace farmland protection, and support innovative ways of producing food.

CHAPTER 9

Working Below the Radar to Create Networks of Green Space

Dakota County, Minnesota, has also experienced an intense loss of farmland, but core rural traditions remain embedded in the community fabric. Several farm families trace their roots through generations, and township governments still control zoning decisions. Development also allowed the County to garner the resources required for long-term planning to protect green space. Environmental leaders living across the Twin Cities metro area, informed in part by community foods activity, forged a broad vision for fostering water quality in the Mississippi River watershed 35 years ago. Knowing the river serves as its eastern border, Dakota County rose to the challenge. One county official worked quietly to implement this strategy, building support from the township level up to county commissioners. Public investments have centered on protecting water quality, preserving wildlife habitat, improving soil health, and fostering recreational opportunities. By acting strategically, this evolved into an extensive network of green corridors. Developers were initially skeptical, but they now embrace these corridors as amenities that add value to nearby properties. Now the County is turning closer attention to fostering innovative agricultural practices and protecting farmland for agriculture.

As the land conservation manager for Dakota County, Minnesota, located just south of the Twin Cities of Minneapolis and St. Paul, Al Singer has devoted the past 16 years to shepherding landowners, community residents, civic leaders, county commissioners, and state bureaucrats through a persistent process of protecting 12,000 acres of farmland and natural areas. Through that experience, he has come to see food issues as an important vehicle for advancing that conversation in the future.

While the County boasts a proud heritage of farming, playing host to historic truck farms, a dwindling number of dairies, and persistent expanses of cropland, it also serves as the center of an emerging core of organic farmers who have shouldered considerable financial risk to sell direct to household consumers. Several of those are part of a cluster of Hmong farmers who lease land from a private owner, market fresh produce collaboratively, and play lead roles in managing the St. Paul Farmers' Market.

However, the County has also documented groundwater nitrate contamination, impaired surface waters, and increased flooding on its farmland, already challenged by sprawling suburban development, an impending generational transfer of ownership, and erratic farm economics. People who moved here decades ago for the wide skies and rural stillness now find themselves facing a complex array of pressures. And it is Singer's job to consider how to balance environmental protection with agricultural uses. He is well aware that policy decisions made by the County today will shape land use for decades to come.

His small office stands in a quiet corner of a massive three-story government building. On the wall is a large map of the county showing interlacing networks of green space, marked in bright colors. Vast reams of scientific reports are piled on the floor. He ignores several phone chimes that sound during our interview. His voice is soft and his recall razor-sharp as he conjures up more than 40 years of tiny steps that have engaged thousands of residents in patient decisions to help understand and protect the land and water they live near, and depend on. Singer's humble demeanor, closely attuned ears, and hospitality offer few clues to the ground-breaking results Dakota County has achieved through this stewardship.

Protecting the Mississippi

Singer is quick to point out that the conservation process was not one he launched; several policy steps preceded his entry. When the last section of the beltway surrounding the metro region was completed in 1985, just as the Farm Credit Crisis erupted, Dakota County was exposed to accelerated development pressure when farms were especially vulnerable. During the 1990s the County approved as many as 3,000 new building permits annually. The natural landscape was devoured, and productive farms were transformed into fields of houses.

Concurrently, expansion of the metro area led planners to consider relocating the region's international airport. A legislative study recommended three potential sites. One was in the center of Dakota County. Residents braced themselves for an onslaught of traffic, noise, and construction, and voiced their concerns. "Many long-time farming families had been taking for granted that their land would always look the way it was," Singer recalled. Now, facing this uncertain future, they called for protecting farmland.

Protection also stood at the heart of two parallel conservation efforts that were launched soon after the airport report was released. First was a regional effort to ensure that natural areas, especially wildlife and ecological corridors, would be sheltered against development. This was part of a broader regional effort to protect the Mississippi River, which flows along the eastern edge of Dakota County. Congress had established a national park along the river in 1988, "to facilitate conversations about development so that it occurs in a way that protects the River's key resources." Ten years later, in 1998, the Minnesota state legislature instituted the $4.3-million Metro Greenways Program, dedicated to creating a network of open spaces and natural areas, connected by green corridors, in the Twin Cities metro area. Al Singer was hired by the state's Department of Natural Resources as the program's first manager, leaving his former role as environmental planner and program manager for the Minneapolis Park and Recreation Board. His primary role was to coordinate local government, nonprofit organizations, and state agencies as they pursued planning and land acquisition.

Second, in that same year, Dakota County attracted state funding to begin developing its own Farm and Natural Areas Protection Plan in response to residents' visions. Singer recalled, "The County had been surveying its residents regularly. During the early to mid-1990s, they were increasingly citing their concerns about urban growth and the loss of natural areas and farmland."

Singer recalled that the Metro Greenways planning process instituted far more sophisticated and precise tools for managing the landscape. Aerial photographs were analyzed to categorize diverse land uses and to calculate the acreage where development had created surface areas that were impervious to rainfall, thus contributing to runoff. These analytical tools were first developed by academic researchers using Dakota County data. Through coordination with state and national protocols, their work eventually became codified as the Minnesota Land Cover Classification System.

Constructing Networks of Greenspace

Having access to these powerful analytical tools meant planners could quickly determine the locations where land had been zoned as residential, commercial, or industrial, or listed as vacant. This allowed them to more accurately understand patterns of development and to identify specific corridors that deserved special protection. These maps showed that wildlife greenways could link areas with similar vegetation, allowing animals to thrive despite disturbance of development. "We began to think in terms of networks, and less about individual land parcels," Singer concluded.

Meanwhile, residential development raced across Dakota County, even as the County deliberated its farmland protection strategies. Yet one significant opportunity for protecting land surfaced near Chub Lake in the southwestern part of the County. Nine siblings had inherited a 192-acre parcel of forests, farmland, and lakeshore, and now they wondered what to do with it. They knew that Dakota County had designated the land to be potential parkland in the early 1970s. But they had also been courted by a developer who wanted to build a golf course there. Residents living nearby wanted it to become a park. However, Singer recalled, "At the time, the county commissioners were not interested in spending funds to protect non-parkland—let alone establishing a new park." Nor had they any precedent of spending public funds to protect land that was not part of the County's park system.

So Singer went to work. He was able to enlist the board of the township surrounding the property, Eureka Township, as well as the Cannon River Watershed Partnership, the local chapter of the National Wild Turkey Federation, and The Nature Conservancy in supporting the effort. The Metro Greenways Program recommended funding a purchase. The Minnesota legislature extended its own appropriation for establishing a proposed state wildlife management area. However, this collaborative funding approach still fell $50,000 short of the $910,000 required. The consortium asked county staff to request that the county board consider contributing the remainder.

Singer noted that he anticipated more resistance than he got. One of the initial skeptics of protecting the land was County Commissioner Joe Harris. A well-known fiscal conservative, he represented all of the rural townships in the county. Harris also had an open mind. He became impressed by this new collaborative approach to land conservation, and he recognized that this project was something that his constituents wanted. Ultimately, the commissioners approved the funding. Their decision proved to be pivotal in putting the County into a leadership position for future land protection efforts.

A County Commissioner Takes the Lead

Singer smiled as he recalled his first meeting with Commissioner Harris. That encounter was the first of a close collaboration that lasted the next 13 years. "He was commissioner for 36 years. Over time, he became *the* county board champion for our conservation work."

By 2002, significant momentum had been built for protecting land. In January, the commissioners adopted a formal Farmland and Natural Areas Protection Plan, with Harris taking the lead. In this plan, the County recognized that residential growth rates in Dakota County were among the fastest in the Midwest and that this was residents' primary concern. They supported public efforts to protect farmland and were willing to pay higher property taxes to make sure it happened. The new plan designated approximately 36,000 acres of natural areas and 42,000 acres of agricultural land, within a half-mile of either rivers and streams or previously protected lands, as worthy of protection.

As a result of these findings, the county board authorized a November 3, 2002, bond referendum that would generate $10 million for protecting farmland and $10 million for protecting natural areas. The measure passed, with 57 percent voting in favor. With this in place, the County applied for state funds to develop a detailed outreach program and set up guidelines and mechanisms for accepting project proposals. A citizens advisory council was formed. Singer elaborated that the broad public discussion leading up to the vote was instrumental. "Previously, Washington County had attempted to pass a similar bond referendum without a strategic educational campaign and it failed."

At this point, Al Singer left his previous job with the Minnesota Department of Natural Resources to join the staff at Dakota County. He brought multiple lessons with him. "At the State, I learned you can't effectively do this work by yourself. You have to collaborate, and be strategic about making public conservation investments." Further, he realized that "working through the counties was the right level. Counties are large enough to have important natural resources, yet small enough to get things done." He was attracted to the opportunities in Dakota County, a complex mix of fully developed cities, rapidly developing suburbs, small rural cities, and a diverse natural and agricultural landscape.

Significantly, he also noted that zoning power was vested at the township level in Dakota County, so the county government would have to encourage voluntary participation, offering incentives rather than writing prescriptive rules. Singer believed that "maybe we could accomplish comprehensive conservation here." If so, "we could have something to share with other people." As an aside, he added, "Frankly, I didn't mind no longer having to go through the legislative process every two years to ensure funding."

At the time, Singer was the County's sole staff for this program. However, the County had appropriated funds that allowed him to contract with two other entities to carry out program goals. One was a nonprofit, The Friends of the Mississippi River, that had been involved in the development of the protection plan, helping to organize the educational campaign for the referendum. The Friends provided outreach services to owners of natural areas who might potentially be interested in enrolling their properties. The second important entity was the Dakota County Soil and Water Conservation District. As a deeply trusted source of information within the agricultural community, the District staff helped solidify this outreach and offered support services.

Singer could also take advantage of broader support statewide. His predecessors had worked with the Minnesota Department of Agriculture to develop a statewide Farmland Protection Plan. Formally adopted in 2003, this allowed county investments to be leveraged with state funding. Enactment of this measure was facilitated by awareness formed through three decades of prior community foods work in Minnesota.

Prioritizing Which Parcels to Protect

As the County's protection efforts matured, it set specific criteria for prioritizing which parcels to protect. These were designed, Singer said, "not just to protect farmland and natural resources, but also to demonstrate the strategic use of public resources and fairness to all applicants. They were meant to clearly delineate the public and private interests in protection, and to ensure accountability to the public." Factors taken into account included a project's location, how much prime farmland or locally significant soil would be protected, the extent of shoreland or other natural areas involved, its proximity to other protected properties, and whether the landowner was willing to donate land or money as part of the process.

Easement value for each parcel was determined through an independent appraisal, largely based on the market value of building rights that were available given the pace of residential development. Singer added, "As these market values increased, we recognized that we could protect nearly the same amount of land if we didn't buy the building rights, but rather clustered new construction along the roadways." This essentially zoned the remaining open spaces out of development. He continued, "This could still allow the majority of the land to be protected at a lower cost, allow the landowner to retain an escalating asset, and minimize potential land-use conflicts if development were to occur."

For more than a decade, Dakota County advanced its farmland protection activities in largely the same fashion. Between 2003 and 2015, when the last agricultural easement was acquired, the County had received nearly $13 million of federal funds that matched local investments. These included land donations valued at $4.9 million and $10 million of County funds, expended to acquire 68 agricultural conservation easements totaling 7,770 acres.

However, federal funding for land protection became problematic when the rules for the 2014 Farm Bill were finalized. Now selection of individual projects to fund took place at the national level, not the state level. The funding formula changed so smaller properties became less competitive. These new requirements made the federal program less relevant to the County's needs, Singer said. The housing market also slowed for a while. The 2008 recession largely eliminated rural residential development, he added. "There was effectively no net loss of agricultural land during that period."

Developers Embrace Grenways

As external factors shifted, and the County gained more experience in its land protection efforts, the program evolved over time. Persisting despite limited federal support, Dakota County acquired 42 natural area easements totaling 1,800 acres. It also provided funds to its 13 cities, and to the state government itself, to protect an additional 2,000 acres in the county. The new County Park System Plan, adopted in 2008, expanded the park system from three paved recreational trails to a 200-mile-long greenway system. In this network, wider corridors provided a combination of habitat, water quality, and recreational benefits all at once. This, in turn, attracted more support from unexpected parties. "Previously, realtors and developers were quite concerned about conservation interfering with their business," Singer explained. "Then they realized that this interconnected network of multipurpose green space was a real amenity. Now, they largely embrace conservation as an asset to the adjacent properties."

Dakota County officials had long recognized that natural resources are not truly protected unless managed carefully. So each farmland protection project requires a stewardship plan. Each agricultural conservation easement must include permanent 150-foot-wide vegetative buffers along all waterways and 75-foot-wide buffers along wetlands. Each plan must include erosion-control measures that document a clear connection to improving water quality and follow best management practices. As an incentive, the County offers initial funds to plant buffer vegetation, install fencing, and the like. However, the County did not specify how natural areas within agricultural easements should be managed; that was left to the owners under the constraints of their own stewardship plan. Now the County is revisiting the management guidelines and may suggest higher standards, while exploring financial and other incentives that encourage private owners to improve natural resources in these areas.

Natural-area conservation easements have similar, but different, criteria. Each requires a natural resource management plan that assesses the current condition of the natural resource, prioritizes recommendations for restoration and enhancement, and estimates costs for such activities as removing invasive species, stabilizing shoreland, or creating more plant diversity. Initially, the County considered this restoration work to be voluntary. But over time it set this as a requirement. Now participating landowners must commit to initial restoration efforts, but with significant financial assistance from the County.

Success Brings New Challenges

Success in land protection and natural resource management also brings new challenges, Singer added. "This continues to be one of the key issues the County's conservation programs face, along with most other public agencies." Initial successes raise new, ongoing questions, such as, "How much protected land should there be and at what cost? Most public agencies are not adequately managing the lands that they already own. Should public agencies restore and manage what they have instead of acquiring more land?" Effective management also requires private cooperation, he added. "Public lands often cannot function ecologically unless they are connected and buffered by managed private lands. So, we ask, How much public financial assistance should private landowners receive for lands that are not publicly accessible, but provide significant public benefits if managed more effectively?"

As he considered the complexity of these deliberations, Singer paused to ponder, "How do we measure success? Is it based on the number of acres or miles of shoreland protected? Do we measure how much water is being infiltrated to protect groundwater quality and quantity? Do we focus on maintaining or improving the number of wildlife species of greatest conservation need? Or do we set a course to find alternative ways to produce more local food, hoping to maintain thriving rural communities while improving soil health and water quantity?"

With a sweep of his arms, he added, "And we have to pay attention to climate change, to increased flooding, carbon sequestration, an aging population and impending transfer of land ownership, as well as keep our eye on global markets." As the County continues to attract new residents, he added, still other concerns emerge: "Affordable housing is becoming a larger issue."

To address these issues and opportunities, the County has nearly completed a comprehensive land conservation plan for Dakota County. This document draws on decades of experience, research, and resident input. In it, the County proposes to define a preliminary set of 24 preliminary Conservation Focus Areas. In each, Singer said, "The County will enter a rich dialogue with landowners, hoping they will integrate their own values and priorities to help guide the future of conserving each landscape."

Then, the County will collaborate with each of its 13 cities to coordinate land protection and increase natural resource restoration, Singer added. He trusts that this will bring new efficiencies in information sharing, allow the partners to share staff and other resources, and reduce costs through joint grant writing and purchasing. He further hopes to create new incentive packages for conservation efforts paid through private donations.

Dakota County will soon reach out to diverse colleagues to gather their comments on this approach. "Our fundamental question is, how to get people to understand the personal value and importance of natural resource protection, and the real challenges we face?" Singer explained. "How do we get the right information into people's hands, and how do we make clear what the consequences will be if we don't take individual and collective action?" He envisions bringing people together for storytelling that helps find "tangible paths" for understanding this complexity. By sharing stories, he added, "People can talk about their heritage with their land. They can describe what is happening today, and their hopes for the future." This is just one strategy that reflects his attempt to understand, "How can we work with systems thinking in a way that does not sound too complicated?"

Food Will Ground the Next Stages

Currently, Singer thinks that one of the ways to cut through this complexity is to ground the discussion in food: "Food has an ecosystem, and everyone can talk about it in very personal terms. It becomes a personal connection with land and water and history and neighbors. There are forces that we cannot control, but there are many things that we can control and influence. It is important to differentiate between the two and realize we can make a difference."

However, he recognizes that this approach is a difficult one to maintain in these polarized times. Singer mused, "It's all about communication, collaboration, and trust. You have to come to these discussions with a clear sense of yourself, and you have to also be thinking about the other person." This means paying attention to what the other person brings to the discussion, where they are coming from and how they experience their life. He thinks Dakota County is well placed to accomplish this. "Fortunately, we have a strong history of collaboration in this County and have been building our credibility over time."

At the end of our conversation, I asked Singer what had surprised him the most. He replied quickly. "It is the success we've had. When I came to Dakota County it was not very well regarded for its natural resource protection and management. Over time and with lots of internal and external assistance and support, the County is embracing its natural heritage as it positions itself for the future. Having a clean environment with quality natural areas is now one of four county board goals, and we're gaining national recognition." The key, he added, was to listen closely, treat people fairly, build trust, use good information, give ample credit to others, and not be afraid to try new things. "We just try to demonstrate good stewardship," he concluded, letting action serve as the example.

County commissioners in Dakota County, supported by a visionary staff, have now formalized their commitment to protecting farmland and natural areas. The foundation for making this commitment was laid decades before, when visionary environmental activists developed effective strategies for protecting water, wildlife habitat, and open space. Acting in concert with other units of government, the County was able to respond fully when residents asked that precious natural areas be protected. Then the County moved into a convening and mobilizing role. Wider public input was sought, and educational campaigns were launched to persuade even more voters to participate. As this gathered momentum, Dakota County engaged wider circles in defining a broader vision, one that is now surfacing as a top County priority, with dedicated funding over the long term.

Once again, the first step was building trust among community members. Officials proceeded with great care, bringing new constituents into a discussion that holds wide implications for the future of the entire Twin Cities metro region. Since the County connects closely with regional, state, and federal officials in the process, they have also built considerable trust among their public peers, fostering a more unified effort across the US.

Here, even green space was configured as a "web." Ecologically, this meant water flowed through protected zones, and wildlife could find both habitat and migration corridors. Connecting green spaces also allowed them to assume greater visibility and importance as recreational networks. This gave the Metro Greenway Corridors approach greater power. Earlier, when the discussion of protecting natural areas revolved around isolated parcels, there was more dissension. Once the entire network of green space became visible, even skeptics had to acknowledge that tremendous amenities had been created. With targeted investments multiple benefits accrued. Natural areas were protected, farmland and soil were preserved for sustainable production, wildlife gained more resilient ecosystems, and housing values increased. Now a broader range of stakeholders hold multiple reasons to protect the network of natural corridors.

Building connections of trust among farmers and those who buy food from them can also provide greater resilience to community food systems. In fact, I would argue that this is the most critical element of success for community food webs. I address this in chapter 10.

CHAPTER 10

Building Market
Power for Farmers

Farmers typically sell the commodities they produce at prices well below the full costs of production. They cannot sustain this; family farms in the US will not survive unless they build greater market power. Some have invented creative ways to step out of the commodity trap and connect directly with consumers. Iowa organic growers negotiated successfully with a grocery chain for a period of time by building loyalty with their customers. Seven siblings in Indiana constructed an innovative farm that reaps exceptional profits by grazing livestock intensively and selling directly to household customers using the farm's original software package. One organic farmers' cooperative in Southwest Wisconsin invited their principal buyers to join their co-op board to ensure greater mutual loyalty. Still, lasting market power for farmers depends on effective public policy.

A Victory for Iowa Farmers

With a playful smile on his face, Pat Garrity rose to stand in the middle of a group of Iowa local food leaders. He had a victory to pass along to the hundred or so who were gathered by the Leopold Center at Iowa State University.

Garrity, a seasoned food broker, had been coordinating a group of organic growers near Woodbury County, Iowa (the county seat is Sioux City). These farmers were determined to carve out an economic niche for organic agriculture in the heart of conventional farm country. Collaborating with the county's director for rural economic development, Rob Marqusee, Garrity had helped organize the growers' group. Each farmer had grown produce organically for several years and wanted to explore collaborating to sell larger quantities. At their request, Garrity approached several food buyers.

One receptive soul was Lori Tatreau, the local farm liaison for Whole Foods in Omaha, a new store that opened in October 2005. A dedicated younger staff person, Tatreau fully embraced the concept of carrying food from nearby farms. She was willing to go the extra mile in urging the firm's buyers to purchase from the co-op, and she made sure the farmers felt valued in the exchange. With her encouragement, the store installed a special display near the front door of the store, featuring Iowa Grown Organic Produce provided by the farmers' group. One of their top-selling products was asparagus, which was especially flavorful in the early spring because the farms' soils were so rich in organic matter.

Whole Foods' Omaha customers warmed to the idea of purchasing vegetables from this special display, because they could see it was fresher and tastier than other options. Plus, the produce conveyed a story—it was grown by farmers within 2 hours of the store, on fields surrounded by conventional corn and soybeans. Omaha shoppers did not mind paying a small premium for a fresher, tastier, and locally connected product. Quality was high, and this special display helped create a sense of connection to the growers. The produce sold well.

The farmers ramped up carefully, not wanting to get ahead of their own marketing, and they delivered a consistent product. As sales grew, they began to relax, planning to convey even more crops to Omaha buyers.

Then, in the middle of the late spring harvest, Garrity received a most unsettling call. He admitted that at some level, he had been expecting it all along, but it still stung. It was Tatreau, the Whole Foods liaison, saying the firm had found a source of organic produce in Wisconsin that was cheaper. Would the farmers' co-op lower their price by one dollar a pound to match this competing source?

Luckily, Garrity was prepared. He suspected Tatreau was working on orders from a manager who was trying to reduce costs, since this was not a position she would have willingly taken. He understood the store had four levels of management that directed her work, starting with her department, then the store, and then regional and national managers. He swallowed hard, adopted his most patient tone, and replied, "I'll tell you what. We've worked together well. Here is what I would ask that you do to honor the relationship we have built. Give us one more week in your special display at the store. Put the Wisconsin asparagus next to ours. Then call me back in a week or so to tell me what happened."

Tatreau agreed. After raising Garrity's proposal to management, the store offered its shoppers a choice of Iowa-grown asparagus at the original high price, or the new Wisconsin product at the lower price. A week later she called Garrity. "We're sticking with your asparagus." The customers preferred to buy from Iowa farmers they knew.

Growers all over the US have told me similar stories about "the call." Many have established a good market niche with a buyer, only to discover months later that the buyer insists they lower their price. This is in fact a strategy that larger retailers have pursued for decades to build a commanding market presence. Indeed, retailers have been known to offer loans to help a small firm expand production, hinting at an ongoing relationship, only to squeeze prices down after the expansion had increased costs of production. The producer is then faced with a dire choice—either to absorb a loss, find a new buyer (which is unlikely), or leave the business entirely. Those who have taken on debt are the most vulnerable.

Garrity was aware of this history, so he had developed a strategy for counteracting it. He knew that since he represented some of the few organic growers in the region, they held a unique position. There were no nearby competitors. Garrity had further taken strong steps to build loyalty among consumers by hosting farmer visits and tasting days at the Omaha store. From these connections he knew his customers were seeking locally raised foods that were organically grown. He also knew his competitors were less experienced at organic farming than the members of his co-op. So he felt somewhat confident that he could exert his influence.

Still, this was also a tremendous risk. Had Whole Foods said no, there was no other store in Omaha that would have been likely to carry the farmers' produce. There were certainly not enough grocers in Sioux City willing to purchase their products. Had Garrity not prevailed, the farmers would have had to look to more distant cities, or retrenched.

This is a classic confrontation for farmers who hold no power in the marketplace. Typically, farmers are price-takers, especially when they are selling undifferentiated commodities. The buyer tells the farmer what they will pay. Yet by creating loyalty among consumers, Garrity's farmers became price-setters: they told the grocer what price they needed to run a sustainable farm business, knowing that their customers supported the farms enough to pay that price. Still, it was a temporary win. Ultimately, corporate managers turned their attention away from supporting the farms nearest them. The loyalty the farmers had built with the store buyer was not enough to sustain sales over the long term. But it was the correct strategy.

Seven Brothers Build a Business Cluster in Indiana

Some farms avoid such difficult negotiations by constructing their own distribution networks. One potent example of such a farm is Seven Sons farm near Roanoke, Indiana. This farm has built a solid market presence by selling directly to customers through a disciplined effort to produce food in innovative ways, and by making their product accessible and convenient for the consumer to purchase.

As the name implies, the farm is owned by seven brothers in one family: the Hitzfields. The vertically integrated collaboration was constructed with the inspiration and help of their parents, who realized that the family's former styles of farming, once quite profitable, would not work in a new era. Seven Sons Farm is actually several different businesses under one family umbrella—a regional business cluster owned by an extended family. The seven families raise grass-fed beef, pastured pork, and eggs. They also sell products, such as chicken and lamb, grown by several partner farms.

Seven Sons Farm generates over $4 million in revenue, selling three-quarters of its products directly to households through its website. This original software platform was constructed by family members. Once a consumer makes a purchase, the farm packs and delivers the orders, either directly to the customer's door or to a remote pickup location not far away. The other 25 percent of sales are earned from a small, on-farm retail store as well as wholesale outlets.

Each separate product is organized under its own business entity. "We have nested and stacked enterprises," business manager Blaine Hitzfield said, "with multiple people per enterprise." Each brother (often with his spouse) takes leadership in the arena where he holds the greatest skill and interest. Each operates with considerable latitude while fitting into the larger plan of the overall enterprise.

By rotating different livestock through the same pastures, the family said it has increased profits dramatically. The family calculates that the farm earns a profit of $400–$500 per acre by raising beef. Chickens are pastured on the same land (typically after the cattle have grazed, in order to clean up insects that have settled on the manure, and also adding their own fertility). So raising chickens is considered both a sanitation strategy and a production strategy—the chickens' main task is to lay eggs. Chickens add profits of about $3,000 per acre above what is earned by raising beef, on the same fields, while also reducing veterinary costs. Raising 200 hogs per year on the same land, pastured after the chickens, adds about $800 profit per acre. Feeding costs for these hogs (Duroc, Large Black, and Hampshire varieties) are reduced by 20 percent since the farm rotates these animals through pasture, rather than feeding them grain continuously. Exercise improves their health and thus the quality of their meat. All told, the brothers claim profits of $4,300 per acre of livestock. The total acreage of their farm (not all in pasture) is 550 acres.

Moreover, the farm washes and packs 500 dozen eggs per day using a small washing device they purchased in Iowa. From their on-farm store, Seven Sons sells cheese from Twilight Dairy, a Hutterite cheesemaker in Indiana, and several other producers. The farm also adds value even to spent laying hens. "We take our spent hens to Greg Gunthorp," Hitzfield said. Gunthorp is a pig and poultry farmer more than an hour north. "He takes the bones out and can process from there to make bone broth and chicken broth." Not surprisingly, Gunthorp also has his own direct sales network, selling hogs and turkeys directly to Chicago and Indianapolis restaurants. To reduce his own costs and gain maximum control over quality, Gunthorp installed a USDA-certified meat processing plant on his own farm.

The Hitzfields further created new efficiencies in marketing. One brother devised an original internet website and ordering platform that allows the farm to sell meat cuts by weight, accurately track live inventory, and manage direct distribution routes. As other farms took note of the software's capabilities, they asked if they could use it as well. Ultimately, several brothers turned the ordering platform into a web-based application that could support multiple users. They now make this platform available to other farmers under another enterprise the brothers created, called GrazeCart, and it is being used by 280 farms across North America. Selling this ordering platform to other farms has provided the brothers additional income.

Seven Sons meat is delivered via FedEx as well as the farm's own vehicles. Most of the farm's customers are centered in a five-state area surrounding Indiana, with Chicago standing out as the most successful. Their files list 5,000 total members who purchase annually. There is no membership fee, but each purchaser pays a minimum $9 delivery fee for each order.

The brothers also partner with three distributors to make their pasture-raised eggs available through both small and major grocers across the Midwest. Currently, Seven Sons eggs are carried in select stores for Kroger, Market District, and Fruitful Yield, as well as every Whole Foods location in the Midwest. While the farm has sold to restaurants, they have found this to be a mixed experience. "Restaurants have always flirted with us," Hitzfield said. "They love having our name on their menus, but they are not always consistent in ordering." The farm has set up a separate ordering channel on its website, however, so restaurants can place orders easily.

Hitzfield said that the concept of the farm was born out of a health crisis in the family. His father, Lee, had bought 70 acres in the 1970s and put up a standard confinement operation (for its time) to raise hogs farrow-to-finish. Yet his mother, Beth, developed rheumatoid arthritis. During the difficult period of overcoming this disease, the family consulted with several experts who advised that they should close the confinement operation because of its health repercussions for Beth. So the family began to explore open-air production, and they refashioned their diet. Through these steps, Beth did overcome her illness.

Moreover, Lee and Beth realized that economic conditions had changed so much that their former style of farming would not work financially. As the farm transitioned, the brothers tried raising chickens inside the old hog barn, after giving the structure a rest and a thorough cleaning. "The confinement barn did not work well for the chickens," Hitzfield recalled. Still desiring evening and winter shelter for their livestock, the family constructed hoop houses where the laying hens could live during cold weather, with separate hoop houses for young pigs.

Seven Sons send their cattle nearly 3 hours north to Byron Center, Michigan, to be slaughtered and processed. A midsized family business with 20–30 employees, the Byron Center shop has won a great deal of respect from local farmers for the quality of their work and their flexibility in dealing with diverse grower needs. "Currently our business is doubling in size," Hitzfield said. "That would not have been possible without Byron Center."

Once the processed meat returns to the farm, the brothers store it for later sale. They have invested heavily in freezer space to ensure that they always have reserve supplies on hand. This means they can promise that bulk meat will always be available when the consumer wants it—not determined solely by the animals' life cycles on the farm. "Any investment we've made in new freezers has paid for itself in a year," Hitzfield added.

As the farm expands, there are always new challenges, but also a wealth of skills and perspectives to draw from in tackling complex issues. Hitzfield noted that "we can keep scaling both our marketing and our distribution quite easily. It is much harder to scale up production." They have scanned their neighborhood to recruit more farmers who can produce under their system, but they have found it difficult to locate producer partners interested in learning these intensive techniques. "Those who were committed to raising only one species of animal did not fit. To work within our system, they need to develop a stacked model of their own (pasturing different types of animals sequentially) that fits their farm and builds the soil on that property. It has to be a combination of a ruminant and poultry to get the maximum benefits to the land," he cautioned.

Hitzfield said that it would be easy for the farm to scale up egg production on their own land simply by building new laying sheds and adding new washing equipment. But their growth in raising chickens for meat is constrained by the region's limited capacity to slaughter and process chickens.

The farm does not rely heavily on advertising campaigns, but has built awareness online by creating original content, including videos that share the farm's story and communicate what makes their product different. Their internet site gets 30,000 hits per month. Hitzfield estimated that 80 percent of this attention comes from within the farm's service area. "Consumers are turning to the internet."

Hitzfield added that the main principle that drives growth in direct marketing has been making access convenient for consumers. The brothers see growing consumer interest in "farm-to-fork" products from shoppers who also want convenience. Creating internet ordering and mounting their own distribution network provides consumers the ease they desire. By combining this with their skill in integrating farm production across multiple species, the family has retained the power to set its own course for the future of their farm.

A Farmers' Cooperative Invites Buyers to Join Its Board

A third path for addressing the challenge of building and keeping market power for farmers was taken by Fifth Season Cooperative in Southwest Wisconsin. This approach is far more complicated to implement and requires far more concerted collaboration across a wider community. It is less tied to the resources at the command of a single family than Seven Sons Farms has been.

Located 2 hours west of Madison and 3 hours southeast of Minneapolis, this "Driftless" region is stunningly beautiful, featuring long, rolling hills of primal rock untouched by glacial action (hence the name, signifying the lack of glacial drift). Wide valleys offer long exposure to the sun, while secluded coulees provide considerable privacy. It is an attractive place to settle, yet job opportunities are sparse. Its remoteness helped fuel the residents' commitment to cooperation.

The region opened a new chapter in 2009. A local environmental organization, Valley Stewardship Network, mounted an 18-month food assessment. I was brought in to compile economic data as one part of that assessment. The findings were sobering: the region's farmers had sold about $403 million of crops and livestock each year for the previous 14 years. Yet they were spending an average of $434 million to raise them. So commodity farmers were enduring losses of $31 million per year. Over half of the region's farms were suffering net losses. One bright spot was the growth of Organic Valley, a cooperative born in this region in 1988 and selling nearly $1 billion of high-quality foods nationwide, but primarily penetrating metropolitan markets.

While federal payments helped make up these losses, these subsidies averaged only $21 million per year and accrued only to those farmers who raised corn, soybeans, wheat, or other subsidized crops. Livestock farmers (including dairy farmers) or produce farmers received few benefits, save from a small number of conservation programs. Farm owners earned more from renting out farmland ($43 million) than they did by farming it.

All of the region's farmers were also dependent on inputs that were critical to their farm operation—fuel, oil, machinery, repairs, feed, and seed—that were increasingly sourced outside of the region. This meant that farmers shipped about $105 million away from the region each year, buying essential inputs they needed to farm—at a loss.

More ironically, in this farming region, where a strong sector of organic produce growers had taken hold since 1970, residents spent about $208 million each year to purchase food that was sourced outside the region. Most farmers produced commodities for export, and most of the food they and their neighbors ate was imported from outside the region. Total outflows ($350 million) totaled 88 percent of the value of all the food products farmers sold in an average year.

As I presented these findings to a packed house at the Vernon Memorial Hospital meeting room in Viroqua, the air was electric. I made the case that building on the strong foundation of local food production the region already enjoyed would be one of the best ways to stem these losses. The executive director of the Vernon Economic Development Association, Sue Noble, who had co-sponsored the event, later told me that these findings played a critical role in persuading local leaders to reshape their region to become a food destination.

Just a few months later, the largest single employer in Viroqua announced it would be moving its operation out of town. The national firm ran a printing facility in Viroqua, but it opted to cut costs by consolidating this factory with a sister unit in another state—where, it turned out, labor was cheaper—even though the Viroqua plant was more profitable. This decision cost Viroqua 85 jobs, which disappeared overnight. Since they were the best-paying jobs in town, it was a severe blow.

Looking for some way to create a positive outcome, Noble called the executive who had made the decision. She reminded him that the community had supported the firm ever since it opened its shop in 1974. She asked what the company was prepared to do to compensate Viroqua for this loss. The executive tried to placate her with boilerplate answers, stating that it was simply a business decision. Not satisfied, she continued to push. After some 20 minutes, he became weary of the conversation. "What would you like me to do?" he asked, exasperated. "Sell us the building so we can start rebuilding this community," she replied. After some discussion, he did just that. Noble began to turn the 100,000-square-foot factory space into a regional food destination.

After 8 years, Noble had sited 16 businesses in the building, thereby replacing all 85 of the lost jobs with new ones in organic production. By 2020, she was up to 20 firms with 90 jobs. She is proud of the fact that "these are owned by local entrepreneurs who are creating their own economic solutions." Almost all source their raw materials locally. Included are firms that make organic beauty products, fermented vegetables, maple syrup, craft-brewed soft drinks using local vegetables in their flavoring, and roasted coffee. The building also houses several small specialty food businesses.

One key tenant is Fifth Season Cooperative, a produce-marketing co-op that has created what I consider to be the most comprehensive approach in the US to building consumer loyalty. This initiative was launched at about the same time as the food enterprise center, after a cluster of several dozen organic growers launched plans to expand their production to meet a burgeoning market demand. The farmers asked Noble to assess the interest of several institutional buyers. She learned that several, "the University of Wisconsin–La Crosse, Western Technical College, Gundersen Lutheran Medical Center, Viroqua Schools, and Vernon Memorial Healthcare, all wanted to buy local food, but they didn't know how to make it happen."

By January 2010, Noble had scored a $40,000 grant to hire a part-time coordinator for the farmers' initiative, with the first priority being to establish a cooperative. This was a natural choice to make because the region holds a deep heritage of cooperation dating back to the 1930s and before. She contacted Margaret Bau, the US Department of Agriculture's cooperative development specialist based in Stevens Point, Wisconsin. Bau had traveled to Europe to visit several of the most renowned cooperative efforts in the world. She brought back inspiration about a business structure that was commonly used in Europe but not often tried in the US: a multistakeholder cooperative. This meant including representatives from several different sectors on the same board. By placing the farmers, workers, food buyers, processors, and distributors into a single entity, the co-op would create a more stable system for local produce trade. Farmers and buyers mutually agreed to a common set of values supporting environmental protection and social and economic fairness for all. They took a common stand in favor of providing nutrient-rich foods. All recognized these agreements might involve valuing food at higher prices. Through these agreements, adopted by their fellow board members, the farmers gained stronger loyalty.

Because of the culture of collaboration that had long been nurtured in the Viroqua region, remarkable partnerships formed. First, the food service director for Gundersen Lutheran Medical Center in La Crosse joined the board of the co-op. He in turn reached out to his squash partner, the CEO of Reinhart Foods in La Crosse, who agreed to join the board as the distributor. The leadership team met frequently for several months to refine the concept and establish procedures. On August 10, 2010, Fifth Season Cooperative was officially formed. The team continued quietly for another year, detailing agreements that specified who could invest in the business with which voting rights, writing a formal business plan, soliciting memberships, and establishing operating policies.

At this writing, Fifth Season engages 47 active produce growers. Most are Amish, Noble said. The co-op is also learning to carry industrial hemp. Its 17 processor-members produce value-added products. In 2019, the co-op sold $290,000 of fresh produce and another $260,000 of frozen goods. In addition to these mainstays, the co-op sells far smaller amounts of cheese, grass-fed meats produced by nearby co-ops, artisan pasta, and dry goods.

Each fall, the co-op's farmers meet together to establish plans for the following growing season. Based on the previous year's sales, each grower signs up on a sheet of paper offering to raise each specific item. When a given sheet gets too full, growers are encouraged to move to the next crop. At first, the farmers and buyers agreed on how much would be produced for the co-op, and they also set minimum and maximum prices. This pricing approach was abandoned over time.

Collaborative discussions also allowed innovative products to be created. When co-op growers asked local schools how to best supply the schools, food service officials described their lunch preparation processes. They were eager to make use of fresh produce, but limited their purchasing because fresh items were not available during the bulk of the school year. So the co-op developed two blends of frozen root crops, tailored for school use. One, The Winter Moon Blend, features butternut squash, potatoes, carrots, and beets grown by co-op farmers. These are partially cooked, then frozen and packaged into 20-pound cases, a quantity suited to institutional buyers. Food service staff can simply open containers and heat the blend in a chafing dish prior to serving, saving considerable labor.

Now the schools receive fresher products than commodity trucks bring, grown on farms they know, tailored to their kitchen's requirements, at a price that has been attuned to what school budgets allow. While acknowledging that the road has not always been smooth for this co-op startup, Noble looks back with satisfaction at how the co-op's vision has flourished: "I can't imagine that there would have been any other way to do Fifth Season than to form a multistakeholder co-op. Having the input and participation from members all along the value chain is critical to success."

Over time, the co-op has progressed through significant changes. The original food service director retired and was replaced by an executive at the Mayo Clinic. Reinhart Foods was purchased by a larger firm, Performance Foods. Fifth Season has developed new relationships with Indianapolis Fruits, Gordon Foods, and Sysco. Each new processor that joins adds to a dynamic process.

Having greater loyalty from buyers does not solve all of the co-op's concerns. Noble emphasizes that the co-op is subject to unpredictable market forces. Demand goes through wild swings, so growers may respond to new market demand by growing more, only to learn that no one wants that product the following year. Fifth Season now hopes that adding industrial hemp will help even out those cycles.

Market Power Requires Trust

Resilient community food systems are built, at core, by creating and nurturing strong connections of mutual trust among farmers and consumers.

Only if people are committed to keeping these connections strong will they flourish over time. It is the broad vision and deep loyalty that allow folks to look beyond their immediate self-interest to take the needs of others into account. To ensure that this trust persists, communities have historically created *cultures* of collaboration.

In each of these three initiatives, people went far out of their way to build mutual loyalties, taking action to improve conditions across an entire network—not simply for themselves. In Iowa, that trust extended across the network of farms that supplied organic produce to Omaha, and to one buyer for a short period of time. In Indiana, trust was embodied in a core group of family members, who then reached out to welcome hundreds of household consumers into their fold. Farmers in Southwest Wisconsin could count on a culture that had taken root widely within the community over generations. Each initiative drew upon the culture available to them, and then deepened the partnerships they forged.

For each of these collaborations to occur, independent farmers had to connect to independent buyers. This could not be done within the confines of a standardized commodity system. Corporate buying programs could support such work for only a short period of time, until some new cost-cutting strategy interfered. Supermarkets with standardized buying procedures determined by distant owners could not do it. It had to be individuals and firms that were rooted in place, at liberty to make their own decisions, and self-directed enough to persist. In each case, farmers asserted their own power to set their own prices, rather than waiting to see what buyers would offer.

There are a wide number of ways to build greater trust among farmers and buyers. Perhaps the most direct is to bring them together for intentional conversations: formal discussions to help both parties realize what they have to gain by working together; agreements to uphold shared values; "speed dating" convenings where people can meet quickly to explore what they might trade with each other; periodic roundtable sessions; and an ongoing "community of practice" where food system practitioners work together over time to construct a more cohesive community food system. Often, members simply visiting each other's farms and businesses can help create lasting awareness of what their partners go through. One produce wholesaler I know convenes all of the farmers that supply the firm each year; this allows the farmers to get to know each other better and also helps everyone understand how the system works—who supplies the wholesaler with which products. Some local organizations build trust by hosting common trainings, such as anti-racism training or conflict-resolution exercises, to help people bond by forging common values and reaching new insights together. To make these sessions valuable, participants have to enter these discussions with a deep interest in learning about each other, keeping self-interest subdued, and challenging their own preconceptions.

Shared physical space, or shared financial risk, can also play a potent role in fostering collaboration. If the farmers' market is adjacent to a group of food processors, conversations among growers and buyers become easier to maintain. Amish and Mennonite produce growers often command market presence by collaborating to build auction halls where buyers will gravitate. At times, food hubs bring farmers and buyers into the same space. If a group of farmers invests cooperatively in a processing plant, the buyer has good reason to remain loyal to the farmer members who supply the plant. Community-supported agriculture farms may hold close conversations with their members to foster a stronger sense of community loyalty. Some institutions, especially food banks, are contracting in advance for food grown on specific farms, and this tends to create a closer connection. Developing tailor-made products in common, as Fifth Season did with food service directors, also helps encourage lasting commerce.

Special events—farm to table meals held on the farm, or chefs preparing food from a specific farm at their restaurant—can also build stronger loyalties, and invite other consumers to join the circle of trust. One chef positioned a table tent on each of his tables, stating clearly how much the restaurant had spent purchasing food from the farms featured in wall photos. A local food summit, if held strategically, can also build considerable group cohesion. Asset-mapping exercises often evoke surprising new perspectives.

Many traditional cultures rely on community rituals or celebrations to bring people together to appreciate their common interests. Weekly services at churches, synagogues, and mosques, or prayer groups, medicine circles, and other spiritual gatherings, often create common bonds among diverse businesspeople. Community choirs, orchestras, theaters, dance events, or even Rotary clubs may do the same. Asian grocery–distribution networks have flourished across the US to supply Asian consumers with specialty foods that were not available at traditional supermarkets.

Finally, organizational umbrellas and common campaigns may foster a strong sense of shared identity. Several states use food charters as a way of enlisting support for a common set of principles. Regional branding campaigns or common production protocols may create a sense of shared identity.

Any of the strategies listed here may work, or fail, in a given context. There is no magic formula for what needs to be done. Rather, the central core, while pursuing any strategy, is to commit to a common vision and values, and engage persistently to build greater trust over the long haul. No tool, strategy, or technology can accomplish this by itself.

Importantly, there are also directions community food initiatives should avoid if they are determined to build market power for farmers. Many farmers simply prefer to spend their time alone in the fields, letting someone else make the decisions about what they should grow, how much they should harvest, and the price at which they should sell. This can be workable if a trusted intermediary represents their interests well—but even keeping such an intermediary close to the farmers' self-interest requires farmers to play a more active role to become price-setters, not price-takers.

Yet each of the creative approaches mentioned in this chapter is vulnerable until public policy creates permanent, but resilient, infrastructure and incentives that sustain market power. The best farm policies the US has conceived to date, from the perspective of rural communities, were the New Deal policies that combined supply management and fair pricing with favorable access to capital, as described in the first chapter of this book. The conditions for implementing those same policies no longer exist today, and they worked better for shelf-stable commodities than they would for perishable produce. Nor did these policies effectively support farmers of color, sharecroppers, or tenant farmers. Over the past 50 years, there has been a growing awareness that new answers must arise through community-based food systems. Yet, as chapter 11 discusses, the essential connection of loyalty between farmers and consumers often gets diluted when well-meaning people work to promote "local" food.

CHAPTER 11

Shifting from "Local Food" to "Community-Based Food Systems"

Many communities find that their efforts to build "local" food opportunities become co-opted by businesses that uphold values inconsistent with local decision making, building local wealth, or stewardship of the environment. In addition to being simplistic, the term "local food" refers to the attributes of a given food item—How far did this tomato travel?—rather than the more systemic issues: What type of food system brought food to us? What is its impact? What kind of food system do we want to build? Framing this work as building community food systems is more effective.

Nancy Matheson and her Montana colleagues (discussed in chapter 2) understood quite viscerally the ways in which the commodity economy extracts wealth from rural areas (shown in chapter 1). As early as the mid-1980s, they envisioned a future in which export agriculture would be balanced by food systems that created opportunity and stronger local regional economies in Montana. The Montanans learned rapidly that calling for "local food" was not enough. They needed to create new community-based food systems.

The phrase "local food" persists, I think, because it is a simple, pleasant, and easy-to-remember concept. Personally, I use it all the time for those very reasons. Yet I also take great care to point out that I use the phrase only as a shorthand: a way to refer to "community-based food systems." I define these as systems of exchange that strive to bring farmers and consumers into affinity with each other, for the purposes of building health, wealth, connection, and capacity.

This places the focus, not on the number of miles food travels, but on the decisions communities make as they define their own menus of food choices. The phrase reminds me that this work involves building *food systems*, not simply inviting consumers to feel happier when something is labeled "local." Constructing stronger connections between farmers and consumers creates new synergies so that more robust and resilient systems can be built. This is not simply a manner of semantics. Different ways of thinking produce different results on the ground. One produce farmer in Indiana holds a particularly insightful view of the twists and turns of "local" that affect his farm's decision making. I describe this next.

When Is "Local" Food Not Local?

In 2013, I met a Southwest Indiana farmer named Bud Vogt who shared provocative insights about the term "local food," and the lack of broader support that farms face when selling to local markets. When I visited his farm near Evansville, I learned about Vogt's struggle to balance exporting food with growing for one's neighbors. He farms land his father tilled, and primarily grows corn and soybeans. Many years ago, the family decided to diversify by raising vegetables. They added a tomato plot and constructed a farm stand so their neighbors could stop by to purchase directly. Working in collaboration with his cousin, Vogt built up this new business slowly, gaining customers primarily by word of mouth. "Somewhere along the line," Vogt said, "We began selling to grocery stores. In fact, we sold to every store in town."

As these grocery stores consolidated into larger chains, "The grocers stopped being independently owned," Vogt added. Local store managers could no longer make the decision to buy from local farms, since policies were set in distant corporate headquarters. Following suit, even locally owned grocers sought to stock the same imported tomatoes the large chains featured. "Little by little we lost business," Vogt recalled.

One generation later, however, consumer priorities shifted. As people wrestled with food-related illnesses, they took stronger interest in buying food from farms they knew. Responding to their wishes, the independent stores near Evansville placed Vogt's tomatoes on the shelves again. When I spoke with him in 2013 Vogt said, "We sell about 20 percent of our tomatoes through our farm stand, and 30 percent to grocers." The remaining half is largely sold at farmers' markets. Some of the household consumers are not entirely local: "Now people drive from far away to buy our tomatoes."

As Vogt sought to supply wholesalers who might value a "local" food item, he was invited to travel several hundred miles to meet with produce buyers at a major supermarket chain. His interest dimmed when officials told him that in order to supply the chain, he would have to invest several thousand dollars in software up front to establish bar codes, allowing his product to be traced throughout the chain. "It just was not worth it to us," he concluded. Further he got no sense from company officials that their purchasing would last. This firm could draw from dozens of growers in many distant places.

This was underscored when he learned how the firm defined "local" produce at the time: anything they could truck within 24 hours or less. When Vogt recalled this meeting years later, he mentioned that one of the growers in the room spoke up, saying that that boundary would cover two-thirds of the US. The corporate rep nodded affirmatively, in silence, with what Vogt called an "awkward facial expression." After hearing Vogt's tale, I did a quick calculation of my own. That limit meant Mexican tomatoes could also be counted as "local" products at the chain's Southwest Indiana stores. It also implied Vogt's farm would be in direct, and undifferentiated, competition with global competitors.

Vogt had accomplished his purpose for the journey. He knew he had little to gain by selling wholesale to this particular firm. He returned knowing that his best wholesale customers would be independent local grocers. He renewed his focus on selling to his neighbors. Yet even here he found complications.

When I interviewed him, Vogt was keenly aware that his tomatoes already competed for shelf space in local stores with tomatoes grown in Kentucky. Growers there benefited from state policies that funneled tobacco settlement money (payments the state received as the result of a successful lawsuit against tobacco companies for selling products they knew caused cancer) into investments promoting sustainable agriculture. While this may seem at first glance to be a positive development, he noted that on the marketing side the Kentucky approach caused some difficulties. "People in Kentucky began selling produce the same way they had sold tobacco. That is, they would drop it off at an auction, and buyers would bid for it. This same idea became the model for produce. Soon, everyone who had a pickup truck would come to the market to buy produce, but only to sell at their own 'farm stand' somewhere else. Semi-trucks would come from Florida and Georgia and dump tons of produce into the auction." Prices plummeted, and buyers had no idea where the products were grown. (In 2020 Vogt told me that Kentucky had finally set more restrictive policies; produce sold at the auctions must now be sourced within 250 miles and could not arrive in semitrailer loads. He added, however, that this did not limit trade to Kentucky: "Obviously, they are still drawing from outside this area.")

As a farmer who farmed with personal conviction, Vogt knew from hard experience that "there has always been an element of the underworld in the produce industry." (For example, in many major metro areas the mafia controlled produce distribution into the 1970s.) His experience of seeing the difficulties inherent in the auction system in Kentucky helped fuel his determination to make sure a similar thing would not take hold in Evansville.

At the farmers' market he helped write policy that would ensure transparency and accountability. "If you want to help make this better," Vogt added, "local regulations have to step in." As a seasoned seller at the Evansville farmers' market, he doggedly pursued a policy that would restrict resellers (those who purchase fresh produce from one market only to resell it elsewhere) from the market. "We went to the Evansville market manager, and said, 'You can't let the resellers dominate here. They will push us out of business.'"

It took many years, but Vogt and his allies pressed the board to adopt a policy that required resellers to abandon the market over a 3-year period. By 2013, he added, "with limited exceptions, you can be banned from the market, for a week, a season, or a year, at the market manager's discretion, if you sell product that is not your own." The contract required each grower who sells at the market to allow an on-farm visit to ensure they were selling only their own produce.

Vogt recalled that, in retribution, "The resellers pulled out [of the market] right away. I think they were trying to show they could hurt us by not showing up." This forced a huge adjustment onto many farmers, who now had to produce significantly larger quantities to meet local demand. "We had to learn how to get enough produce to the market to make up the difference," Vogt continued. The growers succeeded. "Now it is back to what it was, if not better," he told me in 2013.

Tragically, by 2020, his victories had been undermined. New leadership at the farmers' market had "retreated from the notion of locally grown," Vogt lamented. Currently, "they are more concerned with bringing activity to a geographical area than guaranteeing the integrity of the market." Exhausted by the struggle, he stopped selling at the farmers' markets.

Nonetheless, he persisted. Vogt extended his own growing season, installing a greenhouse so he could bring earlier tomatoes to the market. "The market keeps shifting; we have to keep nimble," he noted. Changes in the market have also taught Vogt the value of mobilizing a unified force. "The culture is not the same as it was. Now you have to convince people to value locally produced." To do that, he said, "more than anything else, we need a voice behind us."

One thing I like about Vogt's account is how he speaks, not just from the position of a grower but also as someone who has invested in his community, built connections of loyalty with his neighbors (including grocers), and taken civic leadership to improve conditions where he lives. A connected farmer, rooted in place while also reaching out to global markets, he actively monitors where his farm business can find the highest rewards. He is not dogmatic about feeding only his neighbors, but he recognizes quite pragmatically that they are the people most willing to support him. Moreover, he understands that effective markets require both freedom of choice and thoughtful regulation. The public sector must intervene to balance these competing aspirations. A system of support must be built that nourishes food trade within the community.

Lacking that, Vogt reported in 2020 that he now sells 90–95 percent of his produce directly from his own farm stand. He now supplies only one local grocer, who is increasingly facing competition from national chains. Moreover, Vogt is scaling back the hours he works as he contemplates retirement. He added that there is no one to take over his business when he does retire.

As Bud Vogt learned, food buyers tend to bend the word "local" until it has little meaning. Essentially, supermarket chains define "local" to mean whatever the store can conveniently deliver to its customers in a way that will not invite too much scrutiny. Chefs often fall into a similar trap. One farmer told me of a decade-long effort he had endured to persuade a renowned "local" chef to *remove* the farm name from the menu. The chef had not purchased any food from this farm *for over ten years*. But the chef liked the caché of listing specific farms on his menu, and this apparently drew so many customers that the chef refused to acknowledge the realities of his purchasing.

What Food System Do We Deserve?

In addition to being simplistic, the term "local food" refers to the attributes of a given food item—How far did this tomato travel?—rather than the more systemic issues: What type of food system brought food to us? Who wins through this prevailing system? What food system do we deserve? How do we build it? As a simplistic catchphrase, the term can be co-opted quite easily by those who hold different goals and values.

Certainly, one of the profound reasons our food system is creating faulty outcomes is that producers are so distant from consumers that food buyers can get away with muddling the term. This separation, in turn, affects how people learn how to select, prepare, and eat in healthy ways. To reduce our food's dependence on fossil fuels, and to obtain the freshest foods possible, we need to localize our food supplies. Still, I have come to realize that reducing the miles food travels is more of an *outcome* of making better choices, rather than the *purpose* of food work.

To create a world where the farmer, processor, grocer, and consumer are all in the same locale, sharing purposes and risks, we need to create efficiencies in local food trade and increase coordination among local residents. We are building systems, not simply transporting food items to closer markets. We are engaged in an effort to build new economic structures—or in some cases, to reclaim structures that once existed.

How does one know when one is building a community-based food system? The distinguishing feature is that social and commercial connectivity are being built. This can lower the costs of doing business, reduce turnover, promote innovation, and foster entrepreneurship. It brings multiple benefits. Social connectivity promotes both school learning and lower high-school dropout rates. Even private firms do better. Firms cannot survive economically without a supportive network of personal and financial relationships, as earlier chapters showed.

As community food webs confront global markets and large-scale investors, however, questions arise as to whether all this retail work at the community level can make any difference. Don't family farms have to ramp up to serve larger regional markets and national chains? This is just one of the issues Vogt confronted. I will explore this question in chapter 12, which argues that expanding production is both the problem and the solution.

CHAPTER 12

Scale Is Both the Problem and the Solution

Many growers and food businesses are facing intense pressure to expand their production to meet larger markets. Yet large-scale systems have created many of the problems we face today; growing in size will not resolve them. Getting larger also applies new pressures and new intricacies. Community food webs build on the unique qualities of each region. Right-sizing the work for individual firms must balance the appropriate scale for the community itself. The best approaches find ways to share the advantages that larger firms enjoy with smaller firms, and to keep communications open.

The economic analysis I presented in chapter 1 is, at core, an account of the dilemmas presented by large-scale food production. With access to hundreds of billions of dollars of foreign purchasing power, using the most advanced and mammoth machinery on the planet, sophisticated technical expertise, and considerable public subsidy, farmers have fashioned highly productive farms—yet their net income has declined. As the number of buyers diminished, and as purchasers became less responsive to the uncertainties farmers face, market power was concentrated in fewer and fewer hands, forcing farmers to sell at levels below their costs of production. Trillions of potential wealth was extracted from rural America.

So I am always wary when I hear a farmer, or a food hub, speak too narrowly about "going to scale," that is, expanding the operation to lower the costs of each item produced. Despite considerable cautionary evidence, I hear countless investors, philanthropists, and business owners advocate for this strategy. US Department of Agriculture officials periodically warn farmers to get big or get out of business.

There is merit to scaling up, but one should not go into it blindly. The time-honored strategy of lowering costs and increasing margins has served many firms well. Many smaller growers are certainly saddled with costs that make them less competitive financially because they rely on hand labor and close personal attention. Wholesalers, very reasonably, would rather deal with a single supplier that can deliver several palettes in one order, rather than assembling that shipment from several growers. Creating efficiencies like this is essential to using resources well.

Yet proponents of scaling up assume an economic determinism that believes cutting costs is always beneficial. Clearly this is not always true. I do not choose an auto mechanic, physician, or attorney, for example, based on who charges the least. I want the person who is best for my needs. I consider less tangible characteristics, such as who listens to me the most carefully and responds to my concerns, what is the quality of their work, and who has the strongest reputation with their customers. In sum, Whom do I trust the most to accomplish my goals?

As farmers confront their market choices, they also have intangibles in mind. Farmers typically ask themselves such questions as, What do I enjoy growing? What can I grow best on my land? Which crops fare the best in this climate? What am I called to do as a farmer? These questions are only on the production side. On the marketing side other questions arise. Do I have the equipment needed to convey my harvest to this buyer? Can we negotiate prices and deliveries openly and fairly? If we have a disagreement, will the buyer take my needs into account or retreat to their narrow self-interest? Will they continue to purchase from me as conditions change? These questions are centered on trust and communication. Often, as firms and systems grow larger, there can be so many intermediaries that both trust and communication lapse. Or the voice of any one person or firm becomes so small that it cannot influence how the larger system operates.

Professors Julie Dawson and Alfonso Morales from the University of Wisconsin have an elegant way of capturing this. As they pointed out in their book, *Cities of Farmers*, one cannot build strong communities solely by cutting costs. I would add that community is built through the *investments* we make. Investments always involve risk, with no assurance of return.

Investing in Community Efficiencies

Moreover, what is efficient for a business may not be efficient for a community as a whole. For rural communities that need employment, eliminating work by investing in technology may backfire. A courageous student at the University of Minnesota once wrote a paper for a course I taught. The topic he selected was, "Is it a good thing or a bad thing that my family's farm is the only one left in our township?" His research revealed that there had once been 22 farms scattered across those 23,040 acres. As neighboring farmers retired, or encountered economic trouble, the student's forebears had purchased the 21 farms near the original farmstead. Since the student planned to take over this township-wide farm one day, he wanted to know what his father thought about the process that had left him owning the entire township. The father's answer was nuanced: "Our farm is more efficient, but it gets lonely sometimes."

Following Walter Goldschmidt's lead (in his book *As You Sow*), one can imagine a community of 22 farms, with each family feeling a sense of ownership of the broader community, each paying taxes to support local schools and government, and each sharing life's events with their neighbors. One can also imagine a sole driver working a combine over thousands of acres, noticing how much more corn he or she can produce alone, yet also seeing that the school has shut down because there are so few children living in the area, few mechanics or legal advisers, and no other farmers to support voting for improvements in the farmer's way of life.

That is to say, going to scale is both the problem and the solution. The more difficult call is, when is it best to get large, and when is it critical to remain small? This chapter explains some of the complexities of making these decisions, referencing several community food initiatives where issues of scale have arisen. It will conclude that the level of trust among people in a given community is the limiting factor that determines how effective community food webs can be, whether large scale or small.

From the growers' perspective, one often gains by staying small. Many of the newer generation of farmers stay small because they want to communicate closely with each customer. By selling direct to households they also obtain the maximum value for each food item. For a beginning farmer with limited means, selling direct to households with expendable income is almost the only possible strategy. Smaller growers can also be more responsive to consumers, unless they are strapped for resources. Smaller farms require fewer start-up costs. Smaller growers also take a more independent stance. Small farms at their best can create *livelihoods* more than *jobs*.

But small scale is not always an advantage. Economies of scale do exist. Wholesale buyers can purchase in larger quantities and may be more consistent in purchasing. For many established farmers, the trade-off of accepting a lower price per unit by selling a larger quantity is well worth making. Those farms that choose to grow for wholesale markets can simplify their farm operation, raising a smaller number of crops, say three to six, in larger quantities while limiting their equipment needs and targeting larger buyers. Larger farms may be able to promote their products in wider circles, or hold stronger political influence.

There can also be drawbacks to moving to a larger scale. As several stories in this book discuss, the farmer becomes more dependent on buyers who enjoy a wealth of global options and prioritize cutting their margins. If one is selling to a chain that has several layers of management, decisions may be slow, or agreements made by local buyers could be overruled. There may be no independent local buyer.

On the production side, if hail or disease knocks out a single field with 200 acres of tomatoes, the losses suffered are also greater. While a larger farm with well-established systems in place can produce more, as markets change it will be more limited in its ability to respond. If a farm owns a $400,000 combine for harvesting grain, this will not help much if consumers begin asking for organic vegetables.

Taking the Community Perspective

In my professional work, my role is typically to ask what would make *community* food trade most efficient? Then it is important to remain open to a variety of possibilities within that viewpoint. One solid community response to the scale question would be that we need to take advantage of both large and small, and then make sure that each complements the other.

One larger distributor I worked with, for example, used its market reach to aid smaller farmers. When the firm realized that few farmers were trained in food safety, it began to offer training to its growers. This protected both farmers and buyers. Acknowledging the reasons some farms stay small, the distributor aggregated small shipments into larger loads. This helped both farmers and the distributor by reducing the number of shipments to the warehouse. When certain farmers had difficulty purchasing liability insurance, the distributor purchased a single liability policy that covered all of the growers that supplied the firm. In return, growers allowed the firm's buyer to inspect their farm operation on a regular basis. The distributor's assumption was that any farmer the firm had trained and who had been accepted into its system was low risk. Taking this step often reduced farmers' costs by more than a thousand dollars per farm, while limiting the distributor's liability as well.

By building collaboration and trust among stakeholders, each party can apply their unique skills and advantages to create better outcomes for everyone in the web. This means that the question of scale needs to be posed on multiple levels: When we view the system as a whole, what is the proper scale for our community food system? When we consider individual firms that are part of that system, what are the proper scales for the individual firms that allow us to become as efficient as possible as a food *system*?

Leveraging Market Power by Opening Diverse Channels

One of the best lessons I have learned about balancing the dilemmas of scale came from Matt Russell, an Iowa farmer who was active in the Leopold Center's Regional Food Systems Working Group (RFSWG) in the mid-2000s. Russell supported his farming for years through a professional position at Drake University's Agricultural Law Center. At one of the RFSWG conferences a decade ago, Matt mentioned that he continued to sell directly to household customers at the Des Moines Farmers' Market, even though he had developed a solid cluster of wholesale accounts. In addition to enjoying the chance to build and maintain relationships with families that supported his farm, Matt said it was important for him to establish a high price by selling direct at the market. By so doing, he could remind his wholesale buyers what the full value of his produce was. This was also to imply that he could take his produce elsewhere. By mentioning his direct prices, he minimized the buyers' tendency to squeeze him on wholesale prices.

This balanced market position also prepares Russell for market conditions that change unexpectedly. As wholesale or retail markets ebb or flow, he can place greater emphasis on the appropriate sector. This can be difficult to do in practice, however, because a farm has to plan ahead for each growing season. Moreover, the timing, harvesting, and packaging demands may be different for each market channel, so keeping both open can be difficult. This, once again, is an example of why broader coordination of value networks is integral to covering uncertainties in the market.

Gaining Balance by Relocalizing

One vegetable farm that had fully established itself in national wholesale markets tackled the scale question by moving toward smaller markets. It now strives for a more diversified and resilient farm by selling more food directly to its neighbors, including CSA (community-supported agriculture) members and those who visit its farm stand.

Founded in 1976 in Oaktown, Indiana, Melon Acres grew into an expansive farm decades ago. When I visited in 2012, the Horrall family was operating 2,500 acres of land, with about one-third planted to fruits and vegetables. This makes it an exceptionally large produce farm for its region. The Horralls were also early adopters of advanced technology. The farm harvests approximately 230 acres of cantaloupes, 475 acres of watermelon, 110 acres of sweet corn, 50 acres of cucumbers, and 230 acres of asparagus, selling these through brokers to customers as far away as Florida, Massachusetts, Iowa, Alabama, and Georgia. All told the farm hires 150–200 workers on a seasonal basis to perform fieldwork and operate 20-row melon harvesters and forced-air-cooled packing lines. On about half their land, the family also raises commodity corn and soybeans.

Project manager Norm Conde showed me the operation. The year before my visit, the farm had built 16 immense high tunnels (plastic-covered growing frames) sized 24 feet by 400 feet. That investment was spurred by one daughter's decision to make her living by farming. This established her, Whitney Nickless, along with the family's close friend Melanie Ellis, as managers of a new unit of the larger farm business.

On a bright summer day, these high tunnels sheltered luscious crops of tomatoes, cherry tomatoes, tomatillos, zucchini squash, yellow squash, acorn squash, spaghetti squash, cantaloupe and honeydew melons, asparagus, eggplant, hot and sweet peppers, flowers for fresh-cut sale, and perennials. Beehives were installed inside to ensure that the plants would be well pollinated. "The expense of the high tunnels dictates we need a higher price for the crop, and we can get that higher price locally by increasing retail sales," Ellis said. Conde added, "We want to be the first into the market in the spring, and the last to sell in the fall."

With this expansion, the family was positioning itself for the future by returning to the local markets that allowed them to first establish their business. Conde mused, "The nature and cost of transportation means that local business will become more important." In earlier days, he recalled, the family based its business on selling to nearby retailers. "The small independent grocers would send out a small truck" to pick up melons for their stores. That is now a rarity. Wanting stronger collaboration than the larger wholesalers offered, the family planned to create its own distribution firm to sell products into the Evansville, Terre Haute, and Bloomington markets.

I called Conde early in 2020 to see how the farm business had progressed since my visit. He told me there had been considerable change. In

2013, the Horralls with two other Oaktown melon farms built a brand-new cantaloupe-packing shed, outfitting it with the most advanced food safety technology. This was to position the farm as food-safe in the aftermath of two disease outbreaks traced to other cantaloupe farms. The family had also decided to pull away from several brokers and to serve as its own sales force, finding that external partners were much more expensive than hiring immediate family members. Mike Horrall is the principal owner. His wife Vicki also owns a significant share, as do each of their three children. Son Jake Horrall takes charge of much of the watermelon sales, while his sister Autumn Freeman specializes in selling nearly all the fresh asparagus crop. The younger daughter, Whitney Nickless, manages Melon Acres' CSA and farmers' market sales in close collaboration with Melanie Ellis, who Conde said is considered "family." Working closely with each other, the Horralls have eased away from intermediaries who proved both more expensive and less reliable. This included the local distribution firm they helped start, when it did not deliver the results they had hoped for.

Conde added, "It is the CSA that increased our retail sales the most." The Horralls have also been encouraged by expanding sales at local farmers' markets, and they continue to sell considerable quantities through their own farm stand. Conde said the mix of retail and wholesale income is about the same as it was during my visit. However, pinched by a combination of falling prices and rising labor costs, the family has worked hard to hone its operation to be far more efficient. "Whitney found that many of the crops we were growing in the high tunnels were not making us money," Conde explained, so the family has pared back to growing those that do. "Now we consolidate, reduce, and work more efficiently. If a crop doesn't pay its rent, we stop growing it." He said tomatoes are currently the most profitable high tunnel product. The Horralls raise fewer than 20 crops for the CSA and continue to feature cantaloupe and watermelon. At the time Melon Acres planted its first 60 acres of asparagus, the family had instantly doubled the acreage of asparagus grown commercially in the state of Indiana. Since the farm hopes to harvest more than 250 acres in 2020, they now command an enviable market position. "We're pretty much 'the only game in town' from the middle of April to the middle of May, so some chains send their trucks to the farm every two or three days to pick up freshly picked and packed asparagus," Conde beamed.

Yet Melon Acres also feels pinched by rising costs. Heavily dependent on migrant (H-2A) workers, the farm is required by federal law to increase pay rates 9.5 percent in 2020. Conde added, "The costs of chemicals and equipment have also risen at a rate at least equal to, and probably above, the overall rate of inflation. Meanwhile, fresh produce prices remained relatively stationary over the last decade." He noted that despite the farm's importance as an asparagus supplier to their region, prices dropped 15 percent in 2019. Wholesale sweet corn prices have remained the same for a decade. The silver lining was record watermelon prices in 2019.

In a very real sense, Melon Acres moved in paradoxical directions: it expanded its operation by focusing more intently on local sales, then carved discrete niches where their harvest was large enough to influence local markets. Conde said that four key factors contributed to decision making about the proper level of scale, given the cost squeeze. First was the family's solid reputation in both national and local markets. Second, the farm operation had to be efficient at any operating size they chose, whether across hundreds of acres of melons or inside an intensively farmed high tunnel. Third, the Horralls have expanded by creating subunits that are managed by individual family members, finding that family loyalty was stronger than business connections in the marketplace. Finally, they gained a stronger market presence in specific crops like asparagus when they became the dominant producer in local markets.

The keys to building a resilient farm business, whether at the direct marketing or the wholesale level, are the same. Both depend on developing respect as a quality producer, delivering a safe product, building loyalty with buyers, and responding to changing market conditions. Direct sales come in smaller quantities, but relationships are also more direct. As one moves to larger shipments, the demands of loyalty become different. The buyer may not be the decision maker. Corporate managers are often in distant locations, with more concern for seeking the lowest possible price than for sustaining specific farms. As scale increases, trade becomes more and more commodified. Often "quality," with respect to fresh produce, is defined as good shelf appearance, not better taste or nutritional value, which cannot be known until the product is sampled.

There are extra time pressures when one ships large volumes. Since produce perishes rapidly, trading action is fast paced, and suppliers are changing minute-by-minute. The produce buyers I have met all work within a strict honor system. Each person must be true to their word, or they are cut out of the trade. Written contracts are exceptionally rare.

Even Trusted Firms Get Shocked

Even establishing a solid reputation is not always enough; broader market pressures still create surprises. One firm that has worked equitably with growers and buyers is Red Tomato, formed in the Boston area in 1997. Red Tomato established a hybrid business model that blends philanthropic support (for educational and developmental functions, such as training farmers unable to pay their own way how to stage their products in the most attractive manner) with earned income from brokering food from farms to wholesale accounts. In order to reduce overhead for storage and transportation, Red Tomato primarily forms connections between sellers and buyers without taking physical possession of the products.

Red Tomato has also been a pioneer in establishing an Eco-Apple® label, a marketing brand that allows smaller independent farmers across New England to differentiate their product by featuring their high standards of sustainable production. The growers' apples are offered to consumers via attractive grocery displays and packaging that highlight the brand with colorful graphics. To supplement its product offerings during New England's cold winter, the organization has also represented farmer networks in other regions, including Ojai Pixie tangerine growers in California, and produce from African American farmers in Georgia. For several years in the 1990s, Red Tomato also marketed watermelon for members of the Federation of Southern Cooperatives. Currently it markets pecans for New Communities, in Albany, Georgia.

Red Tomato has built a solid reputation. However, this does not make them immune to disruption. On September 27, 2018, a poignant message came through the Community Food Security listserv. In it, then executive director Laura Edwards-Orr lamented a recent decision by one of the firm's major buyers:

On August 29th, after 13 years of supplying their regional apple program, Red Tomato received notice from our largest customer that they would be sourcing 4 of 5 apple varieties elsewhere. The harvest was under way. Shipping and warehousing contracts were in place. More than $100,000 of custom packaging sat in inventory. The news came in an email. To this day, our voicemails and meeting requests remain unanswered. . . . This is today's wholesale market.

Edwards-Orr then added,

Red Tomato will survive this setback. Our packaging has been resold. Our growers remain loyal. And, in more bountiful years, we built up a reserve for moments such as this. True resilience in this moment, though, will require reinvention. For the last several years, we have been observing an increasingly competitive and rapidly consolidating market. In response, we've tested updates and tweaks to the strategies that have enabled Red Tomato to scale local into the mainstream market over our 20-year history. It wasn't enough.

Grocery retail, which anchors the wholesale market, is fighting for its bricks-and-mortar life in the face of competition from e-commerce, urban migration, and increasing income inequality. As retailers cut and consolidate to bring remaining profits in, they are pushing business externalities up the supply chain—rock bottom prices, inflexible start and end dates, zero tolerance for regional weather or production trends, 100% fulfillment rates, proprietary food safety certifications, lengthy payment terms, and sky-high insurance thresholds. It's true that consumer demand for local, ethical, sustainably grown products has grown year over year. And yet the pressure for wholesale buyers to focus on short-term survival makes it nearly impossible for small and mid-size suppliers to bring to market the very products their shoppers seek.

At Red Tomato, where apples are 50% of our sales, we see the most talented and progressive apple growers in the region struggle to compete against ever-expanding West Coast and global production. They have developed expertise in sustainable production focused on careful monitoring, natural predators, beneficial insects, and targeted, limited use of lowest-risk treatment specifically adapted for the Northeast region. Consumers are more familiar with the organic certification even though most organic fruit is grown on the West Coast. The share of Northeast apples sold wholesale in the Boston Terminal Market has declined from 50% in 1980 to 20% in 1995 and that number continues to drop.

Edwards-Orr's message highlighted what allowed Red Tomato to overcome this surprise. They had built strong loyalty among their producers, more lasting than they held with wholesale buyers. They had also anticipated crises by building financial reserves. In short, they had planned for uncertainty. By building community respect, they kept their producer networks resilient. This is the same strategy that the farmers in Iowa, Indiana, and Wisconsin pursued, as discussed in chapter 10.

In 2019, with the support of its network of growers, Red Tomato once again approached the buyer that had cut them off. It was able to sell three of the four apple varieties it bid on. Now that sales have begun to rebound, the organization continues to strive to diversify its client list. The current executive director, Angel Mendez, explained, "Despite bringing this customer back, the underlying realities remain: Consolidation, centralization of decision making, intense competition, and global supply all make it increasingly difficult for small and midsize growers, and the distributors who represent them, to maintain a foothold."

When Markets Become Impersonal

One risk of "going to scale" is that food becomes simply a commodity to be sold, rather than a life essential that promotes nutrition and community building. The central feature of commodity trade is that it is impersonal, and performed at a distance. When one buys "number 2 corn" one can expect it to have the same qualities whether purchased from Iowa or Ukraine. Similarly, produce has been standardized to the extent that one can purchase, for example, a standard 20-pound box of peaches that are all more or less the same size.

This standardization may obscure the fact that the entire industry is fundamentally dependent on the uncertainties of nature. Groups of people who trust each other closely will find effective ways to respond to surprise. This, then, is another way to determine the appropriate scale. When systems get so impersonal that trust breaks down, they are too large. This is not to say that no large systems can build trust, nor to argue that all small systems do. I have seen plenty of dysfunctional small organizations and neighborhoods riven by mistrust for decades. It *is* to say, however, that one critical limit to scale is how effectively trust has been built, since greater scale requires more complex coordination.

Food Hubs Help Coordinate Value Networks

One of the most common investments communities have made as a way of building localized wholesale trade has been to build food hubs. The concept of constructing such "hubs" became highly visible in the "local foods" discussion in 2009, when Secretary of Agriculture Tom Vilsack announced that hubs were a key element of local foods infrastructure. Although USDA staff did yeoman work defining what a "food hub" involved in very precise terms (as a center that combined aggregation, processing, and distribution), action in the field quickly rendered that rigorous definition moot. Once the agency expressed its support for food hubs, most groups called whatever they wanted to do a "food hub," thinking that it would attract funders' attention. In practice, as use of the concept spread rapidly across the US, the term has come to mean any facility that helps to advance local foods activity. The image of a "hub" that brings together "spokes" of local food activity has resonated with food leaders in countless regions.

However, the USDA eventually realized that it had oversold the concept of food hub. While valuable, they were no panacea. Even exemplary food hubs, in business for decades, were deeply dependent on philanthropic funding. This was primarily because they accomplished tasks that were educational in nature, rather than financially rewarding. Although many played essential roles, food hubs were cost centers rather than profit centers. They were also devising new business models that drew on income from both sales and charitable donations.

Over time, the agency began to focus its publicity increasingly on the essential role that food hubs played, and less on the physical facilities they symbolized. Effective food hubs, the agency pointed out, coordinated local foods activity by forging new social and commercial connections, building greater trust, and creating local efficiencies in food trade. Over the long term, they created long-term relationships, infrastructure, and efficiencies that made localized food trade more likely to succeed. In the short term they were unlikely to be profitable because the prevailing infrastructure was effective at frustrating their missions.

Thus a new term came into use at USDA: "value-chain coordination." Yet "chain" is deeply problematic because it both represents a linear concept and resonates of slavery. It implies that one party at one end of a chain can yank the chain to exert their will over someone at the other end. In particular, it suggests that farmers work at one end of the chain, while buyers hold the power at the other end. As a linear image, the chain metaphor suggests simplicity when in fact relationships are complex. Several colleagues have told me they felt compelled to adopt the language of "supply chain" because it is a term the industry recognizes. Moreover, considerable academic literature is devoted to supply-chain relationships.

But an even more appropriate term, "value-network coordination," was already in use by those in the field. This is more apt in describing the complex contexts in which we actually work. Human relationships cannot be parceled neatly into links of a chain. In most cooperative groceries, consumers own the store. They are not simply the people at the end of the chain who eat. Many dairies and meat-processing firms are partially owned by the member-farmers who supply the company. Several restaurants own a farm that grows some of the foods they serve. In reality, community food systems are networks, and food hubs can play a valuable role in coordinating those networks. I make this distinction so our concepts better reflect reality, and promote pragmatic outcomes, not out of a quest for political correctness.

I do not wish to suggest that food hubs are a bad thing, although I certainly have raised questions about them since 2009. My concern is mostly how the concept was oversold, how that encouraged investment before critical thinking, and how this made the concept easy to corrupt. Food hubs can, indeed, be effective vehicles for building the capacity of their respective regions to grow and eat healthy food items, if they dedicate themselves to the long view and don't expect rapid rewards.

Economic Success Is Socially Created

No food hub, nor any other business, survives without supportive community networks. That is why I have always prioritized strengthening the local culture of collaboration over building any specific facility. Certainly it is also possible that the process of planning, constructing, and operating a food hub or other facility can itself provide an excellent context for building community trust.

So return to the theme of this chapter: Yes, scale is both the problem and the solution. Many of the problems we wrestle with today are the result of economic systems that have become so large that unforeseen problems have developed. People have become so distant from each other that we feel isolated, despite massive communications networks. Millions of people have been marginalized by extractive economic structures. Expanding to become a larger operation is a keen way to reach efficiencies, yet similar efficiencies can also be reached through economies of scope, in which many small efforts, networked together, yield a significant impact.

The interplay of individual and social achievement is a reminder that all capital is socially created. No one earns any wealth outside of some complex system of climate conditions, market realities, cultural traditions, and tax policies. Few in the US, for example, could earn wealth without having favorable tax rates and the ability to write off certain expenses. In my work I have often found that those who have considerable means have forgotten this reality. They assume that their wealth was something they created on their own initiative. More accurately, they are able to enjoy the benefits of that wealth precisely because society has not intervened to insist that the benefits of the wealth that was created by many be distributed among the many. The question of scale is also an issue of justice. It is one that takes us full circle, back to the necessity of building personal trust, as the concluding chapter states.

Building Community Food Webs: Action Networks, System Levers, and Business Clusters

At the heart of every effective community food web is a group of people who trust each other. They share information openly, discuss differences respectfully and honestly, and learn together over time. They learn even from their mistakes, and they value new insight over perfection.

Each of the community foods initiatives featured in this book embodies these traits, but one prime example is Montana. Here, over several decades, a disciplined, creative, and forceful group of women and men living in diverse regions established a foundation of communication, knowledge, and action by fostering small innovation projects designed by farmers. By ensuring that participants shared findings with each other, and reviewed each others' work annually, a statewide network was mobilized. This helped participants thrive spiritually, socially, and economically for decades. One clear mark of their success was that several successive executive directors at the Alternative Energy Resources Association (AERO), each holding strong individual priorities and styles, carried the same body of work forward across decades. The network they constructed created a profound impact, advancing ecologically smart ways of growing and eating food. Although rooted in remote rural communities, their work influenced partners nationally.

The web these visionaries wove was constructed around a single organization at first, but it was also decentralized. AERO responded to grassroots voices across the state, and with every step vested more power among its constituents, rather than in the home office. This meant leadership grew in multiple places at once, spanning a number of food industries, climatic regions, and ethnicities. This work was not accomplished by a single leader, or by a central office. It was not a hub-and-spoke network where information was forced to flow through one point of contact. It was a web, interlaced with myriad connections across its filaments. Its work was inclusive, welcoming diverse points of view and varied strategic approaches.

Coordination Ebbs and Flows

Convergences like this do not last forever; the drive and ability to coordinate so effectively ebb and flow. There are generational shifts, as new leaders enter the network with new visions and respond to changing circumstances. And despite the exceptional impact this network made, billions of dollars have flowed out of Montana since these victories were won, because the broader national economy still extracts wealth from this and other states. Individual Montanans have lost much of the agency they held in the mid-1970s, as more farmers, workers, and businesses find themselves running on a treadmill. Yet they can move forward with greater insight because of what has been accomplished so far.

And the work continues. Community foods initiatives across the US take small, pragmatic steps toward a broad vision of improving our society, and our democracy, by insisting on our right to determine our own lives and produce our own essentials, not to simply act as passive consumers. We know that the most lasting work takes decades, not hours, and that quick victories are ephemeral.

Trust alone, of course, is not enough. Work has to be accomplished. Those community food webs that achieve the most are strategic in thought and targeted in applying resources. They build economic connections that last, dispersing power throughout their communities. They construct new efficiencies in local trade, new commercial loyalties, and new businesses that trade with each other as they deliver essential services to their neighbors.

In particular, effective community food webs build market power for farmers. They give farmers stronger options than being price-takers in impersonal commodity markets. They accomplish this by connecting producers with people who are committed to supporting their farms and families.

Moreover, the most resilient communities are those where these farmers, businesses, and consumers feel deeply connected to nature. These places celebrate the intricate ecological webs that sustain human habitation and go to great lengths to protect them. Whenever possible, they carry forward the insights and practices that Indigenous people discovered over centuries. Cultural rituals are built around the unique qualities of each place, responsive to its strengths and weaknesses.

At a deeper level, those who connect to the intricacies of nature also learn about complexity. Embracing this uncertainty is also an essential quality of effective community food webs. We live in an age that conveys simple concepts rapid-fire across cyberspace, and we work within political cycles that insist on simple "solutions." Yet these straightforward calls for action often create more turmoil over the long term because they overlook important crosscurrents, including the fact that any effort to improve our lives is likely to spark a counterreaction from those who benefit from the structures that have been imposed upon us.

That is why this book offers no easy answers. Each narrative has conveyed both victories and shortcomings. Each is a sparse overview of issues that are far more complex than any single chapter could address. Each story, I hope, invites effective action, based on collaborative strategizing and critical thinking, to create action networks that address the challenges faced in other places.

Moving Systems Levers

At the same time, each community food web has found ways to cut through the complexities they encounter, and to take active steps forward that invoked significant shifts in the opportunities available to their constituents. This is because every complex system that is adapting over time (as food systems do) has "system levers"—elements that can be nudged to create broader outcomes. If this process of shifting levers is managed carefully and strategically over time, positive outcomes can result.

Careful management typically requires that a group of people collaborate openly with each other, because it is nearly impossible for any single person to identify the essential dynamics of a complex and changing system from one individual perspective. Also, because entrenched systems always push back against change, it is important that those managing food systems change prepare themselves for setbacks and dead ends, and keep in the mind the reality that changing systems is a long, drawn-out process. Building trust and equity is critical.

Each of the food-system initiatives discussed in this book held, implicitly or explicitly, some view of the levers that needed to be shifted to move their work forward. Their practical experience with food-systems work offered them deep insights into what works and what does not. As they experienced pushback, they adjusted their strategies. When they disagreed with each other, they worked together to build a sharper analysis, and new unity. Advancing equity has served as a lever.

For the initiatives highlighted in chapter 10, the system lever was to build market power for farmers. The organic farmers in northwest Iowa did this by connecting closely with a group of customers who felt loyal to their product. The family that runs Seven Sons Farms in Indiana built market power by vertically integrating. Raising high-quality meats and eggs, and developing their own custom software to make ordering easy, and delivering their products directly to customers, they built a more immersed type of loyalty among their consumers. Taking that step fostered new opportunities for other farms who sell to their neighbors. For the produce farmers near Viroqua, Wisconsin, building market power centered around inviting institutional customers to become members or directors of the Fifth Season Cooperative.

In Montana, the leaders who instigated the community of co-learning understood that bringing rural people together to learn from each other would shift a system that had been stifled by limited attention to the needs of both the soil and Montana's farmers. Instinctively, these visionary leaders understood that the answers to the dilemmas posed by the farm credit crisis were either in the hands of farmers working their fields or could be devised by the farmers if they were given sufficient support. That support involved (1) encouraging farmers who lived close to each other to form a simple collaboration, (2) insisting that they bring a researcher or technical expert into their deliberations, (3) seeding these grassroots discussions with resource materials and a small bit of funding, and (4) offering opportunities for those working in their own neighborhoods to meet statewide to find common ground with their peers. Over time, this led to building more environmentally attuned farms, creating more market power for farmers raising both commodity crops and fresh foods for their neighbors, and building an effective statewide network of innovators.

Hawaiian food leaders dedicated their work to shifting two levers. First, they returned to traditional Hawaiian cultural practices for stewardship of land and water, farming practices, nutrition, healing, and spirituality. Applying these in contemporary society, they found ways to develop innovative practices among lower-income residents and youth. The second lever they pushed was to build the strongest local and statewide networks possible, so that innovators could learn from each other, be inspired by each other's work, and coordinate more effectively. Hawai'i leaders are now exploring a third lever, whether engaging with public officials will effectively advance this work.

Implicitly, much of this community foods work also assumed that addressing the needs of low-income residents would provoke changes to the regional food system. This turned out to be very true in Tucson, Arizona, as a food bank delved more deeply into the potential for empowering low-income constituents. By engaging low-income residents in broader social advocacy, broader shifts resulted: new food businesses developed, new neighborhood action networks formed, and the food bank itself opened to redirecting its management based on constituents' insights. This, in turn, encouraged other low-income residents to demand further rights, including engaging in electoral and policy work. Once again, effective local work became nationally groundbreaking.

Similarly, a cohesive core of community food leaders in Athens, Ohio, focused their systems change efforts on encouraging worker self-management at first, asserting that by creating a more animated set of community businesses, an economic foundation would be laid for broader community improvement. Then, after discovering that their initial thrust had overlooked many of their lower-income neighbors, ACEnet (Appalachian Center for Economic Networks) raised funds to build a business incubator that could assist budding entrepreneurs to launch their own food businesses. Today, as they reflect on their experience, they also understand that building a strong and resilient network of grassroots leaders was a lever in itself, one that undergirded and sustained all of their efforts.

Meanwhile, in Northeast Indiana, economic developers tackled systems change by connecting farmers directly with food manufacturers. When this did not produce the results they had hoped for, they sought a broader vision. This included bringing farmers more closely into the work of the economic development community, paying closer attention to lower-income residents, and stating their intent to welcome immigrants to their community to keep it vital.

The pressures of housing and commercial development also pose conflicts to community foods efforts, as farmland gets taken out of agriculture, and the remaining land becomes too expensive for farmers to buy. The Phoenix, Arizona, region is just beginning to grapple with this conundrum. In our work there, we found that two levers were critical. First, showing network maps to policy makers so they could see the isolation farmers experienced effectively sparked action. Second, simple steps, such as bringing farmers and policy makers into direct conversation to foster mutual understanding, could open up new possibilities.

Brighton, Colorado, and its surrounding Adams County, shifted systems levers by collaborating across jurisdictional lines, bringing more concerted attention to overall planning, and ensuring that agriculture would not be completely overlooked. A second systems lever was uncovered when a market analysis revealed that these public agencies were the only entities that could purchase farmland for the purpose of farming in the future. Once an initial purchase was made, considerable public dissent dissipated. This nudged still another systems lever: to brand the agricultural district in a compelling way so it would set a tone for future farming and food-related development.

Placing primary attention on the environment fostered systems change in Dakota County, Minnesota, where officials foresaw the need to protect water resources. The strategy they chose was to protect networks of green space where rainfall could percolate and wildlife could thrive amid suitable habitat. Adding a recreational component to this vision (a second lever) helped build a constituency among residents. Since these were conceived as *networks* of greenways, rather than as individual properties (a third lever), political support grew more forceful. Once developers saw the value of their homes rise, they embraced the project. Now this has morphed into a broader effort to protect farmland by fostering food production—still under the goal of protecting water quality.

In each case, local leaders adapted their strategic thinking based on changing conditions in their communities, constituent responses, and the lessons they had learned from early phases of their work. This adaptive management is also part of weaving an effective community food web.

Moreover, nudging systems levers also instills longer-term change. If local leaders have correctly identified the levers that will move a system closer to achieving the outcomes that the food initiative seeks to attain, the effects will ripple outward. Constructing an animated, cohesive network of food leaders carries over into work addressing energy, ecology, inclusion, and spirituality, as well as other arenas. Often the changes wrought in one generation come home for harvest several generations later, as grandchildren pick up the mantles their ancestors have fashioned. This helps to sustain the food work when it encounters dead ends.

Building Economic Multipliers and Business Clusters

Moving one systems lever is particularly critical: changing how we think about economics. In fact, this shift is essential to the survival of American communities, our democracy, and our planet. In most US communities today, the economic development discussion is misleading and simplistic. Calculations of the return on any potential investment are based on two questions: How many jobs will be created? and How much new tax base will be generated?

This framework has the advantage of serving as a simple test to use in public policy discussions. Complex developments can be summarized in terms that a civic leader can easily digest, and votes are taken in response. However, as earlier chapters have discussed, it is often more important to consider creating *livelihoods*, rather than mere *jobs*. People who own thriving businesses, and workers who earn a living wage, can participate more fully in civil society than folks stuck in low-wage jobs. Further, if the new tax base does not actually cover the costs of the development, as is often the case (but seldom considered in pubic testimony) then political leaders have placed themselves on a treadmill—much like the treadmill farmers endure.

This discussion is often made to appear more "scientific" by adding a measurement of an economic multiplier. Using this approach, economists calculate broader impacts that would be generated in the local economy. This is another way to measure return on investment: how much income would be fostered by a proposed development, and how much additional economic output it would generate. Clearly, a new housing development, commercial district, or industrial facility will increase economic activity. This, in turn, will ripple across the community as businesses expand to meet the new demand represented by hundreds of new residents, or thousands of additional shoppers, or scores of new factory workers.

The multiplier calculation is certainly more sophisticated than a simple job count. It takes into account the spending power of the new jobs, and the business activity generated by the new tax base. Yet the calculation is also a bit mysterious, something that only trained professionals can accomplish. This makes it somewhat of a black box to community members, who are asked to trust that a given number means something. I cannot tell you how many municipal officials or legislators I have heard saying something to the effect that, "I have no idea how they calculated this, but I like the high numbers they reported." This is especially problematic in the case of community foods ventures, which are typically so small in scale, and so new, that they cannot effectively be incorporated into modeling software in a satisfying manner. Professional experts do exceptional work to inject more accurate numbers into software databases, but the results still reflect prevailing industries more than the actual firms that are emerging.

In general, a higher multiplier is considered better. The lowest possible value is 1, which would mean that for every dollar of new economic activity that is generated, a single dollar spreads through the local economy. That is, there is no expansion of impact beyond the initial investment. The highest multiplier calculations I have seen range from 2.2 to 2.6. These were measured by the chair of the economics department at the University of Wisconsin–Eau Claire in an earlier era, working in a family farm community in Southwest Wisconsin, where farms typically purchased most inputs from local dealers and sold products to local buyers. These conditions no longer apply, so multipliers are inherently lower.

Ironically, decades of investment based on how large the multiplier will be, with everyone seeking higher numbers, has resulted in lowered multipliers overall, because the economy has become increasingly extractive. Some of the typical multipliers I have seen calculated for suburban areas where commercial malls offer products produced somewhere else to people who earned their money somewhere else range on the order of 1.3 to 1.5.

When I was trained to estimate multipliers in 2012, I had refreshingly honest instructors, several of whom had actually developed the software for making these calculations. One of them pointed out that the multiplier is essentially a measurement of the linkages found in the infrastructure surrounding a given business. "So, it is really a measurement of the network that supports the business?" I asked. He responded with a firm "yes."

Insights such as these helped inform this book, obviously. Independently, my colleague Megan Phillips Goldenberg also studied multiplier calculations in exhaustive detail as part of her graduate program in agricultural economics. She took the lead in writing an academic paper we published called "Building Multipliers, Rather Than Measuring Them." Our thrust was to suggest that since multiplier estimates are only estimates and do not accurately reflect the emergent activity by community-based food firms, it made more sense to spend money building social and commercial networks among local residents, than to hire economists to determine how large the multiplier might be.

In essence, our argument reiterated what Walter Goldschmidt had discovered in his research comparing two rural communities in California in the postwar period. The more family farms and independent small businesses trade with each other while supplying the needs of local residents, the more resilient the community. Ownership, independent agency, and connectivity all play a role in making local communities strong. All are threatened by the extractive economy. And all can be regenerated through community foods activity.

To truly take hold, however, these incipient commercial networks must really become a permanent part of the local landscape. Residents must not only want to trade with each other, they must also be committed to solidifying this trade over the long haul. This means that businesses have to be intentional about clustering with each other. By looking beyond the firm's narrow self-interest (which of course must be considered seriously) to consider the interests of the community as a whole, and to formalize this mutual dependency, is critical to constructing vibrant local economies.

Public policy plays a key role, as well, in sustaining resilient economic trade amid growing uncertainty by creating the appropriate infrastructure and incentives. When investors consider supporting only "what the market will bear" they are often overlooking the fact that policy and infrastructure shape markets. Any firm that is profitable today earns its surplus within a specific policy context, most notably tax incentives. If those shift, different firms will prosper. The food firms of the future will require different infrastructure and better incentives before they can sustain profitability. Some of the investments we need today are to create that new infrastructure.

Imagine, if you will, a hypothetical artisan grain mill located in farm country. The firm grinds fresh flour, exclusively using grains raised on local farms, which is baked into bread by a local shop. Over time, the farmer, the miller, and the baker come to see themselves as a cluster of firms that depend on each other. The health of the fields and farms is clearly linked to the health of the whole network. The three partners communicate frequently and try to grow in concert with each other. One does not expand beyond the point the others can sustain.

But one day, the baker hires new financial advisers, who investigate this collaborative trade and conclude that the bakery could make more money if it purchased commodity grain at lower prices and stopped making a priority of buying from local farms or the miller. The future, management is told, is in supplying multistate markets with a lower-cost product, because consumers won't care that much about losing the local identity.

Decisions such as these are being made daily by bean counters who have been duly trained to focus solely on the profitability of a single firm, rather than prioritizing the economic health of their community. They primarily consider existing laws and incentives, not the economic systems we will need to support healthier living. When this narrow view takes hold the business cluster often breaks up, and the local economy becomes that much weaker. Moving the "systems lever" in the direction of fostering an individual firm's success tends to result in a more extractive economy, while moving it in the direction of a more effective community network can accomplish the opposite. In the future, we will need infrastructure and incentives that create *community* efficiencies.

Striving for Four Balance Points

Each of the community foods initiatives mentioned in this book found balance points amid a chaotic society that often appears to be spinning out of control. Leaders shift the levers they have identified until the lives of their constituents come to a better balance, and shift them again as conditions change over time. Taking into account the goal of building health, wealth, connection, and capacity, community food webs continuously wrestle to bring balance in at least four ways:

1. **Balancing production with consumption** When is it most effective for us to produce for ourselves, and when is it most effective to purchase from other regions?

2. **Balancing internal with external control of value** Are we adopting this strategy because it suits our purposes, or because we are forced into it by external forces or parties?

3. **Balancing private with social success** How do we balance individual achievement with community success and build equity?

4. **Balancing culture with technology** When do we trust our cultural traditions the most, and when do we look to new technology to bring us better solutions?

Tipping too far in one direction—whether to protect private property at all costs, to favor individual whims over long-term results, or to exhort consumers just to keep buying—will damage community over the long haul.

Delicate Webs

Spider webs are constructed from fine filaments, naturally produced, that, once woven together into a fabric, embody phenomenally more strength than the individual fibers would provide. It is just such synergy that makes community food webs influential.

As I write this conclusion, I am secluded at home because of the novel coronavirus pandemic. Although currently fresh organic foods can be delivered directly to my door, nothing is certain about the future. One mill I know is working 24-hour shifts grinding heritage grain into flour to supply home bakers who cannot find flour at the grocery stores. Shuttered gourmet restaurants have begun catering food to deliver to weary hospital workers. My economic development colleagues report that metro areas all over the world are starting to configure more localized supply networks. I experience considerable civility in this time from total strangers.

While I certainly do not make light of the tragedy that befalls us, with more than 200,000 now dead, or the fears that grip me, concrete steps such as these also give me great hope that this crisis will provoke new ways of connecting. I also suspect that those communities which have already forged cultures of collaboration through community food webs will prove more resilient than those that have not. Indeed, the pandemic has made the concept of adaptive management quite popular, and urban consumers now understand more viscerally the uncertainties that farmers face.

Fifty years ago, I could not have imagined having organic romaine lettuce delivered fresh to my doorstep. But some hardy souls with a spark of vision sensed that we would need more organic farmers if my hometown were to stay healthy, thrive, or even survive such a calamity. I owe that direct delivery to them. The food webs that have been built over the past five decades, by those pioneers and others mentioned in this book, are the ark that will help carry some of us through this pandemic, and hopefully to a more resilient future.

Scientists are uncovering solid evidence that our prehuman ancestors were collaborating to gather food. They had, in short, begun to build cultures of collaboration before we were human. This is hardwired into us, invisible as it may be.

Definitions

community food network—A community food network is the cluster of connections people make with each other as they collaborate to create new food systems. This term focuses more on the strength and efficacy of the connections people make and is less encompassing than a community food web.

community food system—This term can be used interchangeably with "community food web," but it implies a slightly different focus on the *structures* of a community food system and less focus on the social and ecological *relationships*. This term appears to have been invented by Nancy Matheson, a food leader in Montana, in the mid-1990s. See Chapter 3 for more detail.

community food web—A community food web is a network of community relationships that conveys food from farms to processors to buyers to consumers, while recycling organic wastes to create fertility for local farms. This term focuses on the quality of the relationships among members of the local food network. At core, community food webs are systems of exchange that strive to bring food producers and food consumers into affinity with each other, for the purposes of fostering community health, wealth, connection, and capacity. The most resilient webs are formed through trusting relationships of mutual respect that extend among the people who live and work in each community, and also protect the natural environment. The most effective are those that disperse strategic power across the web, rather than centralizing control at a hub.

culture—The term "culture" holds multiple meanings. In this book, I strive to use it to convey the concept of the heritage, values, mores, and traditions that communities devise over time in an effort to guide individual choices, codify and promulgate lessons learned by ancestors and researchers, connect people to place, and keep community life resilient. Raymond Williams considers culture "a whole way of life." Lawrence Rosen adds, "cultural concepts traverse the numerous domains of our lives—economic, kinship, political, legal—binding them to one another. Implicitly, culture implies limiting individual choice in favor of a common good. In this book I often refer to a "culture of collaboration," which is such a culture that is dedicated to fostering a balance of competitive and collaborative activity.

farmers—This book places a great deal of focus on farmers, rather than farmworkers, because of the attention paid to building community food systems, which is seldom a challenge that farmworkers are inclined to or able to tackle. This is not to overlook the multitude of issues farmworkers face. That is a subject for another book.

It should also be noted that most commodity farmers do not participate in community food webs unless they devote special acreage to raising foods for their neighbors. While most of the data cited in this book reveals the economics of commodity farming, most of the community stories told here feature farmers who are, at least in part, growing food for community markets.

food system—I define a food system to be the totality of resources, actors, firms, infrastructure, and exchanges that convey food from farmers to consumers, and then recycle organic wastes into new fertility for farmers. This term is more abstract than "community food web" and "community food network" and does not include the term "community," so it covers any food system that can be identified.

While as a shorthand I may discuss the "US food system," in reality there are multiple and overlapping food systems, spanning all the way from a single township to the entire globe. Since each of the players in a food system may interact with all others, and since new firms and relationships are constantly forming and disappearing, food systems are inherently complicated, and therefore difficult to understand or manage. Since their essential structures and functions are adapting to each other, as well as to external contexts, food systems are capable of generating surprising new insights or relationships that could not have been predicted according to the original conditions. At core, each food system also depends on nutrients, typically provided through healthy soil with considerable organic matter, as well as clean air, clean water, and microbes.

infrastructure—Infrastructure is the totality of physical facilities, relationships, knowledge, and worldviews that determine economic trade. A highway is part of our physical infrastructure, and so is a cold storage unit. Less obvious examples of infrastructure are the researchers, their findings that help inform decision making, and public policies we enact to shape our food trade for the greatest benefit.

References

Introduction

Belasco, Warren (1989). *Appetite for Change: How the Counterculture Took on the Food Industry, 1966–1988*. New York: Pantheon Books.

Bethell, T. N. (1982). "Sumter County Blues: The Ordeal of the Federation of Southern Cooperatives." Washington, DC: National Committee in Support of Community Based Organizations. Viewed March 14, 2019 at http://www.federationsoutherncoop.com/fschistory/sumterwordf.htm.

Cooperative Grocer (2013). "Food Co-op History." Viewed October 3, 2018 at https://www.grocer.coop/library/wikis/38602.

Federation of Southern Cooperatives (2017). *Fifty Years of Courage, Cooperation, Commitment and Community.* 2017 Annual Report. East Point, GA: Federation of Southern Cooperatives. Available at http://www.federation southerncoop.com/.

Kansas State University (n.d.). Rural Grocery Initiative. Website. https://www.ruralgrocery.org/resources/.

Steinman, Jon (2019). *Grocery Story: The Promise of Food Co-ops in the Age of Grocery Giants.* Gabriola Island, BC: New Society Publishers.

For specific data citations in the introduction, see references for chapter 1.

Chapter 1. The Extractive US Farm Economy

Allyn, Bobby (2019). "White House Announces $16 Billion in Aid to Farmers Hurt By China Trade Dispute." Washington, DC: National Public Radio, May 23. Viewed May 29, 2019 at https://www.npr.org/2019/05/23/726 117690/white-house-to-announce-16-billion-in-aid-to-farmers-hurt-by -trade-war-with-china.

Caldwell, J. C.; Hughes, Hugh J.; Valentine, James. A.; & Weld, L. D. H. (1913). *Situation in Minnesota with Regard to Agricultural Credit, Marketing, and Co-operation,* St. Paul: State of Minnesota, December.

Cochrane, Willard (1993). *The Development of American Agriculture: A Historical Analysis.* Minneapolis: University of Minnesota Press.

Gardner, Bruce L. (2002). *American Agriculture in the Twentieth Century: How It Flourished and What It Cost.* Cambridge, MA: Harvard University Press.

Goodwyn, Lawrence (1976). *Democratic Promise: The Populist Moment in America.* London: Oxford University Press.

Goodwyn, Lawrence (1978). *The Populist Moment: A Short History of the Agrarian Revolt in America.* London: Oxford University Press.

Goodwyn, Lawrence (1996). Personal communication.

Gurman, Mark; Rojanasakul, Mira; & Sam, Cedric (2018). "How Apple Overcame Fits and Flops to Grow Into a Trillion-Dollar Company." Bloomberg News Service, August 2. Viewed March 13, 2019 at https://www.bloomberg .com/graphics/2018-apple-at-one-trillion-market-cap/.

Meter, Ken (1990). *Money with Roots.* Minneapolis: Crossroads Resource Center. Available at http://www.crcworks.org/roots.pdf.

Meter, Ken (1983). *Green Isle: Feeding the World and Farming for the Banker.* Minneapolis: Crossroads Resource Center. Available at http://www.crc works.org/gi.pdf.

Risser, James (1976). "Why They Love Earl Butz." *New York Times,* June 13. Viewed May 29, 2019 at https://www.nytimes.com/1976/06/13/archives/ why-they-love-earl-butz-prosperous-farmers-see-him-as-the-greatest.html.

Smith, Homer G. (1987). *A Challenge to U.S. Agriculture: Building the Cooperative Production Credit System.* Denver: Graphic Impressions.

Sparks, Earl Sylvester (1932). *History and Theory of Agricultural Credit in the United States.* New York: Thomas Y. Crowell.

Stewart, Charles L. (1914). *An Analysis of Rural Banking Conditions in Illinois.* Illinois Bankers Association. February 12.

Swenson, David (2019). "Dwindling Population and Disappearing Jobs Is the Fate That Awaits Much of Rural America." *Market Watch,* May 8. Viewed May 9, 2019, at https://www.marketwatch.com/.

Taylor, Henry C.; & Taylor, Anne D. (1952). *Story of Agricultural Economics in the United States, 1840–1932.* Ames, IA: Iowa State College Press.

US Department of Agriculture Economic Research Service (series). Agricultural Productivity in the U.S. Available at https://www.ers.usda.gov/data-products/agricultural-productivity-in-the-us/.

US Department of Agriculture Economic Research Service (series). Commodity Costs and Returns. Available at https://www.ers.usda.gov/data-products/commodity-costs-and-returns/.

US Department of Agriculture Economic Research Service (series). Farm Household Income and Characteristics. Available at https://www.ers.usda.gov/data-products/farm-household-income-and-characteristics/.

US Department of Agriculture Economic Research Service (series). Food Insecurity in the U.S. Available at https://www.ers.usda.gov/topics/food-nutrition-assistance/food-security-in-the-us.aspx.

US Department of Agriculture Economic Research Service. Farm Income and Wealth (series). Available at https://www.ers.usda.gov/data-products/farm-income-and-wealth-statistics/data-files-us-and-state-level-farm-income-and-wealth-statistics/.

US Department of Agriculture Economic Research Service. Food Expenditures (series). Available at https://www.ers.usda.gov/data-products/food-expenditure-series/.

US Department of Agriculture Economic Research Service (2017). "Food Security Status of U.S. Households in 2017." Available at https://www.ers.usda.gov/topics/food-nutrition-assistance/food-security-in-the-us/key-statistics-graphics.aspx.

US Department of Agriculture Economic Research Service. Foreign Agricultural Trade of the United States (FATUS). Available at https://www.ers.usda.gov/data-products/foreign-agricultural-trade-of-the-united-states-fatus/calendar-year/.

US Department of Agriculture Economic Research Service. Foreign Agricultural Trade of the United States (FATUS). International Markets & U.S. Trade: China. Viewed May 29, 2019, at https://www.ers.usda.gov/topics/international-markets-us-trade/countries-regions/china/.

US Department of Agriculture National Agricultural Statistics Service (series). Census of Agriculture. Available at https://www.nass.usda.gov/AgCensus/.

US Federal Reserve Bank of Minneapolis. "Consumer Price Index, 1913–Present." https://www.minneapolisfed.org/community/financial-and-economic-education/cpi-calculator/consumer-price-index-and-inflation-rates-1913.

Vieira, Luis (2019). "Brazil's Soybean Success Is Rooted in the U.S." *Successful Farming*, April 11. Viewed May 29, 2019, at https://www.agriculture.com/crops/soybeans/sf-special-brazils-soybean-success-is-rooted-in-the-us.

Wolff, Henry W. (1907). *Co-operative Banking: Its Principles and Practice*. London: P. S. King & Son.

Chapter 2. Co-learning Is Contagious

Alternative Energy Resources Organization (AERO), Helena, MT. (2005). *Sun Times*, Winter, 32, 2.

Baten, Valerie (2002). "Community-Based Food Systems Enterprises." Battle Creek, MI: W.K. Kellogg Foundation "Food for Thought" series, Number 3.

Biello, David (2010). "Where Did the Carter White House's Solar Panels Go?" *Scientific American*, August 6. Viewed January 31, 2020, at https://www.scientificamerican.com/article/carter-white-house-solar-panel-array/.

Carlisle, Liz (2015). *The Lentil Underground*. London: Penguin.

Duce, Stacie (2013). "Agriculture Department Mapping Montana's Food System." *Ravalli Republic*, March 25. Viewed December 20, 2019, at https://ravallirepublic.com/business/article_00e4d0ce-8c01-11e2-89bf-0019bb2963f4.html.

Hassanein, Neva; Ginsburg, Laura; Gilchrist, Kimberly; Stephens, Caroline; & Rocke, Eva (2015). "Collaborative Advantage: A Case Study of the Western Montana Growers Cooperative." Missoula: University of Montana, unpublished paper.

Lutey, Tom (2011). "Local Food Movement Gets Trucking." *Billings Gazette*, May 10. Viewed December 20, 2019, at https://billingsgazette.com/news/local/local-food-movement-gets-trucking/article_ccf4877b-7f5e-5b92-ba05-7cf4 b3ad8a4f.html.

McLeay, Fraser; Barron, Nicola; Matheson, Nancy; McMullan, Crissie; & Hassanein, Neva (2006). "Unlocking the Food Buying Potential of Montana's Public Institutions: Towards a Montana-Based Food Economy." Missoula, MT: Kiwi Trade and Business for The National Center for Appropriate Technology.

Meter, Ken (2011–2012). Farm and Food Economy Studies for five Montana regions. Available at http://www.crcworks.org/?submit=fffc.

Palmer, Warren (1983). *The Montana Food System: First Lessons in Sustainability.* Emmaus, PA: Rodale Press, The Cornucopia Project.

Quinn, Bob, & Carlisle, Liz (2019). *Grain by Grain: A Quest to Revive Ancient Wheat, Rural Jobs, and Healthy Food.* Washington, DC: Island Press.

Rusmore, Barbara (1996). "Reinventing Science through Participatory Research." Doctoral dissertation. Santa Barbara, CA: Fielding Graduate University.

Stegner, Wallace (1969). *The Sound of Mountain Water.* New York: Doubleday.

Tuxill, Jacquelyn L., ed. (2000). "The Landscape of Conservation Stewardship: The Report of the Sustainability Initiative Feasibility Study." Woodstock, VT: Marsh-Billings-Rockefeller National Historical Park, Conservation Study Institute, and Woodstock Foundation.

Wolfe, Emily Stifler (2020). "Homegrown, Part 2: How Small, Community-Based Food Processors Are Building a More Resilient Montana Food System." *Montana Free Press,* August 21. Viewed August 22, 2020, at https://montanafreepress.org/2020/08/21/community-based-food-processors-make-montana-food-resilient/.

Chapter 3. Invoking Traditional Wisdom to Recover from Plantation Agriculture

Fox, Catherine Toth (2018). "These Local Farmers Are Taking Eggs to the Next Level: Local Family Egg Farms Are Stepping Up and Standing Out." *Honolulu* magazine, August 29. Available at http://www.honolulumagazine.com/Honolulu-Magazine/July-2018/These-Local-Farmers-are-Taking-Eggs-to-the-Next-Level/.

Gonschor, Lorenz; & Beamer, Kamanamaikalani (2014). "Toward an Inventory of Ahupua'a in the Hawaiian Kingdom: A Survey of Nineteenth- and Early Twentieth Century Cartographic and Archival Records of the Island of Hawai'i." *Hawaiian Journal of History,* 48.

Ho, K. K. (2016). "Nurturing Waiwai in Kalihi Valley." Honolulu: Kōkua Kalihi Valley Health Center. Progress Report to W. K. Kellogg Foundation.

MacLennan, Carol (2014). *Sovereign Sugar.* Honolulu: University of Hawai'i Press.

Meter, Ken; & Goldenberg, Megan Phillips (2017). *Hawai'i's Food System: Food For All.* Minneapolis: Crossroads Resource Center. Available at http://www.crcworks.org/hifood.pdf.

Chapter 4. Building the Capacities and Voice of Low-Income Residents

Lynch, Jess; Meter, Ken; Robles-Schrader, Grisel; Goldenberg, Megan Phillips; Bassler, Elissa; Chusid, Sarah; & Austin, Coby Jansen. *Exploring Economic and Health Impacts of Local Food Procurement* (2015). Chicago: Illinois Public Health Institute. Available at http://www.crcworks.org/ehimpacts.pdf.

Meter, Ken (2013). "Addressing Hunger by Strengthening Local Foods Logistics." *Journal of Agriculture, Food Systems, and Community Development,* 3(3), June, 17–20. http://dx.doi.org/10.5304/jafscd.2014.044.011.

Meter, Ken (2012). "Field Research for Southern Arizona." Minneapolis: Crossroads Resource Center for the Community Food Bank of Southern Arizona, February 29. Available at http://www.crcworks.org/azsouthfield 12.pdf.

Minkler, Alana (2019). "Tucson School Gardening Movement Sprouts from Manzo Elementary School." Tucson: *Arizona Wildcat,* March 4. Viewed August 13, 2019, at http://www.wildcat.arizona.edu/article/2019/03/n -elementary-garden.

Nabhan, Gary Paul; & Fitzsimmons, Regina, Eds. (2011). *The State of Southwestern Foodsheds.* Tucson: Sabores Sin Fronteras, Southwest Center of the University of Arizona, & Edible Communities.

Natural Grains Tortillas (2019). "How It All Began." June 6 posting. Viewed August 10, 2019, at https://www.facebook.com/NaturalGrainsTortillas/.

Pavlakovich-Kochi, Vera (2018). "Assessing Nogales, Arizona's Major Border Port of Entry (BPOE)." Tucson: University of Arizona Eller School of Management. Arizona-Mexico Economic Indicators, November 20. Viewed August 10, 2019, at https://azmex.eller.arizona.edu/news-article/20nov2018/ assessing-nogales-arizonas-major-border-port-entry-bpoe.

Tucson Unified School District (website). "Green Academy for Garden Based Curriculum Integration." Viewed August 13, 2019, at https://schoolgardens .arizona.edu/green-academy-garden-based-curriculum-integration.

University of Arizona Eller School of Management, Arizona-Mexico Economic Indicators (series). "Pedestrian Crossings." Viewed August 10, 2019, at https://azmex.eller.arizona.edu/border-crossings/pedestrian-crossings.

Chapter 5. Placing Food Business Clusters at the Core of Economic Development

Hackett, Kara (2020). "'A Food Crisis': COVID-19 Reveals Gaps and Opportunities in Indiana's Food System." *Input Fort Wayne.* Viewed August 24, 2020, at https://www.inputfortwayne.com/features/food-crisis.aspx.

Meter, Ken (2012). *Hoosier Farmer? Emergent Food Systems in Indiana.* Minneapolis: Crossroads Resource Center. Available at http://www.crcworks.org /infood.pdf.

Meter, Ken (2016). "Northeast Indiana Local Food Network." Minneapolis: Crossroads Resource Center for Manheim & Associates and the Northeast Indiana Regional Partnership. Available at http://www.crcworks.org/innet works16.pdf.

Northeast Indiana Regional Partnership website (n.d.). Selected comments in this chapter from John Sampson are drawn with his permission from a video, "History of Collaboration in Northeast Indiana," based on an interview of Sampson by Jon Myers, President of Whitley County Economic Development Corporation. Viewed July 10, 2019, at https://neindiana.com/.

Chapter 6. The Cradle of Food Democracy: Athens (Ohio)

Meter, Ken (2011). *Ohio's Food Systems: Farms at the Heart of It All.* Minneapolis: Crossroads Resource Center, with University of Toledo Urban Affairs Center, and Ohio Department of Agriculture. Available at http://www.crc works.org/ohfood.pdf.

Shafer, Jon (1982). *Toward a Sustainable Ohio in Food, Farmers and Land. A Study of the Food System of Ohio.* The Cornucopia Project. Emmaus, PA: Rodale Press.

Chapter 7. Metro-Area Farmers Need Supportive Networks

Davis, Emilly (2020). "'A Raging Crisis': Metro Phoenix Is Losing Its Family Farms and Local Food Sources." *Arizona Republic,* August 16. Viewed August 17, 2020, at https://www.azcentral.com/story/news/local/phoenix /2020/08/16/metro-phoenix-losing-its-family-farms-development/33 15284001/.

Duckworth, Barbara (2018). "Arizona Dairy Manages 12,500 Cows and 52,000 Steers." *The Western Producer*, February 22. Viewed September 25, 2019, at https://www.producer.com/2018/02/arizona-dairy-manages-12500-cows-52000-steers/.

Farmland Information Center (2016). "Cost of Community Services Studies." Washington, DC: American Farmland Trust.

Meter, Ken; Goldenberg, Megan Phillips; and Ross, Paula (2018). *Building Community Networks through Community Foods.* Minneapolis: Crossroads Resource Center, June 23. In partnership with the Maricopa County Food System Coalition Food Assessment Coordination Team and Gila River Indian Communities. Available at http://www.crcworks.org/azmaricopa 18.pdf.

Chapter 8. Municipal Officials Collaborate to Protect Metro Farmland

City of Brighton & County of Adams, Colorado (2016). Special Ag District Plan: Adopted Draft. Produced by Logan Simpson Design Firm, Two Forks Collective, Crossroads Resource Center, HRS Water Consultants, Inc., and Urban Interactive Studio. Viewed August 24, 2020, at https://www.brightonco.gov/DocumentCenter/View/19191/District-Plan _ADOPTED_April-2016.

Chapter 9. Working Below the Radar to Create Networks of Green Space

McCormick, Tori J. (2015). "Think of the Mississippi as a National Park, Too." Minneapolis *Star Tribune*, April 9.

Singer, Al (2019, 2020). Personal communication.

University of Minnesota (2003). "Metro Greenways: Seven-County Twin Cities Region, Minnesota." Minneapolis: University of Minnesota Metropolitan Design Center. Case Study.

Chapter 10. Building Market Power for Farmers

Fellowship for Intentional Community (2016). "Wiscoy Valley Community Land Cooperative." Viewed March 27, 2018, at https://www.ic.org/directory /wiscoy-valley-community-land-cooperative/.

Garrity, Pat (2019). Personal communication.

Meter, Ken (2016). "Northeast Indiana Local Food Network." Minneapolis: Crossroads Resource Center, for Manheim & Associates and the Northeast

Indiana Regional Partnership. Available at http://www.crcworks.org/innet works16.pdf.

Meter, Ken (2008). "Southwest Wisconsin Local Farm & Food Economy." Produced for Valley Stewardship Network by Crossroads Resource Center. Available at http://www.crcworks.org/crcdocs/wiviroquasum08.pdf.

Renwick, Danielle (2017). "Twenty-five Years Later, 'The Town That Beat Walmart' Is Back on the Map." *The New Food Economy*. July 11. Available at https://newfoodeconomy.org/viroqua-wisconsin-local-food-renaissance/.

Tatreau, Lori (2019). Personal communication.

Chapter 11. Shifting from "Local Food" to "Community-Based Food Systems"

Born, Branden; & Purcell, Mark (2006). "Avoiding the Local Trap: Scale and Food Systems in Planning Research." *Journal of Planning Education and Research* 26:195–207 DOI: 10.1177/0739456X06291389.

Caton Campbell, Marcia (2004). "Building a Common Table: The Role for Planning in Community Food Systems." *Journal of Planning Education and Research* 23:341–355.

Lynch, Jessica; Meter, Ken; Robles-Schrader, Grisel; Goldenberg, Megan Phillips; Bassler, Elissa; Chusid, Sarah; & Austin, Coby Jansen (2015). *Exploring Economic and Health Impacts of Local Food Procurement.* Chicago: Illinois Public Health Institute. Available at http://www.crcworks.org/EH impacts.pdf.

Meter, Ken (2013). "Snapshots of the Southwest Indiana Farm and Food Economy." Minneapolis: Crossroads Resource Center for the Welborn Baptist Foundation, Evansville, Indiana, November 15. Available at http://www.crc works.org/crcdocs/inswstory13.pdf.

Meter, Ken; Goldenberg, Megan Phillips; & Ross, Paula (2018). *Building Community Networks through Community Food.* Minneapolis: Crossroads Resource Center for Maricopa County Food System Coalition Food Assessment Coordination Team. Available at http://www.crcworks.org/azmaricopa 18.pdf.

Putnam, Robert (1993). *Making Democracy Work.* Princeton, NJ: Princeton University Press.

Putnam, Robert (1993). "The Prosperous Community: Social Capital and Public Life." *The American Prospect* 13 (Spring), 35–42. Available at http:// www.prospect.org/cs/articles?article=the_prosperous_community.

Snyder, Brian; Smith, Leah; Meter, Ken; Goldenberg, Megan Phillips; Miller, Stacy; & Amsterdam, Rob (2014). *The Real Deal: How Do We Define "Local" in a Meaningful and Measurable Way?* Harrisburg, PA: The Pennsylvania Association for Sustainable Agriculture. Available at http://www.crcworks.org/realdeal.pdf.

Chapter 12. Scale Is Both the Problem and the Solution

Dawson, Julie; & Morales, Alfonso (2016). *Cities of Farmers: Urban Agricultural Practices and Processes.* Iowa City: University of Iowa Press.

Meter, Ken (2012). *Hoosier Farmer? Emergent Food Systems in Indiana.* Minneapolis: Crossroads Resource Center. Available at http://www.crcworks.org/infood.pdf.

Red Tomato (2018). "Can the Good Food Movement Make It to Market?" September 27. Viewed October 10, 2018, at https://www.redtomato.org/can-the-good-food-movement-make-it-to-market/.

Shields, Dennis A. (2010). "Consolidation and Concentration in the U.S. Dairy Industry." Congressional Research Service 7-5700, R41224. April 27.

Conclusion. Building Community Food Webs: Action Networks, System Levers, and Business Clusters

Goldenberg, Megan Phillips; & Meter, Ken (2019). "Building Economic Multipliers, Rather Than Measuring Them: Community-Minded Ways to Develop Economic Impacts." *Journal of Agriculture, Food Systems, and Community Development,* 8(C), January 23, 1–12. https://doi.org/10.5304/jafscd.2019.08C.010.

Goldschmidt, Walter (2006). Interviewed by Ken Meter in Turin, Italy, July.

Goldschmidt, Walter (1972). *As You Sow.* Montclair, NJ: Allanheld, Osmun.

Meter, Ken (2019). "Assessing Food Systems as Complex Adaptive Systems: Conceptual Views and U.S. Applications." In Blay-Palmer, Alison; Conaré, Damien; Meter, Ken; Di Battista, Amanda; & Johnston, Carla, Eds. (2019). *Sustainable Food System Assessment: Lessons from Global Practice.* London: Routledge UK. Open source.

Meter, Ken (2007). "Evaluating Farm and Food Systems in the U.S." In Williams, Bob; & Imam, Iraj (2007). *Systems Concepts in Evaluation: An Expert Anthology.* Point Reyes, CA: EdgePress, for the American Evaluation Association.

Meter, Ken (1990). *Inside the Empire: Dependence and Self-Determination in Rural America.* Minneapolis: Crossroads Resource Center. Available at http://www.crcworks.org/empire.pdf.

Further Reading

Berger, John (1979). *Pig Earth.* New York: Pantheon Books.

Boggs, James; Boggs, Grace Lee; Payne, Freddy; & Payne, Lyman (1978). *Conversations in Maine.* Boston: South End Press.

Brand, Caroline; Bricas, Nicolas; Conaré, Damien; Daviron, Benoit; Debru, Julie; Michel, Laura; & Soulard, Christophe-Toussaint, Eds. (2019). *Designing Urban Food Policies: Concepts and Approaches.* Springer. Open source.

Case, Martin (2018). *The Relentless Business of Treaties.* St. Paul: Minnesota Historical Society Press.

Cronon, William (1991). *Nature's Metropolis: Chicago and the Great West.* New York: Norton.

Cronon, William (1983). *Changes in the Land: Indians, Colonists and the Ecology of New England.* New York: Hill and Wang.

Gable, Medard (1981). *Empty Breadbasket? A Study of the U.S. Food System. Cornucopia Project.* Emmaus, PA: Rodale Press.

Koehler, Rhiannon (2018). "Hostile Nations: Quantifying the Destruction of the Sullivan-Clinton Genocide of 1779." *American Indian Quarterly* 42(4), 427–453. DOI: 10.5250/amerindiquar.42.4.0427.

Mamen, Katy; Gorelick, Steven; Norberg-Hodge, Helen; & Deumling, Diana (2004). *Ripe for Change: Rethinking California's Food Economy.* San Francisco: International Society for Ecology and Culture, 27.

Meter, Ken (2020). *New Mexico Farm and Food Economy.* Minneapolis: Crossroads Resource Center for New Mexico Healthy Soil Working Group. Available at http://www.crcworks.org/nmfood20.pdf.

Meter, Ken (2019). *New Hampshire Farm, Fish, and Food Economy.* Minneapolis: Crossroads Resource Center. With National Family Farm Coalition. Available at http://www.crcworks.org/nhfood.pdf.

Meter, Ken (2009). *Mapping the Minnesota Food Industry.* Minneapolis: Crossroads Resource Center. Available at http://www.crcworks.org/mnfood.pdf.

Meter, Ken (1981). "Who Produces Minnesota's Food?" *The Farmer*, July 18, 22. Available at http://www.crcworks.org/mnfoodimp81.pdf.

Meter, Ken; & Goldenberg, Megan Phillips (2014). *Food Security in Alaska.* Minneapolis: Crossroads Resource Center for the State of Alaska Department of Health and Social Services. Available at http://www.crcworks.org/akfood.pdf.

Meter, Ken; & Goldenberg, Megan Phillips (2013). *Making Small Farms into Big Business: A Plan for Infrastructure Investments to Connect Small Farms in South Carolina to Local Markets.* Minneapolis: Crossroads Resource Center for the South Carolina Department of Agriculture, South Carolina Department of Commerce, Palmetto Agribusiness Council, Coastal Conservation League, Carolina Farm Stewardship Association, and Bank of South Carolina. Available at http://www.crcworks.org/scfood.pdf.

Nabhan, Gary P. (2018). *Food from the Radical Center: Healing Our Land and Communities.* Washington, DC: Island Press.

Philpott, Tom (2020). *Perilous Bounty.* New York: Bloomsbury.

Philpott, Tom (2013). "A Brief History of Our Deadly Addiction to Nitrogen Fertilizer." *Mother Jones*, April 19. https://www.motherjones.com/food/2013/04/history-nitrogen-fertilizer-ammonium-nitrate/.

Richardson, Heather Cox (2020). *How the South Won the Civil War: Oligarchy, Democracy, and the Continuing Fight for the Soul of America.* Oxford, UK: Oxford University Press.

Rodale Center Cornucopia Project (1980–1984). Food System Studies. Emmaus, PA: Rodale Press. Partial listing available at https://crcworks.org/?submit=rodale.

Viljoen, André; and Wiskerke, Johannes S. C., Eds. (2012). *Sustainable Food Planning: Evolving Theory and Practice.* Wageningen, the Netherlands: Wageningen Academic Publishers.

Index

About the Author

Ken Meter is one of the most experienced food system analysts in the US, integrating market analysis, business development, systems thinking, and social concerns. Meter holds 50 years of experience in inner-city and rural community capacity building. His local economic analyses have promoted local food networks in 144 regions in 41 states, two provinces, and four tribal nations. He was commissioned to create statewide food system assessments for New Mexico, New Hampshire, Hawai'i, Alaska, Mississippi, South Carolina, Indiana, Ohio, and Minnesota, and developed strategic plans for 16 regional food systems. Meter served as one of 14 coauthors of the USDA Agricultural Marketing Service and Colorado State University's toolkit for measuring economic impacts of local food development, and served as national review panel manager for the USDA Community Foods Projects Competitive Grant Program. He was coeditor of *Sustainable Food System Assessment: Lessons from Global Practice* (Routledge, UK) in 2019. Meter taught microeconomics at the Harvard Kennedy School midcareer program, and the economic history of US agriculture at the University of Minnesota. As an independent journalist in the 1980s and 1990s, he wrote first-hand dispatches from 12 countries and a weekly column on agricultural trends for Reuters. Meter's work can be found at www.crcworks.org

Island Press | Board of Directors